D1391894

The Extinguished Flame

For Emily and Oliver on their engagement.
May your lives be long and full of love and interest.
No greater love do two people share.

The Extinguished Flame

Olympians Killed in The Great War

Nigel McCrery

Pen & Sword
MILITARY

First published in Great Britain in 2016 by
Pen & Sword Military
An imprint of
Pen & Sword Books Ltd
47 Church Street
Barnsley
South Yorkshire
S70 2AS

ISBN 978 1 47387 798 6

Typeset in 10pt Dante by
Mac Style, Bridlington, East Yorkshire

Printed and bound in the UK by CPI Group (UK) Ltd, Croydon, CRO 4YY

Pen & Sword Books Ltd incorporates the imprints of Pen & Sword
Archaeology, Atlas, Aviation, Battleground, Discovery, Family History,
History, Maritime, Military, Naval, Politics, Railways, Select, Transport, True
Crime, and Fiction, Frontline Books, Leo Cooper, Praetorian Press, Seaforth
Publishing and Wharncliffe.

For a complete list of Pen & Sword titles please contact
PEN & SWORD BOOKS LIMITED
47 Church Street, Barnsley, South Yorkshire, S70 2AS, England
E-mail: enquiries@pen-and-sword.co.uk
Website: www.pen-and-sword.co.uk

Contents

Acknowledgements   x
Preface   xii

1914

Henri Edmond Bonnefoy, 09.8.14   2
Felix Lucien Roger Debax, 25.8.14   3
Robert Merz, 30.8.14   5
Oszkár Demján, 04.9.14   7
Jean Latrie, France, 5.9.14   8
Carl Heinrich Goßler, 09.8.14   9
George William Hutson, 14.9.14   11
Eduard von Lütcken, 15.9.14   14
Louis Desire Bach, 16.9.14   16
Charles Devendeville, 19.9.1914   18
Leopold Mayer, 21.9.14   20
Alexandre Bouin, 29.9.14   21
Georges de La Nézière, 9.10.14   24
Thomas Gillespie, 18.10.14   26
Árpád Pédery, 21.10.14   30
Béla Zulawszky, 24.10.14   31
Joseph Racine, 28.10.14   32
Alphonse Meignant, 04.11.14   33
Gerard 'Twiggy' Anderson, 11.11.14   35
Jenő Szántay, 11.12.14   37
Richard Francis Yorke, 22.12.14   38
André Six, 1914   40

1915

Georg Krogmann, 9.1.15   42
Max Herrmann, 29.1.15   43
Georges Adam Lutz, 31.1.15   44
Kenneth Powell, 18.2.15   45
Edward Radcliffe-Nash, 21.2.15   47
Adolf Kofler, 13.3.15   49
Wyndham Halswelle, 31.3.15   51
Geoffrey Barron Taylor, 24.4.15   54
Gilchrist Maclagan, 25.4.15   56

William Anderson, 26.4.15   58
Ralph Chalmers, 08.5.15   60
Henry Mills Goldsmith, 09.5.15   61
Anthony Wilding, 09.5.15   63
Herman Donners, 14.5.15   66
James Duffy, 23.5.15   67
Henry Alan Leeke, 29.5.15   70
Oswald Carver, 07.6.15   72
Alfred Mickler, 14.6.15   74
George Fairbairn, 20.6.15   75
Amon Ritter von Gregurich, 28.6.15   80
Jakob Person, 15.7.15   81
Edward Gordon Williams, 12.8.15   82
Rudolf Watzl, 15.8.15   84
Edmond Wallace, 18.8.15   85
Paul Kenna, 30.8.15   86
Fritz Bartholomae, 12.9.15   90
Arthur Ommundsen, 19.9.15   92
Renon Boussière, 25.9.15   94
Michel Soalhat, 25.9.15   95
Ismael de Lesseps, 30.9.15   96
Heinrich Schneidereit, 30.9.15   98
Joseph Caulle, 1.10.15   100
Béla von Las-Torres, 12.10.15   101
Alfred Staats, 22.10.15   103
Dragutin Tomašević, 10.15   105
Lajos Gönczy, 4.12.15   107
Edmund William Bury, 5.12.15   109
Georg Baumann, 1915   110

1916

Hugh Durant, 20.1.16   112
Arthur William Wilde, 21.1.16   114
Geoffrey Horsman Coles, 27.1.16   116
Jules Aristide Jenicot, 22.2.16   117
Walter Jesinghaus, 22.2.16   119
Alan Patterson, 14.3.16   120
Karl Braunsteiner, 19.4.16   122
Guido Romano, 18.6.16   123
Maurice Raoul-Duval, 5.5.16   124

Contents

John Somers-Smith, 1.7.16   125
Alfred Edward Flaxman, 1.7.16   127
Béla Békessy, 6.7.16   129
William Philo, 7.7.16   131
Pierre Six, 7.7.16   133
Josef Rieder, 13.7.16   134
Hermann Bosch, 16.7.16   135
Maurice Salomez, 7.8.16   136
John Robinson, 23.8.16   137
Robert Finden Davies, 9.9.16   139
Justin Pierre Vialaret, 30.9.16   141
René Victor Fenouillière, 4.11.16   142
Frederick Septimus Kelly, 13.11.16   143
Léon Honoré Ponscarme, 24.11.16   146
Louis de Champsavin, 20.12.16   148
Andrei Akimov, 1916   150
Nikolai Kynin, 1916   152
Wilhelm Lützow, 1916   153

1917

Leon Flameng, 2.1.17   156
Feliks Leparsky, 10.1.17   158
Henry Ashington, 31.1.17   160
Charles Vigurs, 22.2.17   162
Alister Kirby, 29.3.17   164
Prince Karl of Prussia, 6.4.17   166
Herbert Wilson, 11.4.17   169
Gordon Alexander, 24.4.17   172
Robert Powell, 28.4.17   174
Issac Bentham, 15.5.17   176
Percy Courtman, 2.6.17   178
Harold Hawkins, 16.6.17   180
Herbert Gayler, 23.6.17   181
Percival Molson, 5.7.17   183
Louis Octave Lapize, 14.7.17   185
Waldemar Tietgens, 28.7.17   187
Noel Godfrey Chavasse, 4.8.17   189
Wilhelm Brülle, 5.8.17   193
James Roche, 25.8.17   194
Claude Ross, 19.8.17   196

George Albert Hawkins, 20/22.9.17   197
George Butterfield, 24.9.17   198
Bernhard von Gaza, 25.9.17   200
Duncan Mackinnon, 9.10.17   202
Harry Crank, 22.10.17   204
Alexander Decoteau, 30.10.17   207
Ivan Laing, 30.11.17   209
Gori Nikitin, 1917   211

1918

Juho Halme, 1.2.18   214
Reginald Pridmore, 13.3.18   216
Hermann Plaskuda, 21.3.18   218
Ronald Sanderson, 17.4.18   219
Kurt Bretting, 30.5.18   221
István Mudin, 22.7.18   222
Albert Rowland, 23.7.18   223
Ernest Keeley, 23.7.18   225
Henry Macintosh, 26.7.18   227
Hans Sorge, 6.8.18   229
Thomas Raddall, 9.8.18   230
Frederick Kitching, 11.8.18   232
Bertrand de Lesseps, 28.8.18   233
Cecil Patrick Healy, 29.8.18   235
Joseph Frank Dines, 27.9.18   237
Hanns Braun, 9.10.18   239
Imre Mudin, 23.10.18   242
William Lyshon, 13.10.18   244
Alfred Motté, 31.10.18   245
Arthur Yancey Wear, 6.11.18   247
Heinrich Burkowitz, 11.18   249
Andre Corvington, 13.12.18   250
Victor Willems   251
Hermann Bönninghausen, 26.1.19   253

Bibliography and Sources   255
Appendix 1: Olympians in Order of their Date of Death   257
Appendix 2: The Number of Olympians who Died in the First World War by Nation   261
Appendix 3: Olympians by Nation   262
Appendix 4: History of the Olympic Games   270
Appendix 5: Casualties Who Won Olympic Medals   279

Sing we now the glorious dinner
Served in grand Freemason's Hall;
Welcome loser, welcome winner,
Welcome all who've rowed at all:
Oarsmen, steersmen saints and sinner,
Whet your jaws, and to it fall …

Thus in generous emulation
Cam and Isis both are one;
Thus each passing generation
Earns the meed to duty done;
Thus the glory of OUR NATION
Shines wherever shines the sun.

Acknowledgements

The author wishes to thank the following for helping throughout the researching and writing of this book:

Rowena Ackney, London Medal Company, for her continual help and advice to say the least; Mathias Aerts, for all his help with various matters; Trevor Bailey and Bill Hazley, Northamptonshire County Cricket Club, for their time, trouble and expertise; Jill Barlow, Cheltenham College Archives; Richard Black, London Medal Company, for his help, advice and loan of books and Cecilia; Alan Clay, collector and researcher who has, as ever, done all he could to help and that was a lot. I'd like to say he never complains but I'd be lying; Eleanor Cracknell, Eton College Archivist, for her time and trouble; John Eagle, researcher, collector and specialist in the London Scottish, for allowing me to reproduce photographs of Richard Yorke and for the wonderful photograph of Yorke's medals; Roddy Fisher, keeper, Eton College Photographic Archive; Norman Franks, leading air war expert, writer and researcher, for his continual help; the late Hal Giblin, gentleman, historian, writer, my inspiration; the late and much missed Dennis Ingle, researcher and medal dealer; William Ivory and Phil Nodding, for keeping me going; Glenn Jewison, for his time and research; Jane Jones, WWI photos, obituaries and service records database, for providing many of the photographs and obituaries; Matt Jones, Pen & Sword, for his continual understanding, calmness and friendship; Jack Langley; Medals Forum; David O'Mara, of Croonaert Research Services, a first class researcher and very generous man; Ashley McCrery, for his help and advice; Pearce Noonan, Nimrod Dix medals, for his continual help and advice; Ken Scheffler, Great War Forum, a superb researcher; Robert Smith, collector and researcher, without whose generous help some of the information would have been wrong and photographs not discovered; Richard Steel, for his help, friendship and advice; Richard Taylor; Jan Vancoillie, for his time, trouble and effort – much appreciated; Jon Wilkinson, for once again coming up with a beautiful book jacket.

Forums
Great War Forum, a superb research tool, which everyone interested in the subject should be a member of; Medals Forum, a first class online research tool, well worth joining.

Schools, Colleges and Museums/Archives
Balliol College, Oxford; Bedford School; Cambridge University; Eton School, who provided much information and many photographs of old boys; Charterhouse School; Corpus Christi College, Cambridge; Guards Museum, London; Jesus College,

Cambridge; **King's College**, Cambridge; **Magdalen College,** Oxford; **Marlborough College**; **Merton College,** Oxford; **New College**, Oxford; **Oxford University**; **Radley College**; **Royal Military Academy**, Woolwich; **The Royal Military College**, Sandhurst; **Rugby School,** who helped in the finding of several photographs and information on their old boys; **Stonyhurst College**; **Trinity College**, Cambridge; **Winchester College**, who provided a number of photographs and a wealth of information on their old boys.

Websites
The Blue and Gold Trust Website – www.thelinnets.co.uk

To anyone who I may have forgotten a big apology, and please let me know I will put it right in the next edition.

Nigel McCrery,
July 2016

Preface
'The Extinguished Flame'

For this book I have chosen to examine, be it briefly, those Olympic athletes who died during World War One. It is difficult to read into the lives of these extraordinary people and their breathtaking achievements, lives that were so sadly cut short by war. Their drive, their tenacity, their will to win. Not just that but their will to get up again and again no matter how many times they get knocked down. The sheer pleasure they take in what they do. Imagine, if you can, waking up almost every day for over four years to discover that yet another champion sportsman had been killed. Someone you had shouted for from the stands, applauded as they walked in from a record innings or having taken several wickets for few runs, run a mile in a record time, swum through choppy waters, jumped, or thrown a disc or a javelin or shot-put an impossible height or distance, or scored a remarkable goal.

I have only been able to draw a brief sketch of the lives of these Olympians and we need to know so much more. To try and help remedy this I'm going to set up a web page dedicated to sportsmen who died during the First World War One. I hope to have this up and running by next year, so watch out for it and any contributions will be gratefully received.

I have tried to add photographs to go with each of these Olympians, but this has not always been possible as, after so many years, many have been lost and destroyed. Many countries' archives were destroyed by war and political upheaval, and entire families and their records have vanished. Where I have found a photograph, I have included it, my motto being, better a poor photograph than no photograph at all. I have also, in some cases, included team photographs, where I know the person concerned is in the picture even if over the years the names have been lost and I have no idea which one he is.

This has probably been the hardest of the books I have written due to the various languages I have had to read through. Also finding and ploughing through foreign archives is never easy. If with my poor grasp of these languages I have made a mistake in interpretation I apologise. Please do feel free to point out my mistakes and I will correct them in the next publication of the book. The same goes for the research. If I have made any errors – and my experience is that despite my best efforts I will have made a few – please feel free once again to point them out (as long as you are not rude about it!). If I feel you are correct I will alter and acknowledge in following editions. Although I hope I haven't missed anyone out, if I have please make their case and I will add them to further editions of the book. I have gone as far as early 1919 in allowing for Olympians who died of wounds received in the war to be included. Again if you can make a case for others I will add them to future editions.

The Extinguished Flame

I want *The Extinguished Flame* to be an ongoing work. I want each edition to contain new and fresh information, new and better quality photographs, and I rely on my readers to help provide that and keep this work as up-to-date as we can.

My biggest thanks have to go to all the people who have helped and supported me in writing my books. To all of them a very big 'thank you' for taking the time and trouble to make them as good as I can make them. Books like this are a labour of love; any money you are paid is quickly spent buying photographs, travelling to various sites, telephone bills, ink and, most of all, time. However, despite all this, it's worth it. As the poem says, 'At the going down of the sun and in the morning, we will remember them.' People are not numbers on some casualty list, so many lost on this day, so many on that, they are people who had jobs and lives, and who loved and were loved. I do not want their lives or their extraordinary achievements to be forgotten. It is something my father Colin George McCrery, who served with the RAF for over twenty-five years, taught me, and a lesson I have never forgotten. Most of all, I hope you enjoy the book and it helps you remember some of the men who for a moment in their lives were Olympians and reached the very pinnacle of their chosen sport.

1914

Lieutenant Henri Edmond Bonnefoy
1908 London
France
Shooting (small-bore rifle) team, 50 and 100 yards
Bronze Medal (Team)
133rd Regiment
Died 9 August 1914 aged 26

'The First Olympian to Die'

Henri Edmond Bonnefoy was born on 17 October 1887 at Le Tremblois, Haute-Saône, France. A crack shot and director of the Henri Bonnefoy School of shooting in Chalons.

He was selected to shoot individually and in the team events during the 1908 Olympic Games in London. The French team finished third in the lagskyting rifle 50 and 100 yards team shooting event behind Great Britain and Sweden, winning a team bronze. Bonnefoy scored 166 points, the weakest score in the French team. The other team members were as follows. Paul Colas, who went on to win two gold medals in Stockholm in 1912 and a silver medal in the 1924 games in Paris. He died in 1956. Leon Lecuyer, who also took part in fencing events. He died in 1915, but not as a result of the war. And André Regaud who died in 1945. Bonnefoy also took part in the individual stationary target and small-bore rifle event finishing nineteenth.

He enlisted into the 85ᵉ RI (Sdt 2 Cl) on 9 October 1906. A year later, on 17 October 1907, he was posted to the Special Military School at St Cyr. He was promoted corporal on 19 October 1907 and sergeant on 19 March 1908 before being commissioned six months later on 1 October 1908. He transferred to the 133ᵉ RI on 11 July 1909 and was promoted to Lieutenant on 1 October 1910. Mobilized on 2 August 1914, he was killed with his regiment (133ᵉ RI) on 9 August 1914 during the battle of Alsace. For his bravery during the battle he was later mentioned in despatches for his 'remarkable qualities in the campaign'. He was the first Olympian to die in the war. Originally buried at Thann, his remains were eventually buried in Cernay, Haut-Rhin, France.

**Chef de Bataillon, Félix Lucien Roger Debax
Chevalier de la Légion d'Honneur, medaille
Militaire, Croix de Guerre avec Palme, Chevalier
de l'Ordre du Danebrog du Danemark
1900 Paris
France
Fencing
240th Infantry Regiment
Died 25 August 1914 aged 49**

A Hero of France

Félix Lucien Roger Debax was born on 28 September 1864 in Toulouse. He was the son of Gervais Achille Francois Alexandre Debax and Blanche Chemineau. After leaving school at 18 he decided on a career in the army enlisting on 24 October 1882 on an initial five-year commission, becoming an officer cadet at the École Speciale Militaire de Saint-Cry. The Militaire de Saint-Cry is France's foremost French military academy, established by Napoleon Bonaparte in 1802, and it was considered an honour to go there. He became a corporal-cadet on 3 November 1883, eventually commissioned as a sub-lieutenant into the 83rd Regiment in October 1884 before being promoted to lieutenant into the 57th Regiment in February 1888. Promoted to Captain he joined the army gymnastics school in 1889 (École Normale de Gymnastique) and became a gymnastics instructor. After two further years with the infantry he returned to his college and resumed his duties as an instructor until 1901. During this time Debax was appointed an officer of the Danish Order of the Dannebrog on 19 March 1898 and an officer of the French Order des Palmes Academiques on 22 January the same year. He also became a knight of the Swedish Order of the Sword on 2 May 1900 and an officer of the Turkish Order of Osmanieh. It was during this time that Debax also took part in the 1900 Olympics in Paris.

Debax competed in the Men's Foil, individual competition. Fifty-four fencers took part in the competition from nine different countries. In 1900 the first round, quarterfinals, and repêchage, skill and art with the foil was more important to advancing than actually winning the bout. The first bout was held on 14 May 1900. Debax faced the experienced Spanish fencer Mauricio de Ponce de Leon. Both Leon and Debax fought well and impressed the jury and, with thirty-seven other fencers, passed through to the quarter final stage of the competition. In the quarterfinals Debax faced fellow Frenchman Jean-Joseph Renaud. Once again both men acquitted themselves well and passed through together with ten other fencers to the semi-finals. Of the fourteen that were sent to the repêchage, six eventually went through to the semi-finals. The semi-finals were the first round of the foil tournament to use actual match results in determining advancement. The sixteen fencers were divided into two pools. Each fencer then faced each other fencer in his pool once. The four fencers with the best record in each pool moved on to the finals, with the other four competing in the consolation. Once again Debax did well and fought his way through to the final. The final was held on 21 May 1900. The top four fencers in each of the two semi-finals competed against each other, each fencing the other seven once. Debax managed to win four of his competitions and lost three making him fourth overall, missing out on a bronze medal by one place. Of the eight top places, seven were French including the gold medal winner Émile Coste.

On 12 October 1901 Debax was transferred into the 18th Infantry Regiment. He was further appointed a knight of the Spanish Order of Isabella the Catholic and a first class member of the Order of Military Merit. In October 1902 he was attached to the Gymnastics Institute in Stockholm. He later published books on the teaching of gymnastics and fighting with the bayonet. In June 1906 Debax returned to the 18th Infantry Regiment becoming their adjutant. In May 1907 he was appointed Chevalier of the Legion of Honour and the French Medaille Militaire.

He became chef de bataillon for the 19th Infantry Regiment in June 1908 before transferring to the 14th Infantry Regiment in 1909. He was mobilized on 2 August 1914 while stationed in Nîmes and transferred to command the 240th Infantry Regiment. He was killed in action at Saint-Maurice-sous-les-Côtes, Meuse on 25 August 1914. According to an account of his death he was 'killed by rifle fire emanating from German infantry under the cover of a talus to the west of the village of Boinville [Boinville-en-Woëvre] – 2 miles SE of Etain – at 05:15 am'. He was one of 881 casualties, 58 dead, 518 wounded, and 305 missing, between 24 and 25 August 1914.

He is commemorated on the war memorial at Falga not far from where he was born, and the Rue Félix Debax in Blagnac near Toulouse is named after him.

Leutnant Robert Merz
1912 Stockholm
Austria
Football
Reserve Infantry-Regiment Nr.28
Died 30 August 1914 aged 26

'Fastest Feet in Austria'

Robert Merz was born on 25 November 1887 in Vienna, Austria. He began his footballing career for the team Währing in 1902. In 1904 he joined the Schwerathletik Wiener Sportvereinigung, a predecessor of today's very prestigious Wiener Sports Club. Playing alongside the legendary Austrian footballer and later journalist Willy Schmieger, Merz won the Challenge Cup defeating Magyar AC 2–1 (a team from Budapest). In 1907 Merz began to play for the Jewish club DFC Prague and it was

Merz is pictured here although it is unknown which of these footballers he is.

while playing for them that he made his first international appearance. He made his debut against England playing inside right on 6 June 1908, a match played to celebrate the Jubilee of the Emperor Franz Joseph. In front of a crowd of 3,500 at Vienna's Cricket Platz, England beat Austria 6–1. Merz scored his first international goals against Hungary on 7 May 1911, when he knocked in two of three goals in a 3–1 victory over the Hungarians. England went on to win the gold medal.

Selected to play in the national side during the 1912 Olympic Games in Stockholm, he turned out in four of their five matches, scoring two goals against Germany in the first round in Austria's 5–1 victory. Austria then went on to defeat Norway 1–0 before losing to Hungary 3–0 and the Netherlands 1–0. Merz also managed to score two goals in a consolation tournament.

However the team failed to progress and missed out on a medal. Merz was capped thirteen times for Austria and scored five goals. His final match was against the old enemy Hungary on 3 May 1914, a match Austria won 2–0. On the declaration of war Merz was commissioned as a lieutenant into the Infantry Regiment Nr.28. He was killed in action on 30 August 1914 while fighting in Poturzyn, Tomaszow, Poland.

Private Oszkár Demján
1912 Stockholm
Hungary
Swimming
Breaststroke 200 and 400 metres
Nr.43 Infantry Regiment
Died 4 September 1914 aged 22

'A fine swimmer but not a fine competitor'

Oszkár Demján was born on 28 December 1891 in Budapest, Hungary.

In the 1912 Olympics he competed in the 200 and the 400 metres breaststroke. In the 200 metres he was eliminated, and in the 400 metres he was disqualified because he touched the wall with only one hand at the second turn.

In the First World War he was wounded while serving with Nr.32 Infantry Regiment. Later while serving with Nr.43 Regiment he was killed in action in Sianky near Lviv in the Ukraine.

Opening ceremony of the 1912 Olympics.

Captain Jean Marie Pierre Xavier de Mas Latrie
Chevalier de la Légion d'Honneur, Croix de guerre
1908 London; 1912 Stockholm
France
Fencing (1908) Modern Pentathlon (1912)
15e Chasseurs á Cheval
Died 5 September 1914 aged 34

'Two different Olympics two different events'

Jean Marie Pierre Xavier de Mas Latrie was born on 23 November 1879 in district VII, Paris, France. He was the son of René Mas Latrie and Marie Dawans. On 23 November 1905 he married Margueritte of Canolle at St-Louis des Invalides, Paris VII.

A well-known and established fencer he was selected to take part in the 1908 London Olympics as part of the French fencing team specializing in the sabre. Knocked out during the qualifying events. Jeno Fuchs of Hungary took the gold with fellow Hungarian Béla Zulawszky taking the silver, and the Bohemia fencer Vilém Goppold z Lobsdorfu Sr the bronze.

Four years later, in 1912, he was selected once again to compete in the Olympic Games, this time being held in Stockholm. However this time it wasn't as a fencer but in the modern pentathlon. He came fifteenth in the shooting, twenty-seventh in the swimming, second (not surprisingly) in the fencing, tenth in the riding and nineteenth in the running. He came sixteenth overall.

Deciding on a career in the army and rising to the rank of captain he served with distinction with the 15ᵉ Chasseurs à Cheval, being decorated with both the Chevalier de la Légion d'Honneur and the Croix de guerre. He was mortally wounded on a reconnaissance whilst on attachment to the British Army on 5 September 1914 (the first day of the Battle of the Marne) dying of wounds the same day at Rebais (Seine et Marne).

He is buried in the cimetière militaire of Signy-Signets, Seine et Marne (grave number 47).

Lieutenant Carl Heinrich Goßler (Gossler)
1900 Paris
Germany
Rowing (Coxed Four)
Kaiser Wilhelm 2nd Grand Ducal Hessian No 116 in Gieben
Died 9 September 1914 aged 29

'One of the youngest men ever to win an Olympic Gold Medal'

Carl Heinrich Goßler was born on 17 April 1885 in Hamburg, Germany. He was the son of Carl Oscar, a lawyer and chairman of the Hamburger Seeamts, and his wife Elizabeth. He had two brothers, Oskar Goßler (1875–1953) and Gustav Ludwig Goßler (1879–1940) both Olympic rowers. Both his brothers became merchants but this wasn't for Carl and he decided on a career in the army taking a commission on 27 January 1907.

As helmsman of the German coxed four, being rowed by his two brothers Gustav and Oskar, together with Walther Katzenstein and Waldemar Tietgens, he took part in

Goßler is seated on the far right.

the 1900 Olympic Games in Paris as coxswain of the German boat, *Germania Ruder Club, Hamburg*. Der Hamburger und Germania Ruder Club (DHuGRC) is a rowing club from Rotherbaum, Hamburg, Germany. It was founded in 1836 as Der Hamburger Ruder Club and is the fourth oldest rowing club in the world. The competition was dogged by problems from the very start involving a dispute over which boats should have progress to the final. In an attempt to resolve the controversy the Olympic Committee made one of the strangest decisions it has ever made. They decided to hold two separate finals for the same event. Each of the winners, from both finals, were considered Olympic champions by the International Olympic Committee. The coxed fours event was held on 25, 26 and 27 August 1900 on the River Seine. Ten boats, involving fifty rowers from four nations, competed. In Semifinal 3, Germania Ruder Club, Hamburg defeated two French boats, the *Cercle de l'Aviron Roubaix* and *Club Nautique de Dieppe*, and the German boat, *Favourite Hammonia* in a time of 5 minutes 56.2 seconds. In final A, the French boat, *Cercle de l'Aviron Roubaix*, took the gold medal in a time of 7 minutes 11 seconds defeating another French boat, *Club Nautique de Lyon*, and the German boat, *Favourite Hammonia*. In final B, *Germania Ruder Club, Hamburg*, coxed by Carl Goßler, took the gold in a time of 5 minutes 59 seconds defeating the Dutch boat *Minerva Amsterdam* and the German boat, *Ludwigshafener Ruder Verein*.

It was the first time a German boat and crew had won a gold medal at the Olympics. At the time of the event Goßler was still a student and only fifteen years old.

Lieutenant Carl Heinrich Goßler was killed in action serving with Kaiser Wilhelm 2nd Grand Ducal Hessian No 116 in Gieben on 14 September 1914.

L/9097 Sergeant George William Hutson
1912 Stockholm
Great Britain
5,000 metres/3,000 metre team event
Two Bronze Medals
'B' Company 2nd Battalion Royal Sussex Regiment
Died 14 September 1914 aged 25

First British Olympian to be killed

George William Hutson was born on 22 December 1889 in Lewes, East Sussex, the son of George William and Frances Hutson of Heathfield, Sussex. Deciding on a career in the army, he enlisted into the ranks of the 2nd Battalion Royal Sussex Regiment in 1908. In May 1914 he married Kate Elizabeth Hutson, of 19 Neville Rd, St Anne's, Lewes.

Quick on his feet his talent as a distance runner soon came to notice especially after he beat all-comers at a regimental cross-country race. Described as the 'most promising British distance runner of his generation' in 1914 he become the AAA champion of England at both 1 mile and 4 miles and set a new British record for the three-quarter

Hutson pictured third from the left.

Hutson is pictured third in line with the Union Jack visible on his shirt.

mile. His greatest achievements however were to come during the 1912 Olympic Games held in Stockholm, Sweden. He came in third winning a bronze medal in the 5,000 metres being beaten by the 'Flying Finn' Hannes Kolehmainen (who had won the 10,000m two days earlier) and the French runner Jean Bouin, both of whom smashed the world record. He next competed in the 3,000 metre team race together with his friends, William Cottrill and Cyril Porter once again taking the bronze medal.

On leaving school George became a gentleman's outfitter, and then, on 5 March 1908, he attested for six years' service with the Uckfield Special Reserves Royal Sussex Regiment. Deciding on a full time career with the army he enlisted on 12 August 1908, was promoted to corporal on 1 May 1912, and then sergeant on 5 August 1914. Shortly before sailing to France on 12 August 1914 he learned that his wife was expecting their first child. His daughter was born days before his death, so he might well have known of her birth but alas never got to see her. He was killed in action during the battle of the Marne on 14 September 1914. It was a bad day for the battalion, losing fifty-nine officers and men, including the commanding officer, Lieutenant Colonel Montresor, Major Cookson, Lieutenants Daun and Hughes, the Hon Herbert Lyttleton Pelham, son of the 5th Earl of Chichester, and Captain Durnford-Slater. George was initially posted as being missing in action. It was known he had been wounded and left behind during his battalion's fighting retreat, so hope that he had survived and was a prisoner of the

Germans was high. It wasn't until a year later when no trace of him could be found that it was assumed he had died from his wounds on 14 September 1914. His widow was later granted a pension of sixteen shillings a week for herself and her daughter. His body was never recovered or identified and he is commemorated on the La Ferté-sous-Jouarre memorial. The *Sussex Express* wrote on Friday, 27 August 1915:

FAMOUS ARMY RUNNER. LEWES SOLDIER'S DEATH. THE LATE SERGEANT G. W. HUTSON.

Although so far back as last September Sergeant G. W. Hutson, of the 2nd Batt. Royal Sussex Regiment, was reported to be missing, it was only last week that his wife, who lives at 3, Roseland-cottages, Cliffe, Lewes, received an official notification of his death. It was in 1908 that Sergeant Hutson joined his Regiment, and he soon became famous in the Army as a runner, his first noteworthy event being in a regimental cross-country race whilst stationed at the Curragh, when he beat all favourites. From that time he had a very successful career as a runner. Among his chief successes were: Two third prizes at the Stockholm Olympic Games; three years in succession the four-mile A.A.A. champion of England; one mile champion (A.A.A.) of England; three-quarter mile world's record holder; two years in succession champion of Austria; three miles champion of Sweden; and twice winner of the Atlanta Cup. He was a member of the Surrey Athletic Club. Sergeant Hutson, who leaves a widow and child, with whom much sympathy is felt, was most popular among a large circle of friends. His mother and father live at 12, Harley-lane, Heathfield, and he was their eldest son.

He is also commemorated on the Lewes and Heathfield War memorials.

Lieutenant Eduard von Lütcken
1912 Stockholm
Germany
Equestrian Single and Team Event
Silver Medal
Royal Saxon Ulan Regiment Nr.17
Died 15 September 1914 aged 31

'Captured a Russian general during the early months of the war'

Eduard von Lütcken was born on 26 October 1882 in Syke, Niedersachsen, Germany. He was the only son of Eduard von Hermann von Lütcken, a local magistrate and Frida (née Meding). He was educated at the University of Heidelberg where from 1903 he joined the Corps Vandalia Heidelberg where he took part in 'student duelling', being scarred on one cheek as a result. He later settled in Oschatz.

An outstanding rider, he was selected to compete for the German side during the 1912 Olympic Games. Riding Blue Boy, he came eighth in the individual jumping event. However in the team event, together with Carl von Moers, Richard von Schaesberg-Tannheim and Friedrich von Rochow, he came second taking a silver medal, the Swedish team taking the gold.

Shortly before the outbreak of the war he was serving as an instructor at the riding school in Dresden. On the declaration of the war he was transferred to the Royal Saxon Ulan Regiment Nr.17 serving as oberleutnant. Fighting on the Eastern Front in Szumsk in Lithuania he captured a Russian general officer, staff captain and a number of Russian soldiers during a patrol. He was killed in action on 15 September 1914 while on patrol at Szumsk (Kowno). Encountering a superior Russian force on a reconnaissance patrol on the Wilkowitzki–Mariompol road, he had his horse shot from under him and was subsequently killed in the following action. An account of his death and its interesting aftermath was reported later:

> 'Whilst the Unteroffizier lay like dead with several wounds, the Oberleutnant [Lütcken] fought on with several remaining troopers against ten to 15 Russians, he with his Browning pistol and when the last round had been expended with his sabre, until finally cut down by the Russians with his two remaining comrades.

The severely wounded NCO survived and managed to return to his regiment and report on the death of Eduard v. Lütcken and his lancers.'

Interestingly, through the Red Cross, the family received a post card at the end of November 1919 from a Russian Guards cavalry lieutenant by the name of Boris Genischta with the following message:

'Oberleutnant v. Lütcken found his death on 2 September 1914 (Russian calendar). Fighting to the end, he died with his weapon in his hand. He astounded us by his courage and spirit. As a witness to his death, I feel compelled to have you inform his relatives.'

Private 2nd Class Louis Desire Bach
1900 Paris
France
Football
Silver Medal
128ᵉ Régiment d'Infanterie
Died 16 September 1914 aged 31

'The youngest player at the Olympics'

Louis Desire Bach was born on 14 April 1883 in Paris France. He played for Club Français Paris (founded in 1890, disbanded 1935). The team were selected to represent France in the Olympic football competition in Paris in 1900, representing Union des Sociétés Françaises de Sports Athlétiques (USFSA). The team consisted of Pierre Allemane,

Bach is believed to be standing on the back row, second from the left.

Louis Bach, Alfred Bloch, Fernand Canelle, R. Duparc, Eugène Fraysse, Virgile Gaillard, Georges Garnier, René Grandjean, Lucien Huteau, Marcel Lambert, Maurice Macaire and Gaston Peltier. Bach was the youngest member of the team at only 17 years of age.

France defeated Belgium easily in the opening game 6–2. The Belgium team was very inexperienced and was made up of players from various Belgium clubs, as well as students from the Universities of Liège, Louvain, and Brussels. The British team represented Upton Park Football Club. They were by far the best team of the three teams that played at the Paris Olympics. Playing a 2-3-5 system they defeated the French 4–0 in a very one-sided affair. It was their only match and they did not play again. England took the gold, France the silver and Belgium the bronze.

Bach enlisted into the ranks of the 128^e Regiment of Infantry in 1904 leaving two years later in 1906. However he remained on the reserve. At the outbreak of the war he was called up again on 2 August 1914 rejoining his old regiment. He was killed in action on 16 September 1914 in Servon-Melzicourt, Marne, France.

Louis Bach was buried in the Nécropole Nationale de Saint Thomas-en-Argonne, Marne, grave number 1953.

6867 Private 2nd Class Charles Devendeville
1900 Paris
France
Swimming (Underwater) – Water-Polo (Team)
Gold (Water Polo)
151ᵉ/1ᵉ Infantry Regiment
Died 19 September 1914 aged 32

'The Only Gold ever awarded in Underwater Swimming'

Charles Devendeville was born on 8 March 1882 in Lesquin in northern France. After a basic education he became a house painter. He had always been a powerful and enthusiastic swimmer, playing water polo for the French club Tritons Lillois.

Aged 18 he was selected to represent France in two events during the 1900 Olympics in Paris: underwater swimming (no longer an Olympic event) and water polo. To succeed in the underwater swimming competition swimmers had to earn points for various aspects of the event. These were allocated, two points for each metre swum underwater and one point for each second the swimmer was able to remain submerged. The event took place in Paris on the Seine between the Courbevoie Bridge and the

Devendeville is believed to be one of the swimmers pictured here.

2nd Class Private, Alexandre François Étienne Jean Bouin
(better known as Jean Bouin)
1908 London; 1912 Stockholm
France
Bronze Medal (1908) Silver Medal (1912)
Running
3 Mile Team (5,000 metres) (1908) 5,000 metres (1912)
141st Infantry Regiment 163rd Infantry Regiment
Died 29 September 1914 aged 25

'The fastest man in France'

Jean Bouin was born on 24 December 1888 in Marseille, France. His father died shortly after his birth and his mother remarried a man by the name of Galdini who Jean never got on with. The family moved to 111 rue Consolat in the district of Chartreux, Marseille, where Jean was also educated. Jean enjoyed most sports but specialized in both fencing and gymnastics. In 1903 he met the famous French runner Louis Pautex during a training session at the local Borely Park. Seeing something in the teenager Pautex agreed to train Jean who now began to specialize in athletics. On 28 February 1904 Jean won his first race, a 10,000-metre cross-country event, and he established an athletics club at his school. Offered a job as a courier by a banker working for the General Society of Canebier he left his small athletics club and joined the more prestigious 'Phocaea Club Marseille'. Running for his new club throughout 1904, he won fourteen of the seventeen races in which he ran.

At the beginning of January 1905 Jean took part in his first race outside the Marseille district. Running in the 11 km Lyon Ayçaguer challenge he came ninth. After this his stepfather persuaded Jean to take part in a race in Genoa, Italy. Jean won the race by a good distance only to discover that his stepfather Galdini had already claimed his purse and spent it. For Jean it was the final straw in an already tempestuous relationship. He left home and moved in with his old school friend Joseph Granier and his sister Rose whom he later married. Despite the family problems Jean continued with his winning ways taking a 5,000 metre race in August 1905 in a time of 18 minutes and 20 seconds before going on to win the Criterium de Provence. In 1906 he improved his winning time in the 5,000 metres to 16 minutes and 38 seconds. In 1907 he came third in the National Cross Country Race and thirteenth in the Cross of Nations, the first time France had ever taken part in the race. After finishing first in the 18 km Nice–Monaco race he was selected to run for France in the 3-mile race during the 1908 Olympic Games in London. Not for the first time in the games, controversy surrounded placings in the final. The French team came in third and Jean broke the French record. However as a punishment for an unauthorized night out, the French federation refused to recognize the award of the bronze medal or Jean's record. To this day it is unclear whether the bronze medal was awarded to Jean or not.

In 1909 Jean became France's cross country champion. He came second in the Cross of Nations behind Edward Wood before going on to break several French records and receive a gold clock from his many supporters in his home province of Marseille, engraved with the initials 'JB'.

The following year, 1910, Jean was called up to do his national service and was enlisted into the 15th company of the 141st Infantry Regiment, then stationed at Fort de la Revère not far from Nice. He also changed his club to the 'Athletic Club of the General Society of Marseilles' and won the cross country national championship with them for the second year running. It wasn't all good news however and due to a fall early on in the race Jean was obliged to retire from the Cross of Nations race.

His running success continued in 1911 and he once again became the French Cross Country Champion before going on to become the World Champion. In November 1911 he set the first of his world records, this time in the 10,000 metres (a record he would keep for ten years).

In 1912 he was selected to take part in the Olympic Games in Stockholm. Running in the 5,000 metres Jean won the silver medal being beaten to the gold in the very last second of the race by the Finnish runner Hannes Kolehmainen. Remarkably both men broke the world record.

In 1913 Jean moved to Paris with his wife Rose Granier and began running for the 'Athletic Club of the Société Générale de Paris'. On 6 July 1913 while running in Stockholm Jean broke yet another world record, this time in the one hour run (19,021 metres) becoming the first person to exceed the nineteen kilometres in one hour. He also began writing for the French sports magazine *La Vie au grand air* (launched in 1898 under the editorship of the press baron Pierre Lafitte) and took part in a four-minute film called *Pommery Parc de Reims*.

On 2 August 1914 Jean was mobilized into the 141st Regiment in Nice. Although he had the opportunity to remain behind at base in a training capacity he refused, insisting on being sent to the front with his regiment on 13 September. Jean Bouin was killed by shrapnel during a French bombardment on 29 September 1914 during an attack on 'Mont Sec' during the last days of the first battle of the Marne. He posthumously received the Military Medal.

Tragically, Rose Granier was sent for to identify his body. A great French hero, all of France mourned his death. He was buried at the castle of Bouconville-sur-Madt. In his will Jean left everything to Rose Granier. However his stepfather contested the will demanding that all Jean's properties be handed over to him. After a lengthy legal process Rose was finally awarded Jean's effects.

After the war on 27 June 1922 the body of Jean Bouin was exhumed and buried with full military honours in the cemetery of Saint-Pierre, square 30 grave 81. A bust of Jean Bouin sculpted by Constant Roux now sits above his grave, a permanent reminder of one of France's greatest athletes.

As well as having several sports stadiums and races named after him, in 1960, on the occasion of the summer Olympics, a stamp with the effigy of Jean Bouin was issued.

Alexandre Étienne coming second to the Finn Hannes Kolehmainen in 1912.

Corporal Georges de La Nézière
1896 Athens
France
Athletics
26ᵉ Infantry Regiment
Died 9 October 1914 aged 36

Athlete and rally driver

Georges de La Nézière was born on 18 July 1878 in Paris. His parents were Philip Ernest Daviel, *counselor du prefecture*, and Marie Therèse (née Massé). He had two brothers, both painters and illustrators, Joseph and the more famous Raymond. Raymond was a well-known illustrator and writer who worked under various names such as Raoul, René or Robert de la Nézière. He was an early French comics artist best known for his drawings of horses and his anthropomorphic animals.

Georges was a difficult child, unkindly nicknamed 'the devil in flesh' because of his continual bad behaviour. In the end his parents, despairing, sent him to boarding school in the hope it might calm him down. In 1892 he was sent to a Dominican-run boarding school, Alberto Magno Arcueil. It was to be the making of him. One of the teachers at the school was Father Didon. Didon saw great sporting potential in Georges.

In 1895 Nézière ran the 2,000 metres in 5 minutes and 53 seconds, and the 1,000 metres in 2 minutes and 52 seconds. He became the college cross country champion and the Paris all schools and colleges champion.

In 1896 he was selected to run for France in the 800 metres during the Olympic Games held in Athens. With Father Didon as escort, together with twenty other

24

students from his college and his brother Raymond, he travelled to Athens. Running in the 800 metre dash he was placed third in the preliminary heats but failed to advance.

In 1899 he joined the army and because of his interest in engineering started to work on armoured cars, attempting to show how you could put a Maxim machine gun onto a military vehicle. After leaving the army he joined Rouen Business School and took part in the Paris to Berlin race in 1901. The race, which took place in June, was broken down into three parts, Paris to Aachen 263 miles (in which he came 27th), Aachen to Hanover 278 miles (28th) and finally Hanover to Berlin 186 miles (29th). Over a hundred cars entered the race, which was eventually won by the French pioneer motorist Henry M. Fournier in a time of 16 hours and 5 minutes at an average speed of 44.12 miles per hour, quick for the time.

In 1903 Georges married Hélène Laborde with whom he had two children.

At the outbreak of the First World War he was recalled to the territorials serving as a corporal in 11 company, 26e Infantry Regiment, which formed part of the 84 division. He was shot and killed by machine gun fire on 9 October 1914 in the forest of Mouchy ten miles from Arras.

Lieutenant Thomas Cunningham Gillespie
1912 Stockholm
Great Britain
Rowing
New College Men's Coxed Eight
Silver Medal (Team)
2nd Battalion King's Own Scottish Borderers
Died 18 October 1914 aged 21

'A man who saw duty before he saw life'

Thomas Cunningham Gillespie was born on 14 December 1892 in Alvington, Gloucestershire. He was the younger son of Thomas Paterson Gillespie and Elizabeth (née, Chambers) of Longcroft, Linlithgow. He was educated at Cargilfield Preparatory School, Cramond Bridge and Winchester College. He entered Kingsgate House and later became a Commoner Prefect. He was President of the Boat Club in his last year, played in Commoner XV and took a leading part in the work of the Natural History Society. He went up to New College Oxford in 1911 where he was a member of the College VIII for three years, being part of the crew that was Head of the River twice. In 1912 he was part of the crew that was selected to attend the Olympic Games in Stockholm, rowing number three. Two Oxford boats took part in the Olympics, New College and Leander/Magdalen College. In heat 4, held on 17 July, New College beat the Norwegian boat *Christiania* in a time of 6:42.5. In the quarter finals New College defeated the Swedish boat *Roddklubben* of 1912 in a time of 6:19.0. They rowed alone in the semi-final going through to meet Leander/Magdalen College in the final. The Stockholm course, much like the Oxford and Cambridge Boat Race course, was not straight, so winning the toss and getting the better lane was important if victory was to be secured. In time-honoured tradition the two captains tossed to decided which side of the river they would get. New College won the toss and following gentlemanly tradition offered the choice of lanes to their opponents. In their turn and in a gentlemanly fashion Magdalen were supposed to turn this offer down and allow New College to decide which side of the river they wanted. However on this occasion the Magdalen captain acted like a 'bounder' and accepted New College's offer taking the better side of the river. As a result Leander/Magdalen went on to win the race and take the gold medal, leaving New College with the silver. King Gustav V of Sweden was so angry at this breach of protocol and ungentlemanly conduct that he presented his colours to New College. Ever since this date, New College have raced in purple and gold, the colours of the royal house of Sweden. To add to this, a toast made by New College Boat Club on the evening of the race, 'God Damn Bloody Magdalen!', which were the words spoken by the New College stroke Robert Bourne as he watched Magdalen take the gold, is repeated to this day. The abbreviation GDBM has been used commonly ever since, and is still on the bottom of the NCBC letterhead.

Gillespie was also a leading member of the University OTC and obtained a university commission in the King's Own Scottish Borderers, joining the 2nd battalion at the outbreak of the First World War. He left for the front almost immediately. He served a couple of weeks on the Aisne under continuous shell fire and then orders were given to try and advance eastwards across the La Bassée Canal. It was during this operation that Gillespie was killed near La Bassée on 18 October 1914.

A few days before he was killed he wrote his last letter home to his father:

October 16, 1914

My Dear Daddy,

We have been moved from the Aisne right round to the North, and are now operating in the region we were originally intended for.

We had a soft time during our transit, and were kindly treated, so we knew we were in for something stiff. Nor have we been mistaken. We marched up country for several days, and did 30 miles of the way in French motor transport wagons, which showed us there was some hurry. They packed us very close; it was fearfully dusty, and the springs were very bad. I have had more comfortable and clean drives.

We spent one night in a house in which some N. French refugees, quite good class men, were also stationed. They have to get out when the Germans come anywhere near, as they are one of the reserve classes, and may be wanted. If they stayed, and the Germans got into their towns, they would all be made prisoners. We all had dinner together in style and were very friendly.

We moved on the next day and were billeted that evening at a castle, where we were entertained most hospitably by a French lady and her daughters, and I actually got a night between the sheets. It was a paradise there. Heaven and Hell are close together sometimes; we were in the latter not many hours after leaving the castle.

Next day we attacked the Germans in the afternoon and advanced a considerable way. They gave us a pretty hot time though, any amount of bullets flying, and one company lost two officers killed dead and one wounded. At dusk I found myself with two platoons rather ahead of the rest of the line (I had started in reserve, but things got mixed) near a cottage and a trench of French soldiers. There were German snipers loosing at us close ahead. We entrenched there by night. I had the Frenchmen under my command too, as all their officers had been killed. I found two poor fellows lying fearfully hurt in a ditch with several dead, and managed to get a bottle of wine out of their packs for them without the sniper getting me.

Fortunately a captain came and took command. Next day, having been about all night digging, I was shifted to make room for some other company.

I advanced to a cemetery to defend it and stayed there most of the day. It is a beastly thing to have to do, digging trenches among graves and pulling down crosses and ornamental wreaths to make room. One feels that something is wrong when a man lies down behind a child's grave to shoot at a bearded German, who has probably got a family anxiously awaiting his return at home.

We were at the edge of a village and the Germans were entrenched about 200 yards on. One could see heads in the trench sometimes, and sniped at them. There was a large brown barn door behind one man, a look-out, I think. I and a corporal had several shots at him, and later in the day I noticed through my glasses a white cross scratched on the door. It is a grim thought, but you have to think of individual Germans as a type of German militarism even if they are not.

The church tower also was fired at by us, the belfry windows being our object. If everyone agreed only to treat churches as such, one would feel more comfortable.

We slaughtered a lot of Germans in the failing light, who advanced in close order along the road. Then we had to quit, as the post was too advanced for the night, and the Germans came in.

It was a miserable day, wet, and spent in a cemetery under those conditions. There was a large crucifix at one end. The sight of the bullets chipping Christ's image about, and the knowledge of what He had done for us and the Germans, and what we were doing to His consecrated ground and each other, made one feel sick of the whole war (or sicker than before).

The next day we spent lying in the trenches there, with little to do except lie low, as shells from the Germans and, I fear, our own guns too were dropping near us. Towards evening a party of about forty Germans charged the left of our line from about 300 yards away. They made a noise like 'All, All', when they came out of the wood, 'Deutschland über alles,' I suppose.

Mad fools they were to charge like that across a wet beetroot field. They must have thought about ten of us were there. Barely ten of them struggled back wounded. All that night we spent expecting to be attacked. Nothing came though, our bayonets were not inviting. In the early morning we were relieved by French troops. The last I saw of that place was the shattered crucifix standing up against the dawn, and the glare of a score of burning homesteads all round.

We were marched back, a muddy, wet, tired, and hungry crowd, to rest. We lost two officers killed, one died of wounds, and three wounded, besides a large quantity of men. But our reward was to come when we got into billets — a letter from Sir Charles Fergusson,

Com. 5th Division, saying that the Corps Commander wished him to express his great appreciation of our conduct and grit and courage, saying how proud he was of us and thanking us.

A friend later wrote of him: 'Tom was a great strong, fearless, affectionate fellow: his men must have believed in him and loved him for what he obviously was to the eye. But there was much more to him than that …'

His body could not be recovered or identified, and he is commemorated on panel 15 of Le Touret Memorial.

His brother Alexander Douglas Gillespie, who was also killed in the war, on 25 September 1915, describes in letters home how he unsuccessfully searched the area his brother was known to have fallen in an effort to find his body. See *Letters from Flanders* by the Right Reverend Hubert Burge a former Headmaster of Winchester and published by Smith Elder in 1916. Thomas Cunningham Gillespie is also commemorated on his school memorial.

During an edition of the BBC TV programme *Countryfile* it was revealed that Gillespie was the great uncle of presenter Tom Heap.

Árpád Pédery
1912 Stockholm
Hungary
Gymnastics
Silver
Austro-Hungarian Army
Died 21 October 1914 aged 23

'Destined for Athletic greatness from an early age'

Árpád Pédery was born on 1 February 1891 in Budapest. He trained with and represented NTE, Budapest. A keen, keep fit enthusiast, he began his gymnastics training while still at school.

In 1912 he was selected as part of the Hungarian gymnastics team to take part in the Olympic games being held in Stockholm. The team event was held on 11 July 1912 at the Stockholm Olympic stadium. It was the first time this event had

The Hungarian team at the Stockholm opening ceremony.

ever been staged at the Olympics (it would appear in the Olympics on only one more occasion, in 1920 in Belgium). Five teams from five nations took part: Germany, Great Britain, Luxemburg, Italy and Hungary. Between sixteen and forty athletes formed each team. There was a time limit on their performance of one hour including the march in and march out. The Swedish Olympic Committee provided the fixed apparatus, which consisted of four horizontal bars, four parallel bars, four pommelled horses, and four Roman rings. Each team had to provide their own hand apparatus for the freestanding exercises. Exercises on the horizontal bar, parallel bars, and pommelled horse were compulsory. A maximum of 58 points could be scored. The Italians won the gold medal with a score of 53.15 points, the Hungarians came second with 45.45 points and Great Britain the bronze with a score of 36.90.

During the First World War Árpád Pédery served with the Austrian-Hungarian army and was killed in action early in the campaign in Luzsek, Galicia on 21 October 1914.

Major Béla (Vojtech) Zulawszky
1908 London; 1912 Stockholm
Hungary
Fencing
Silver Medal (1908)
(individual Sabre)
Died 24 October 1914 aged 45

'One of the finest blades in Hungary'

Béla Zulawazky was born on 23 October 1869 in Tokaj, Borsod-Abaui-Zemplen, Hungary. On leaving university in 1897 he became a gymnastics teacher at a military academy in Koszeg. He also taught, sabre, épée and sword and dagger. He was a member of MAC (Hungarian Athletics Club). As a result he became a member of the very successful Hungarian national fencing squad between 1908 and 1914. He competed in the 1908 Olympics held in London winning a silver medal in the individual sabre, being beaten to the gold by fellow Hungarian Jeno Fuchs (1882–1955) whose overall Olympic record was 22 wins, 2 losses, and 1 draw. He won two gold medals for fencing during the 1908 Olympics, individual sabre and team sabre. The Hungarian team won eight medals for fencing during the 1908 games coming second to France who won one more bronze than them. In 1982 he was finally inducted into the International Sports Hall of fame. He competed again in the 1912 Olympics but failed to qualify in any of his events.

In 1912 he was commissioned into the Hungarian Army rising to the rank of major. He was killed in action during the early months of the First World War on 24 October 1914 in Sarajevo. His ashes were interred in the cemetery of Koszeg.

2982 Private 1st Class Joseph Racine
1912 Stockholm
France
Cyclist
113ᵉ Infantry Regiment
Died 28 October 1914 aged 23

France's fastest cyclist

Joseph Racine was born on 18 July 1891 in Clichy, Hauts-de-Seine, France. A keen cyclist he was selected to represent France in the 1912 Olympics to be held in Stockholm. He came 40th in the individual road race in a time of 11 hours 50 minutes and 32.7 seconds. Although low down the field he was still the fastest French man riding at the event. The winner and gold medallist was the South African cyclist Rudolph Lewis (1887–1933) in a time of 10 hours 42 minutes and 39 seconds. Second and silver medallist was the British cyclist Freddie Grubb (1887–1949) in a time of 10 hours 51 minutes and 24.2 seconds, third place and the bronze going to Carl Schutte (1887–1962) of the USA in a time of 10 hours 52 minutes and 38.8 seconds. Racine came tenth in the ten-mile team event in a time of 49 minutes 44.53 seconds. The event was won by Sweden in a time of 44 minutes and 35.33 seconds, Britain came second in a time of 44 minutes and 44.39 seconds, and the USA third in a time of 44 minutes and 47.55 seconds.

Racine enlisted into the army at Seine Bureau 2 in October 1912 and was posted to 113ᵉ Infantry Regiment with whom he was still serving when war was declared in 1914. He was killed in action on 28 October 1914 in the Argonne Forest Meuse, France.

3834 Private 2nd Class Alphonse Adrien Meignant
1912 Stockholm
France
Rowing (Men's coxed four)
31ᵉ Bataillon de Chasseurs à Pied
Died 4 November 1914 aged 32

'A fine rower and man'

Alphonse Adrien Meignant was born on 27 March 1882 in Paris. He enlisted into the army in Paris (Seine 3rd Bureau) in October 1903 and served until 1905 with the 31ᵉ Bataillon de Chasseurs à Pied.

Always a keen rower, on returning to Paris after his national service he began to row for the Paris-based Société Nautique de Bayonne. Such was his progress that he was selected to row for France in the men's coxed fours during the 1912 Stockholm Olympics.

1912 Olympic opening ceremony at Stockholm, Sweden.

The Extinguished Flame

The men's coxed fours with inriggers, also referred to as the coxed four with jugriggers, was one of the rowing events held for the one and only time during the 1912 Olympics. It took place on Wednesday, 17 July to Thursday, 18 July 1912. Thirty rowers from four nations took part: Denmark (*Nykjøbings paa Falster Roklub*), France (*Société Nautique de Bayonne*), Norway (*Christiania Roklub*), Norway (*Ormsund Roklub*), Sweden (*Göteborgs Roddförening*), and Sweden (*Roddklubben af 1912*). The French crew consisted of Charles Garnier (bow), Alphonse Meignant (number two), Auguste Richard (number three), Gabriel Poix (stroke) and Francois Elichagaray (cox). The French boat was eventually knocked out of the competition by Norway in the quarter-final. The gold was finally taken by the Danish boat *Nykjøbings paa Falster Roklub*, the silver by the Swedish boat *Roddklubben af 1912*, and the bronze by Norway in *Ormsund Roklub*.

On 2 August 1914, at the outbreak of the First World War, Meignant was called up from the reserve and rejoined his old regiment, 31e Bataillon de Chasseurs à Pied, as a private second class. He was killed in action at chapel St Éloi, Belgium, on 4 November 1914 during the First Battle of Ypres. His burial place is unknown.

2nd Lieutenant Gerard Rupert Lawrence Anderson (Twiggy)
1912 Stockholm
Great Britain
Hurdler
1st Battalion Cheshire Regiment
Died 11 November 1914 aged 25

'He had wings on his heels'

Gerard Rupert Lawrence (Twiggy) Anderson was born on 15 March 1889 in Twickenham. He was the son of David Anderson, an Anglican prebendary, and Blanch Alice May. He had one older brother and a sister, Arthur Emilius David and Mona Constance Anabel. He was educated at Eton College where he picked up the nickname 'Twiggy', and was Captain of the Oppidans and President of 'Pop'. After Eton he went up to Trinity College Oxford. Twiggy was a notable athlete and was the AAA champion at the 120-yards hurdles in 1909–10 and 1912. While at Oxford he won blues in 1910 and 1912 (he was ill in 1911). The first to perfect a new style of hurdling and using this to good effect on 16 July 1910 at the Crystal Palace, Anderson set the first IAAF world record in the 440-yards hurdles with a time of 56.8 seconds. As a result of his success

he was selected to take part in the 1912 Olympic Games in Stockholm and was favourite to win a medal. However due to an accident in the men's 110 metres Anderson was disqualified. Anderson's brother Arthur Anderson, a Cambridge blue, was also a well-known runner at both 100 and 200 metres. Although he took part in the 1912 Olympic Games he failed to win a medal. Anderson took a first in Greats and in 1912 won a Prize Fellowship at All Souls. After graduating from Oxford, Anderson became a manager at the Cammell Laird shipyard in Birkenhead.

Three days after the outbreak of war Anderson enlisted into the ranks before being commissioned on 16 October 1914 as a second lieutenant into the 3rd Battalion Cheshire Regiment, being attached to the 1st Battalion. Travelling

612 Sergeant Richard Francis Charles Yorke
1908 London; 1912 Stockholm
Great Britain
Athletics
14th Battalion London Regiment (London Scottish)
Died 22 December 1914 aged 28

'Run for the game not the prize'

Richard Francis Charles Yorke was born on 28 July 1885 in Kensington, London. He was the son of Charles Vincent George Yorke, who died in 1908, and Martha of 24 Woodstock Rd, Bedford Park, Chiswick. On leaving school he became a bank clerk.

York showed early promise as an athlete and joined the Blackheath Harriers on 31 October 1903. He came second in the Nichols Cup in 1904 and second in the club 10-mile championship in 1905. He left the Harriers in 1907. In 1908 he was selected to run for Great Britain in the 1908 London Olympics. Running in the 3,200 metre steeplechase, Yorke was eliminated in the first round.

Selected once again to run in the 1912 Olympics this time being held in Stockholm. Unfortunately he was eliminated from both the 800 and the 1,500 metres in the first rounds and failed to win a medal.

Richard Yorke winning yet another race.

Richard Yorke enlisted into the ranks of the 7th Middlesex Volunteer Rifle Corps (London Scottish) in 1906 joining 'B' company. Continuing with his running he won the Territorial Army National Mile Championships in 1909, 1910 and 1911. On 25 September 1909 he won the London Athletic Club Challenge Mile, defeating the holder, F.A. Knott, by fifteen yards in a time of 4 minutes and 28 seconds. He also won the Dr Voelcker prize for the most points during the year's sports. In 1909 he came third in the AAA's mile and the following year, on 12 March

Richard Yorke on the Western Front, 1914.

1910, Yorke won the six mile cross-country race against the Gordon Highlanders at Aldershot helping the London Scottish defeat the Gordons' 92 points to 118. On 9 July 1910 he helped the County of London win the Grand Aggregate Cup at the National Championships by winning the one mile race. On 19 September he was elected Captain of the London Scottish Athletic Club. He set a new record for the 1,000 yards at the London Athletic Club on 24 June 1912 in a time of 2 minutes and 17 seconds. He won the one mile against Cambridge University Freshers on 15 November 1913. During all this activity Yorke also found time to marry Lillian Maud McNee in Westminster on 6 July 1914 and they later moved to Fairlawn Court, Chiswick Park, Middlesex.

On the outbreak of the war Yorke volunteered for overseas service, was promoted to sergeant, and together with his battalion travelled to France on the SS *Winifredian* on 15 September 1914. He survived the fighting at Brown Road Wood and Messines where the London Scottish covered themselves in glory. Yorke took command of the Machine Gun Section after Lieutenant Ker Gulland was killed in November 1914. Sergeant Yorke was shot in the head and killed by a German sniper concealed in a haystack at Givenchy on 22 December 1914 while he was positioning his machine gun.

He is buried in Arras Road Cemetery, Roclincourt, grave ref: III. N. 29.

Richard York's 1914 trio and memorial plaque.

Corporal André Jules Henri Six
1900 Paris
France
Underwater Swimming
Silver Medal
24e Section du COA (*Commis et ouvriers d'administration*)
Died 1 April 1915 aged 26

'Accidentally killed after a life of service'

Olympic swimmers in Paris, 1900.

Commemorative card for 1900 Olympics and World's Fair.

André Six was born on 15 July 1879 at Nord on Lambessart. A keen swimmer he swam for the French Tritons Lillois swimming club. In 1900 he was selected to compete for the French swimming team in the underwater swimming event. It was the one and only time in Olympic history that this event was held. The swimmer was awarded two points for each metre he swam underwater and one point for each second the swimmer was able to remain submerged.

André Six swam the 60 metre underwater course in a time of 65.4 seconds scoring 185.4 points taking the silver medal. His friend and fellow countryman Charles Devendeville (died 19 September 1914) took the gold.

Six enlisted into the army in Lille in 1910 serving until 1912. At the beginning of the war he was called up from the reserve in August 1914 and served in the 24e Section du COA. He was killed in an accident on 1 April 1915 while serving as a corporal at Fort de Chelles, Seine et Marne.

1915

Lieutenant Georg Krogmann
1912 Stockholm
Germany
Football
61st Infantry Regiment Reserve
Died 9 January 1915 aged 28

Member of the highest scoring football club in Olympic history

Georg Krogmann was born on 4 September 1886 in Meldorf, Schleswig-Holstein, Germany. A gifted footballer playing centre half he established himself with Holstein Kiel, 'The Storks'. He was in the loosing squad when the Storks were defeated by Karlsruher FV in the final of the German Cup. However playing them in the German Cup again on 26 May 1912 the story was different, with Kiel taking the honours 1–0. The month before his cup success on 14 April 1912 Krogmann was selected to play for Germany in the match against Hungary. In a hard-fought match the final score was 4–4.

In 1912 he was selected as part of the German football squad to play in the 1912 Stockholm Olympics. The tournament attracted a record eleven European entries with over 135 footballers taking part. Germany's first round match was played on 29 June 1912 at the Råsunda Stadium, Stockholm. They were defeated 5–1 and knocked out of the main competition. During the consolation matches Germany lost to Austria 5–1 and to Hungary 3–1 before defeating Russia 16–0. The German player Gottfried Fuchs equalled the record for most goals scored in an international match (set by Sophus Nielsen of Denmark during the 1908 Olympics) scoring ten goals during the match against Russia. Hungary finally won the consolation tournament. England took the gold in the main tournament defeating Denmark 4–2. Netherlands took the bronze by defeating Finland 9–0.

During the First World War Krogmann served as a lieutenant with the 61st Infantry Reserve. He was killed in action on 19 January 1915 in Warsaw.

Reservist Max Herrmann
1912 Stockholm
Germany
Athletics
100 metres, 200 metres, 400 metres, 4×400 Relay Team
No.7 Company 41st Infantry Regiment
Died 29 January 1915 aged 29

First World Record Holder at 4×100 Relay

Max Herrmann was born on 17 March 1885 in Gdansk, Pomorskie, Germany. Herrmann was a sprinter who ran for Berliner SC, Berlin. He was German champion in 1911 and 1913 in the 400 metres, and was also runner-up seven times in the 100 and 200 from 1910 to 1913. His personal bests were outstanding in their day. In the 100 metres it was 10.8 seconds

German team at the 1912 opening ceremony.

which he achieved in 1910, 21.9 in the 200 in 1914, and 49.9 in the 400 achieved in 1913.

He took part in the 1912 Stockholm Olympic Games competing in the 100, 200 and 400 metres as well as in both relays. The team reached the semi-final of the 4×100 metres, the first time this event had been run in the Olympic Games. Thirty-three runners from eight nations competed. Only Germany replaced one runner, replacing Karl Halt with Otto Röhr. Running together with Röhr, Erwin Kern and Richard Rau, the team set a world record time of 42.3. Great things were expected of them in the final but unfortunately the team was disqualified after a fault with its second baton passing, the British team going on to win the event in a time of 42.4. Their disqualification left the event without a bronze medallist, making it the only athletics event to award only two medals. It was also the first official world record for the 4×100 metres relay. Alas it wasn't a good games for Herrmann. He was knocked out in the first round of the 400 metres. In the 200 metres he made it as far as the semi-final before being eliminated.

Joining the German army at the outbreak of the war he served on the Eastern front. On 29 January 1915 he was sent out on a snow-shoe patrol and was initially reported as missing, however it was later established that he had been killed while a prisoner of the Russians.

Corporal Georges Adam Charles Lutz
1908 London
France
Cyclist
Men's 20 and 100 kilometres
106e Régiment d'Infanterie
Died 31 January 1915 aged 30

'Ill luck stopped him being the finest cyclist in France'

Georges Lutz was born on 3 November 1884 in Paris France. He cycled for CASG Paris and took part in two events during the 1908 Olympics in London, the first being the 20 kilometres held at the White City on 14 July 1908. The race was finally won by the British cyclist Clarrie Kingsbury with Ben Jones, another British rider, taking the silver and the German rider Joseph Werbrouck the bronze. Lutz next took part in the 100 kilometres. This race was considered to be the premier race in the round of cycling events to such an extent that the Prince of Wales donated a cup to be presented to the winner. On the day of the final, a heavy rainstorm saturated both riders and course. The race was also marred by multiple punctures and accidents. It was finally won by the British rider Charles Bartlett, with Charles Denny, another British rider, taking the silver and the Frenchman Octave Lapize the bronze. Georges Lutz finished tenth.

Lutz enlisted in the army at the Seine 6th Bureau, Paris, in October 1905, serving until 1907 but remaining with the reserve. He was recalled from the reserve on 2 August 1914 being promoted to corporal. He died of typhoid fever in the Hôpital Mixte at Bar-le-Duc, Meuse on 31 January 1915. He is buried in the Nécropole Nationale of Bar-Le-Duc, grave number 1202.

Private Kenneth Powell
1908 London; 1912 Stockholm
Great Britain
Tennis/110 metres hurdles
Honorable Artillery Company
Died 18 February 1915 aged 29

'Determined to the end'

Kenneth Powell was born on 8 April 1885 in Hampstead, London, the second son of James and Mary Powell of Ivanhoe, Aldersyde, Reigate, Surrey. He had five brothers and sisters, Hilda, Leslie, Vera, Doris and Douglas.

He was educated at Rugby School where he shone at most sports. A fine all-round sportsman he captained the school fifteen at Rugby and was honoured as Victor Ludorum for his athletic ability two years running. He was a very fine rackets player reaching the final of the public schools competition in 1903, and was a prominent member of the school's gymnastic eight.

After leaving school he went up to King's College Cambridge where he concentrated on athletics and tennis. He won his athletics blue in the 120 yards hurdles against Oxford in 1907–08 and a further blue for lawn tennis. In the AAA championships he had the remarkable record of being placed in the first three for six successive years (1909–14) without ever winning the title and in 1907 he twice set the British record.

Quick and energetic he stood a little over six feet tall and played tennis left-handed. His main asset was his break service together with an excellent volley, which made him a formidable opponent. It was said that his only weakness was his backhand, which he never really mastered. He was a member of the 1905 Cambridge University Lawn Tennis Club which was then captained by one of the finest tennis players ever to hold a racket, Tony Wilding (Wimbledon singles champion, killed in action 9 May 1915). Kenneth Powell became team captain in both 1906 and 1907, and in 1908 he defeated Major Ritchie to the singles title at the

Queens Club Championship, Richie retiring in the second set. In the same year he also went on to win the Covered Court Championships in Sweden.

Between 1905 and 1913 Powell competed in eight Wimbledon championships. His best singles result came in 1913 when he defeated the favourite Charles Percy Dixon (four-time Olympic medallist who led the British team to Davis Cup victory in 1912 as well as being a finalist in the singles at Wimbledon and winner of the men's doubles). He finally lost to the German Oskar Kreuzer in the quarterfinals.

He took part in the 1908 Olympic Games in London, competing in the singles but losing to the German Otto Froitzheim in the first round. In the men's doubles, together with his partner Walter Crawley, he was eliminated in the quarterfinals. Surprisingly he also participated in the 110 metres hurdles competition but was once again eliminated in the first round.

Four years later in 1912 he took part in the Stockholm Olympics, this time coming a respectable fifth in the 110-metre hurdles final, the Americans taking the first four places. He had led for most of the way but faded towards the end.

On leaving Cambridge he joined the family firm of leather factors in London. On 2 September 1914, shortly after the outbreak of the war, he entered the ranks of the HAC (Honorable Artillery Company) having previously seen service with the Territorials and was sent to France with them on 18 September 1914. He was seriously wounded by a gun shot at Kemmel on 17 September 1915, succumbing to his wounds on the 18th.

He is buried in the Commonwealth War Graves section of the churchyard in the small Belgian village of Loker, grave reference II. D. 7. He left an unsettled personal estate with net value of £11,257.

Captain Edward Radcliffe-Nash
1912 Stockholm
Great Britain
Equestrian
16th Lancers
Died 21 February 1915 aged 26

'A better horseman you will never see'

Edward Radcliffe-Nash was born on 9 June 1888 in Ballycartee, Tralee, Co. Kerry the son of Lieutenant Colonel Edward Nash JP, late of the Essex Regiment, and Constance, daughter of John Radcliffe JP of Moorfield, Withington. He was first educated at Mr Bull's Preparatory School, Westgate on Sea between 1898 and 1902 before going up to Eton where he remained between 1902 and 1905. While there he distinguished himself as not only a long distance runner but also as a 'wet bob' winning the Junior Sculls in 1905 and stroked his Junior House Four to Head of the River.

Deciding on a career in the army he won a place at the Royal Military College, Sandhurst, and while there proved himself to be a remarkable athlete, winning the equivalent of the Victor Ludorum cup, quite a feat in one so young. On 29 August 1906 Edward Radcliffe Nash was gazetted as 2nd Lieutenant into the 16th Lancers. He was promoted to Lieutenant on 15 January 1909 and then Captain on 10 October 1914. While with the regiment he ran twice in the Army Championship for the mile, coming second on both occasions.

His main passion however was riding. He was first and second in successive years at the Grafton point-to-point, won his Regimental Light Weight Steeplechase twice, and was 'placed' at numerous other meetings.

He was selected as part of the British Equestrian team to take part in the 1912 Olympic Games to take place in Stockholm. Riding his horse 'Flea' he failed to finish in the individual eventing or the team eventing. However, still riding Flea in the individual jumping event, he managed to finish twenty-ninth.

In August 1914 he was sent to France with his regiment. He took part in the retreat from Mons, the battle of the Marne and the Aisne, and the First Battle of Ypres. He was later mentioned in Sir John French's despatches (8 October 1914) for his courageous work during the BEF fighting retreat. He became acting adjutant of his regiment before being killed in action when the trench which he was occupying was blown up on 21 February 1915.

A brother officer later said of him: 'As conspicuous for dash, energy and endurance in War as in sport, he was the ideal cavalry officer and appeared to have a distinguished career before him. His exuberant vitality found expression in all that he said or did, and one who knew him well, observed on hearing that he had been killed: "Of all the deaths in this war, his death is the hardest to realize".'

Captain Edward Radcliffe-Nash is buried in the Ypres Town Cemetery, West-Vlaaderen, Belgium, Row G, Grave 4.

Captain Llewellyn Charles Nash, King's Royal Rifle Corps, Edward Nash's younger brother, died of wounds seven months later on 28 September 1915.

Private Adolf Kofler
1912 Stockholm
Austria
Cycling
Cyclist Company of the 24th Infantry Battalion
Died 13 March 1915 aged 23

'The bravest cyclist in Austria'

Kofler in the middle of photograph
with the white cap.

Adolf Kofler was born on 12 January 1892 in Graz, Steiermark, Austria. A gifted and popular cyclist, on 2 June 1912, Adolf qualified to cycle for the Austrian team in the 1912 Olympics to be held in Stockholm. He finished fourth in the selecting competition held on a street track between Purkersdorf, Rekawinkel, St Pölten, Sieghartskirchen and Purkersdorf (three laps, total 291 kilometres) in a time of 11 hours 17 minutes 44 seconds.

Much was expected of the young cyclist, however despite his best efforts the Austrian team only managed to come seventh in the team event. The team event consisted of twelve riders per team, with the top four finishers from each team counting towards the team's total time. The race was held on 7 July 1912 in Stockholm over 196 miles (315.385 km). The event was won by Sweden, with Great Britain taking the silver, and the bronze going to the American team. In the individual time trial Kofler only managed thirty-first. There were 151 entrants, 123 of whom eventually started. The riders set of at two-minute intervals, the first at 7 am. The South African Rudolph Lewis took the gold in a time of 10-42:39.0. The silver was taken by the British rider, Freddie Grubb in a time of 10-51:24.2. The bronze went to the American Carl Schutte in a time of 10-52:38.8. Adolf Kofler came home in a time of 11-39:32.6.

During the war he served with the Austrian army being killed in action on 13 March 1915 in Monte Piano, Bolzano-Bozen, Italy.

The Extinguished Flame

The following obituary taken from an Austrian paper of the time probably explains his career, military service and death best:

The Styrian Champion Racer Adolf Kofler Has Fallen

On April 13, the same day that the congenial young racer Hans Griebler, who had fallen in the southern theatre of the war, was being carried to his grave, Adolf Kofler, his brother-in-law, had died a hero's death for his Fatherland in the Ampezzo Valley. With much sorrow the Austrian cycling community mourns the death of one of its best and most promising racers, one who did not shy away from foreign competitions and every time was prepared to don Austria's colors and to bring honor upon it. The champion racer also regularly participated in large Austrian road races and his name was constantly to be found on the winners' list. Also within the Viennese racing circle the Styrian enjoyed much respect. As the lone Styrian participant, Kofler successfully competed in the cycling race at the last Olympics in Stockholm. Examples of his more notable successes are the following: multiple alpine and road cycling championships for Styria; the Austrian alpine championship in 1913; first place in the Graz—Semmering—Graz road race in 1913 (record time), two-time winner of the tour of Graz (record time), winner of the Graz—Marburg—Graz road races for 1911 and 1912, Graz—Mureck, tour of the Niederung, Fehring—Feldbach—Fehring, as well as various road races covering shorter distances. Kofler earned second or third place in: the Wien—Graz—Wien endurance race, the tour of the Gletscher, the tour of the Hochschwab, the tour of the Görzer Karst, the tour of the Winerwald, etc. The Styrian champion racer met his hero's death while in his third year of military service. He joined the Graz Hausregiment, 27th Infantry Regiment, as a recruit, and in order to better devote himself to racing, eventually managed to secure a transfer to the Cyclist Company of the 24th Field Jäger Battalion, which was commanded by the well-known military sportsman, Captain Jalic. Right from the beginning of the war Kofler demonstrated his bravery in the northern theatre and was thus awarded the Silver Bravery Medal. Having fallen ill with dysentery, he recuperated for several weeks in his hometown and then departed for the southern theatre of the war, from where time and again his spirited cycling exploits were reported, and because of which the aspiration for a Golden Bravery Medal was realized. Now he had to atone for his daredevil conduct, for in the valiant fighting during an attack along the Schluderbach he sacrificed his young, promising life. Just as he had always been a dear comrade for his fellow athletes, so too had he faithfully sacrificed his life for the Fatherland.

Captain Wyndham Halswelle
1906 Athens; 1908 London
Great Britain
400 metres
Gold-Silver-Bronze
1st Battalion Highland Light Infantry
Died 31 March 1915 aged 32

'The only man in Olympic history to win by a walkover'

Wyndham Halswelle was born on 30 May 1882 in London (although considered Scottish) to Scottish parents, Edinburgh-trained artist Keeley Halswelle (who exhibited at the Royal Scottish Academy and was a member of the Institute of Painters in Oil Colours and contributed to the *Illustrated London News* as well as illustrating several books including Wordsworth's poems and Scott's poems) and Helen Marianna Elizabeth Gordon.

He was educated at Charterhouse School where he became a noted athlete. While there he decided on a career in the military going on to the Royal Military College, Sandhurst. He was commissioned into the Highland Light Infantry in 1901 and travelled with them to South Africa to take part in the Boer War in 1902. While serving with the regiment in Africa his sporting prowess came to the notice of Jimmy Curran, a former professional athlete and coach, and under his direction began to take athletics seriously. He became the army champion in the 880 yards in 1904 and in 1905 he won the Scottish and AAA 440 yard titles. During the Intercalated Olympics in Athens in 1906 he took the silver medal in the 400 metres and a bronze in the 800 metres. In the same year he won the 100, 220, 440 and 880 yards races at the Scottish championships held in Powderhall. An injury to his leg ruined his 1907 season, however he came back with a vengeance in 1908 when he set a world record 300 yards, winning the race in a time of 31.2 seconds, and later achieved a British record in the 440 yards in a winning time of 48.4 seconds.

Because of his remarkable form, Halswelle was selected to race in the 1908 Olympics in London. The 1908 Olympic Games were originally supposed to have taken place in Rome, but a particularly violent eruption of Vesuvius in 1906 caused severe financial problems for the Italian government and the games were moved to London. Halswelle reached the final of the 400 metres with the fastest qualifying time and an Olympic record 48.4 seconds. In 1908 the 400 metres was not run in lanes as it is today and this was to cause a serious problem and change Olympic rules forever. The race got away to a quick start, however the American runner William Robbins baulked Halswelle within the first fifty metres. Coming off the final bend, Robbins led by a yard, with Halswelle waiting to pass him in the last straight, a tactic that had worked well for Halswelle previously, but another member of the American team, John Carpenter, ran wide and using his right elbow to stop Halswelle passing forced Halswelle to run wide almost forcing him of the track. His actions didn't go unnoticed and one

of the umpires screamed 'foul!' As a result of Carpenter's actions the race was declared void. It was clear that Carpenter had in fact blocked Halswelle but US rules allowed this so in Carpenter's eyes he had done nothing wrong. Olympic events were run under stricter rules (British rules did not allow for this either).

There had been problems between the American and British authorities from the start of the games. The row started by the omission of the American flag from the stadium at the opening ceremony, and intensified when the American standard bearer, discus thrower Martin Sheridan, refused to dip the flag on passing the royal box. To add to these problems, the Irish athletes, wanting to draw attention to demands for home rule, boycotted the games, and the opening ceremony descended into farce, with a series of rows over flags involving Sweden, and Finnish athletes who objected to running under the Russian flag. The result caused an unseemly spectacle as American athletes and officials remonstrated publicly and heatedly with the British officials. The partisan crowd spilled onto the field and for a time it looked like a full-scale riot was about to take place. However the intervention of the London police, truncheons drawn, eventually managed to restore calm.

The Olympic committee ordered the race to be run again two days later, this time without Carpenter who had been disqualified. As a result, and in support of their teammates, the other two American races refused to run, so Halswelle ran the race by himself, although Halswelle had no taste for it and only ran because the three AAA officials insisted. As the only runner he won the gold medal in a time of 50.2 seconds. It is the only time in Olympic history where the final was a walkover. From the 1912 Olympics onwards, all 400 metre races were run in lanes. The fiasco also helped lead to the foundation of the International Amateur Athletic Federation, to establish uniform worldwide rules for athletics. Halswelle retired from athletics in 1908 still feeling bitter about what had happened during the Olympics.

At the outbreak of the war Captain Halswelle travelled to France with his battalion and while attempting to save the life of a brother officer on 31 March 1915 during the battle of Neuve Chapelle was shot though the head by a sniper and killed. Halswelle had been wounded by shrapnel earlier in the action (although some accounts say he had been shot by the same sniper who eventually killed him) while leading his men across an area known as Layes Brook. In the earlier action, despite his wounds he refused to be evacuated and continued at the front, heavily bandaged. He was shot and killed while trying to get a wounded brother officer into cover. For his actions on this day he was mentioned in despatches.

The Highland Light Infantry regimental magazine described in some detail the action in which Halswelle, together with seventy-nine other members of the regiment, were killed to gain fifteen yards of ground:

> 'I called on the men to get over the parapet... There is great difficulty in getting out of a trench, especially for small men laden with a pack, rifle and perhaps 50 rounds in the pouch, and a bandolier of 50 rounds hung around them, and perhaps four feet of slippery clay perpendicular wall with sandbags on the top. I got about three men hit actually on top of the parapet. I made a dash at the parapet and fell back. The Jocks then heaved me up and I jumped into a ditch – an old trench filled with liquid mud – which took me some time to get out of.'

Halswelle was initially buried close to where he fell, his grave marked with a wooden cross, with his name written in charcoal. Later his remains were reinterred in the Royal Irish Rifles Graveyard at Laventie near Armentières, grave reference III. J. 2.

One of the battalion's greatest heros, the Royal Highland Fusiliers still award the Wyndham Halswelle Memorial Trophy to the winner of the 400 metres at the Scottish under-20 championships. He remains the only British athlete to have won gold, silver and bronze medals in individual Olympic events. In 2003, he was posthumously inducted into the Scottish Sports Hall of Fame. His Olympic medals and other trophies are displayed there and are well worth a view.

Lieutenant Geoffrey Barron Taylor
1908 London; 1912 Stockholm
Canada
Rowing
Bronze Medal Coxed Eight – Bronze Medal
Coxless Four
15th Battalion Canadian Infantry
Died 24 April 1915 aged 25

'The first Trinity member from the dominion nations to fall in the war'

Geoffrey Barron Taylor was born on 4 February 1890 in Toronto Canada. He was the son of William John Mahaffy and Stella Bertha Taylor, of 49 Heath St West, Toronto. While at school he excelled at rugby, football and rowing and served as his school's athletics director in his final year. Of all the sports he excelled at, it was rowing that was to bring him the greatest distinction.

Rowing for the Argonaut Rowing Club, Toronto, he was selected to row stroke for Canada in the coxed eight and coxless fours at the 1908 London Olympics. Together with his crew, which was made up of Gordon Balfour, Becher Gale, Douglas Kertland, Walter Lewis, Charles Riddy, Irvine Robertson, Julius Thomson and Joe Wright, they managed to take the bronze in the coxed eight after being defeated in the semi-finals by the eventual gold-medal-winning Leander crew from Great Britain. Although the coxless four were eliminated in the opening round they were still awarded the bronze medal as there were only four teams in the event.

On leaving school in 1910 he went up to the University of Toronto where he obtained a degree in applied science. He came close to obtaining a Rhodes Scholarship in 1912 but attended Trinity College Oxford anyway.

He was selected once again to row in the coxed eight for Canada in the 1912 Olympics held in Stockholm. His crew was once again defeated by the British Leander crew who went on to win the event and take the gold.

When the First World War broke out Taylor remained at Trinity College taking a commission in the 15th battalion (48th Highlanders of Canada) Canadian Expeditionary Force on their arrival in England in February 1915. On 22 April 1915 Taylor found himself in the line at St Julien, opposite Langemarke, where chlorine gas was used for the first time in Flanders. Geoffrey Taylor was reported missing on 24 April 1915, one of 6,000 casualties suffered by the British army, one third of whom died. According to an eye witness account, Taylor 'was last seen making his way to a deserted farm house a short distance back from the trenches'.

Geoffrey Barron Taylor was the first Trinity member from the dominion nations to fall in the war. His body was never discovered or identified and he is commemorated on the Ypres (Menin Gate) Memorial, panel 18-24-26-30.

Lieutenant Gilchrist Stanley Maclagan
1908 London
Great Britain
Rower
Gold Medal
3rd attached 1st Battalion Royal Warwickshire Regiment
Died 25 April 1915 aged 35

'Small in stature, large in heart'

Gilchrist Stanley Maclagan was born 5 October 1879 in London the son of Dr and Mrs T.J. Maclagan. He was educated at Eton where he steered the second eight but it wasn't until he went up to Magdalen College Oxford that his undoubted talents came to notice. While at Oxford he obtained his blue and steered the Magdalen crew Head of the River in 1900. He also coxed the Oxford boat in the Boat Race for four years between 1899 and 1902, being a member of the losing crew on three occasions and the winning crew on one (1900). He joined the Leander Club and coxed their boat at Henley Royal Regatta from 1899 to 1908. He set the record of being the only man to be in the winning crew in the Grand Challenge Cup six times. He was Honorary Secretary of the Amateur Rowing Association at the outbreak of war. In 1904 he became a member of the London Stock Exchange.

In 1908 he was selected as cox of the Leander eight at the London Olympics, defeating the much-favoured Belgium crew and winning the gold medal (Canada and Great Britain taking the bronze). He was one of six old Etonians that made up the Leander crew.

In September 1914 Maclagan was commissioned into the 3rd battalion the Royal Warwickshire Regiment, later being attached to the 1st. In December 1914 he went out with a draft of officers to make up the 1st battalion's heavy casualties. He served in the trenches for the next four months until he was finally killed in action during the Second Battle of Ypres at Pilkem Ridge, West-Vlaanderen, Belgium, on 25 April 1915. It was a disastrous day for the battalion: 17 officers and 500 other ranks were killed, wounded or missing.

The day before the attack, 24 April, Sir John French ordered counter-attacks towards Kitchener's Wood and St Julien to restore gaps that had been created in the line. The official history describes the 10th Brigade attack:

'The battalions of the 10th Brigade were able to pass the wire of GHQ Line under cover of the mist but, before they could open out, they came under rifle and machine-gun fire…and it was at once obvious that snipers were out in the rye grass and other crops that gave cover from view, and that some of the farms between Wieltje and St Julien were in the hands of the enemy. The brigade, therefore, shook out into fighting formation somewhat earlier than intended. Its advance, visible from many points, was carried out in faultless order… The fire now came mainly from machine guns hidden in the houses of St Julien and the upper stories of farm buildings, with cross fire from Kitchener's Wood, and particularly from two farms south of it (Oblong and Juliet) … By rushes the leading lines advanced more than quarter of a mile till they were within one hundred yards of the outlying houses of St Julien. Then…the lines paused and became stationary and for twenty minutes the Germans deluged them with machine-gun fire, very effective and very heavy. A few men tried to crawl back into cover, but the majority of those in the leading lines never returned; mown down, like corn, by machine guns in enfilade, they remained lying dead in rows where they had fallen. The following lines were pinned to the ground by fire and, after several efforts to advance…rose and surged back to cover in the folds of the ground and hedges behind them… A new line was quickly organized… The losses of the 10th Brigade in its magnificent but hopeless attempt had been heavy … mostly irreplaceable, well trained men … In compensation for the disaster that had overtaken them, the battalions had the satisfaction of knowing later that they had stopped any possible enemy advance in the St Julien quarter.'

The 10th Brigade front lines had in essence been wiped out.

Maclagan's body was never recovered or identified and he is commemorated on Ypres (Menin Gate) Memorial, West-Vlaanderen, Belgium, panel 8.

21563 Private William Davidson Anderson
1906 Athens
Great Britain
400 and 800 Metres
5th Battalion Canadian Infantry (Saskatchewan Regiment)
Died 26 April 1915, age not known

'Billy Whizz'

William Davidson Anderson was born in Ireland but at the tender age of six months moved to Scotland with his parents and settled in Glasgow. A talented runner he joined the Glasgow-based Olympic Harriers and later the Bellahouston Harriers. In 1905 he became the Scottish AAA champion. In the same year he won the 880 yards race in the Scotland vs Ireland games.

Selected to run in the 1906 Olympic Games in Athens he competed in both the 400 and 800 metre events. Anderson qualified for the 400 metres final after winning the

British Olympic Team, 1906.

repêchage race in 53.0 seconds, the equal fastest time of the Games, but was off form for the final two days later and ran a poor race coming eighth and last. He failed to qualify for the final of the 800 metres.

At some point after the Olympics, Anderson emigrated to Saskatchewan in Canada. On the outbreak of the First World War he enlisted into the ranks of the 5th battalion, Canadian Infantry and travelled to France with them. He was killed in action during the Second Battle of Ypres on 26 April 1915. He is buried in Boulogne Eastern Cemetery, grave VIII. A. 31.

Captain Ralph Chalmers
1908 London
Great Britain
Fencing
2nd Battalion Suffolk Regiment
Died 8 May 1915 aged 24

A view of the Ypres Menin Gate Memorial.

'Mentioned for bravery on the day he was killed'

Ralph Chalmers was born on 13 January 1891 in Fitzroy Road, Primrose Hill, London. He was the elder son of the first Baron Chalmers, of Northiam, and Maud Mary (née Pigott) of Peterhouse Lodge, Cambridge. He was educated at Bradfield College before going up to Oriel College Oxford in 1908. Deciding on a career in the Army he attended the Royal Military College Sandhurst before being commissioned into 2nd battalion Suffolk Regiment in 1910. He was aide-de-camp to the Governor of Ceylon between 1913 and 1914.

A talented fencer, he took part in the individual épée fencing competition during the 1908 Olympic Games in London. He was only 17 years old. However he didn't advance beyond the first round.

At the outbreak of the Great War he returned to the 2nd battalion, Suffolk Regiment rising to the rank of captain. He was killed in action during the Second Battle of Ypres at West-Vlaanderen on 8 May 1915. He was mentioned in despatches for his bravery on the day he was killed.

His body was never recovered or recognized and he is commemorated on the Ypres Menin Gate Memorial Panel 21. He is also remembered in the memorial book at St Stephen's Church, Gloucester Road, London SW7.

His brother Lieutenant Robert Chalmers was killed a few weeks later on 26 May 1915. With both his sons dying in the Great War and only a daughter, Mabel, remaining (died in the 1960s), on Lord Chalmers death in 1938 the title became extinct.

Chalmers War Memorial St Stephen's Church, Gloucester Rd, London.

Lieutenant Henry Mills Goldsmith
1908 London
Great Britain
Rowing (Men's Coxed Eight)
Bronze Medal
3rd Battalion Devonshire Regiment attached 2nd
Battalion Lincolnshire Regiment
Died 9 May 1915 aged 29

'Considered to be one of the outstanding oarsmen of his day'

Henry Mills Goldsmith was born on 22 July 1885 in Compton Gillord, Plymouth, Devon, the second son of John Philip Goldsmith, solicitor of Devonport. He was educated at Sherborne School before going up to Jesus College Cambridge. Nicknamed 'Rosie' he was considered to be one of the outstanding oarsmen of his day. He rowed number five in the college first boat from 1906 and in the same year was elected president of the Cambridge University Boat Club, an honour not afforded to a Jesus man for twenty years. He took part in the Oxford and Cambridge Boat Race rowing number three in the winning boat in 1906, repeating this in 1907 by a winning by a margin of four and a half lengths. He also rowed number three in the famous victory against the Harvard boat on 8 September 1906 winning by a little over two lengths in a time of 19 minutes and 58 seconds. Later a profile of Goldsmith in the Cambridge magazine said of his leadership qualities:

> '…the tact he showed in negotiations with Harvard and the way his genial presence inspired the crew in the sweltering heat of Bourne End and Putney, these things are not written' (*The Granta*, 13 October 1906, pp 13 & 14).

Because of his outstanding form he was selected to row in the British boat at the 1908 Olympic Games to be held in London. This time instead of taking seat number three, his usual position, he was seated five. Britain were beaten in the semi-final by the Belgian boat *Club Nautique de Gand* and took the bronze medal.

Graduating in 1908 he missed out on Jesus becoming Head of the River in 1909, something at which he later expressed regret. However in May 1911 he returned to the college boat and defeated the *Club Nautique de Grand* in the famous race at Terdonck. It was a fine revenge as the Belgians had beaten them in the Olympics and forced them out of the final. In a hard-fought race honour had finally been satisfied. He later wrote of events: 'You can't imagine what good fellows these Belgians are. Their great ambition is to be like English "sportsmen" in the best sense of the word.' It was to be a cruel irony that of the crew that went to Belgium, six were to die during the First World War defending the neutrality of Belgium.

In 1909 he was commissioned into the 5th (Territorial) battalion Devonshire Regiment. In 1913 he met and married Sybil Elizabeth Perrens, the daughter of the late Mr W. King Perrens of Torquay, and they settled at Rockmoor, Yelverton, Devon. They had one daughter, Elizabeth, born in August 1915, alas several months after Harry met his death.

He was promoted to lieutenant in 1910 and on mobilization was appointed ADC to the general commanding the Wessex Division. Keen to get to the front, he was transferred first to the 3rd battalion Devonshire Regiment going to the Front in March 1915. He was then attached to the 2nd battalion Lincoln Regiment and appointed machine gun officer of the battalion, later becoming machine gun officer to the headquarters of the 25th Brigade. Harry was killed in action on 9 May 1915 at Fromelles during the Second Battle of Ypres, one of more than 11,000 casualties sustained on the British side on that day.

The Dean of Jesus, writing in the *Cambridge Review* wrote of him: 'Tall and apparently slightly built he was an oarsman of unusual power, not only because of his easy and graceful movements, but on account of the immense strength he put into every stroke. Absolutely unaffected and modest in everything, he is a type of man whose loss makes us feel more poignantly the sacrifices that our struggle with Germany demands.'

His remains were never recovered or identified and he is commemorated on the Ploegsteert Memorial, Panel three. He is also commemorated on the war memorial at Marker and the Crapstone War Memorial.

Captain Anthony 'Tony' Frederick Wilding
1912 Stockholm Olympics
Australia
Tennis
Bronze Medal
Royal Marines
Died 9 May 1915 aged 31

'He had displayed the greatest bravery'

Anthony (Tony) Frederick Wilding was born in Christchurch, Canterbury, on 30 October 1883, the second of five children born to Frederick Wilding and Julia Anthony. Both his parents were British and had emigrated to New Zealand from Hereford in England in 1879. His father Frederick practised law in Christchurch and was also a fine sportsman, playing cricket for New Zealand. Anthony Wilding was brought up in some comfort in a large house called 'Fownhope', which had a swimming pool, tennis courts, a croquet green and a cricket wicket.

Anthony, like his father, was a good all-round sportsman, excelling at cricket, tennis and swimming. He was sent to Mr Wilson's school in Cranmer Square, Christchurch, for three years where his sporting prowess soon became obvious. As well as cricket he excelled at tennis and, in October 1901 at the age of 17, won the Canterbury Tennis Championships. Wilding left New Zealand in 1902 to attend Cambridge University where he hoped to gain a blue for cricket. However, once there he began to play more tennis than cricket. During the summer holidays of 1903, Wilding decided to play tennis on the tournament circuit with players who had enough of a private income to allow them to spend their time playing the game.

Despite his sporting activities, he still managed to pass his law examinations, graduating with a BA in 1905. In the same year he made his debut in the Davis Cup as a member of the Australian team.

Returning to New Zealand, he joined his father's law firm but after winning the New Zealand national tennis title in 1906, he returned to England and was admitted to the Bar at the Inner Temple. In this year he also won the Australian Open singles and doubles titles. Between 1907 and 1909 he helped the Australasian team win the Davis Cup and won his second Australian Open in 1909, the same year he qualified as a barrister and solicitor at the Supreme Court of New Zealand.

Returning to England, between 1910 and 1913 he won four successive Wimbledon titles, losing the 1914 final to Norman Brookes. He also won four doubles crowns, and in 1914 returned to Davis Cup competition, leading the Australasian side to another success.

Anthony also represented New Zealand in the Stockholm Olympics of 1912. In the men's singles covered court he defeated Silfverstolpe (Sweden) three sets to love in round one, Gronfors (Sweden) three sets to love in round two, and in the quarter finals he beat Caridia of Great Britain by three sets to love. However in the semi-finals he was defeated by Dixon (who was defeated by the French player Gobert three sets to love in the final) of Great Britain three sets to one. In the final round Wilding defeated Lowe of Great Britain three sets to love to take the bronze medal.

Unusually for the times, Wilding did not smoke or drink alcohol, and followed a strict training programme to keep up his level of fitness. He was not regarded as a naturally brilliant player but succeeded because he worked hard on improving his game, and was more consistent in his play than other players. In 1912 he wrote a book describing this life called *On the Court and off.*

At the outbreak of the First World War Winston Churchill advised Wilding to join the Royal Marines and in October 1914 he was gazetted as a second lieutenant in the Corps. He was attached to the Intelligence Corps before joining the Royal Naval Armoured

Wilding sitting in his military car in 1914.

Car Division in northern France, where he had thirty men, three guns, and armoured cars under his command. He was promoted to lieutenant and then in February 1915 served under the Duke of Westminster as an officer in a new squadron of Rolls Royce armoured cars. On 2 May Wilding received his captaincy and on 8 May wrote home to his parents, it was to be his final letter:

> For really the first time in seven and a half months I have a job on hand which is likely to end in gun, I, and the whole outfit being blown to hell. However, if we succeed we will help our infantry no end.

The following day, 9 May, he was killed in action at 4.45 pm while taking part in the battle of Aubers Ridge at Neuve Chapelle when a shell exploded on the roof of the dugout in which he was sheltering. A description of his death was later outlined in a report from his commander, Reginald Gregory, RN:

> The gun's crew was sent to the trenches for shelter, Captain Wilding and three Army officers retiring to a dug-out close by.
> This was, however, shortly afterwards struck by a large shell, which killed the officers there, Captain Wilding dying in such a manner that his death must have been instantaneous.
> I beg to draw your attention to the fine work carried out by this officer. His loss will be greatly felt from a technical point of view, as he was carrying out experiments of great importance. On every occasion he had displayed the greatest bravery, exposing himself to every risk whilst working the armoured cars with the advanced forces of the Army. His loss is much regretted by the officers and men of the Armoured Car Division under my command.

Captain Tony Wilding was buried the following day at the front but was later reinterred at the Rue-des-Berceaux Military Cemetery in Richebourg-l'Avoué, Pas-de-Calais, grave reference II. D. 37.

Shortly before leaving for the front he had become engaged to the famous Broadway actress Maxine Elliott.

After the First World War the Canterbury Lawn Tennis Association bought land in Woodham Road for tennis courts and named their new centre for Canterbury tennis Wilding Park. In 1978, Wilding was elected to the International Tennis Hall of Fame.

**135/51553 Private 2nd Class Herman Louis
Clement Donners
1908 London; 1912 Stockholm
Belgium
Water Polo
Silver Medal (1908) Bronze Medal (1912)
1e Grenadiers 2/3 (7e Comp)
Died 14 May 1915 aged 26**

'Two Olympics, Two Medals'

Herman Louis Clement Donners was born on 5 August 1888 in Antwerp. He was the son of Jean Henri Edmond Donners and Celence (née Verspreuwen). They resided at Antwerpen Schildersstraat 53.

A keen swimmer and water polo player he swam successfully for the Antwerpsche Zwem Club, Antwerpen. He was first selected to play in the Belgian water polo team during the 1908 London Olympics where the Belgian team came second and Donners won a silver medal. He was selected again in 1912, travelling to Stockholm to take part in the Olympics. This time he won a team bronze.

He enlisted into the army on 1 January 1914 and died of wounds received in action on 14 May 1915 in Calais.

Donners can be seen standing, furthest on the right.

29437 Private James (Jimmy) Duffy
1912 London
Canada
Marathon
91st Argyle Regiment/16th Battalion Canadian
Expeditionary Force
Died 23 May 1915 aged 25

'The king of marathoners'

James Duffy was born on 1 May 1890 in Lisacoghil, County Leitrim, the son of James and Mary Duffy. While Duffy was still a child the family moved to Scotland settling in Edinburgh (12 St Mary Street). After leaving school he was apprenticed as a stonecutter. He began cross-country running while at school and continued distance running after leaving. He began to race for Edinburgh Harriers winning the Scottish junior cross-country title in 1909 and gained the Scottish national record for five miles (25 minutes 52 seconds) in 1910. He also represented Scotland three times in the international cross-country championship. In 1911 he emigrated to Canada joining the migration of young, single Scots and Irish-Scots to Canada. Settling in Toronto he took a job as a porter with T. Eaton Company before continuing his trade as a stonecutter and sometime tinsmith. Becoming a keen member of the Central YMCA he represented them in the twenty-mile Ward Marathon (Marathon races had yet to be standardized) in 1911. The course followed the Lake Shore Road from the exhibition grounds (there and back). Duffy ran well and came second, this despite the fact he stopped half way through the race to argue with the supporters of another runner. The following year 1912 he raced in the 19 mile 186 yard Spectator Marathon in the Hamilton, Ontario 'Around-the-Bay' course. Twenty-five runners took part in the race in hot and humid conditions. Leading for most of the race Duffy, running in the colours of the Eaton's Athletic Association, was overtaken in the final mile by the American runner Harry Jensen who went on to win the race by twenty seconds. Only eight runners managed to finish the race. As the marathon was a qualifier for the Olympics, by coming second he was automatically selected to represent Canada in the 1912 London Olympic Games.

The Olympic distance was 24 miles and 1,725 yards. Running in the colours of the Eaton Athletic Club, Duffy's early pace was slow and by the half-way point he had been

1912 Around the Bay Road Race in Hamilton.

left far behind. With ten miles to go Duffy began to move up the field, although he had left it much too late to have any chance of being placed. The race was eventually won by the South African runner Kenneth McArthur, Duffy finishing a credible fifth, in 2 hours 42 minutes 18 seconds. It is still the best placing by a Canadian runner in the Olympic marathon to this day. The race wasn't without tragedy: in hot and humid conditions the Portuguese runner Francisco Lazaro died.

Returning to Canada, Duffy won both the Ward Marathon and the *Hamilton Herald*'s race around Hamilton Bay in a record time of 1 hour 46 minutes 15 seconds, a course record that would stand for 46 years.

Keen to improve, Duffy accepted full-time coaching from the famous athletic trainer Tommy Thomson. Relocating to Hamilton he joined the Ramblers Bicycle Club. Running for his new club Duffy won seven consecutive marathons, including the Yonkers Marathon in New York. On 20 April 1914, Duffy won the Boston Marathon in 2 hours 25 minutes and 1 second. Such was his fame by this time that Boston bookmakers would not take bets on Duffy winning. Duffy only had one rival – fellow Canadian Édouard Fabre. Fabre matched Duffy step for step throughout the race and it was only in the final mile that Duffy was at last able to pull ahead of Fabre going on to win the race by a narrow fifteen seconds.

The *Boston Post* described the event as 'the most sensational race ever held' and proclaimed Duffy 'the king of marathoners'.

After Boston, Duffy became a professional but didn't do well. Unfortunately people had lost interest in long distance running and Duffy only took part in a few races losing his first professional race to his old rival Édouard Fabre.

At the outbreak of the First World War Duffy enlisted into the ranks of the 91st Argyle Regiment, later transferring to the 16th battalion of the Canadian Expeditionary Force (Manitoba Regiment) and travelled with them to France. Private Duffy was among the first Canadian soldiers to see combat when the Manitoba Regiment took part in heavy fighting near Ypres, Belgium on 23 April 1915. This was part of a larger battle that saw the Canadians courageously hold the front line after the Germans used poison gas for the first time. Sadly Duffy was killed by shrapnel during a night-time counter-attack against German positions at Kitchener's Wood. He was one of the 278 members (out of 305) of the 16th Infantry Battalion (the Canadian Scottish) who were killed in the midnight assault. Ironically, on the day Duffy was killed, Édouard Fabre won the 1915 Boston marathon, becoming the new champion.

He is buried in Vlamertinghe Military Cemetery, grave reference I. F. 14.

Lieutenant Henry Alan Leeke
1908 London
Great Britain
Athletics
Men's Shot-Put, Discus Throw, Discus Throw
Greek Style, Hammer Throw, Javelin Throw,
Javelin Throw Free Style
'D' Company 9th Battalion Royal Warwickshire
Regiment
Died 29 May 1915 aged 35

A pioneer of athletic field events

Henry Alan Leeke was born on 15 November 1879 in Weston Hall, Stafford. He was the only son (although he had five sisters) of Mr and Mrs Henry and Elizabeth Leeke of Southdown Cottage, Seaford, Sussex. His father was a successful field athlete in his own right and was one of the pioneers of British hammer throwing, had been the AAC champion three times in 1868, 1870 and 1872, and had been the winner for Cambridge against Oxford in the Varsity games of 1868. He was also the grandson of the Reverend William Leeke, a well-known Waterloo historian who, at only 17, was the youngest ensign at Waterloo and became famous for carrying the Colour of the 52nd Light Infantry during the battle.

Henry Leeke was educated at Leamington College and Corpus Christi Cambridge between 1899 and 1902. In 1898 he married Catherine Herbert, younger daughter of Charles G. Fullerton. They had one son, Alan Charles Herbert and one daughter, and resided in Hill, Warwickshire. Associated with the London Athletic Club he was a fine all-round thrower, winning the AAA hammer in 1906 and coming second in the shot three times: 1903, 1906 and 1910. He won his blue 1901–03 in the shot put and hammer and won both events against Cambridge's old rivals Oxford in 1903. He was one of the first British athletes to take up the discus and set a British record with it in 1908.

At the 1908 Olympic trials, Leeke won the freestyle javelin with a throw of 135 feet 8½ inches (41.37 metres), but as the method used is not known this mark was never recognized as a UK record. Selected for the 1908 Olympics in London Leeke participated in no less than six events: the shot put, the discus, the Greek style discus, the hammer, the free style javelin and the javelin, but he failed to qualify in the top three in any of them.

On 22 September 1914 Leeke was commissioned into the 9th battalion Royal Warwickshire Regiment and became D Company's machine gun officer. Taken ill in France he returned home and was hospitalized at the Thornhill Isolation Hospital Aldershot. He died there on 29 May 1915 and was buried with full military honours in Aldershot military cemetery, AH 339.

Captain Oswald Armitage Guy Carver
1908 London
Great Britain
Rowing (coxed eight)
Bronze Medal
1/2nd (East Lancs) Royal Engineers
Died 7 June 1915 aged 28

'His widow later married Bernard Montgomery later Field Marshal'

Oswald Armitage Guy Carver was born on 2 February 1887 in Marple, Greater Manchester. He was the son of Oswald William and Katherine Armitage Carver. His father was a cotton goods merchant who owned Hollins Mill at Marple. He had been successful enough to buy Cranage Hall, near Holmes Chapel, Cheshire. Oswald was educated at Charterhouse School and Trinity College Cambridge. While at Trinity he rowed not only for his college but took part in the 1908 Oxford vs Cambridge Boat Race rowing number three. It was a Cambridge victory by two and a half lengths in a time of 19 minutes and 20 seconds.

Carver was selected to represent the Cambridge University Boat Club in the 1908 London Olympics, once again rowing at number three. Coached by Mr C.W.H Taylor and Mr W. Dudley Ward, they trained at Henley for three weeks to improve their general style of rowing. Unfortunately things didn't go well and the crew never really gelled. As a result on the day of the semi-finals they were below par and were comfortably beaten by the Belgian crew. They were however awarded the bronze medal together with the Canadian coxed eight.

On leaving Cambridge, Oswald became a director of his father's cotton company and in his spare time became very active in the scouting movement, introducing scouting to Marple. In the later months of 1911 he married Elizabeth Hobart at St James's Church Tunbridge Wells and they moved to The Hollies in Marple. They had two children, John Hobart Carver born on 30 November 1912 and Richard Oswald Hobart Carver born on 26 May 1914.

The East Lancashire Company of the Engineers was part of the Territorial Army. There seems to be uncertainty as to when Oswald took a commission with them, but on 3 September 1914 a few weeks after war was declared Lieutenant Carver volunteered to serve overseas. Unusually for the time his application was rejected by the Army's Medical Board at Bury because of his hearing. However a month later he applied again and this time was accepted. Whether strings were pulled or his condition was just a temporary one we will never be sure. On 10 September 1914 the Lancashire Territorials left England bound for Egypt and on 31 December of the same year Oswald was promoted to captain commanding one of the company's four sections.

At the beginning of May 1915, the Lancashire Territorials left Egypt and headed for Gallipoli. They were mainly employed preparing and repairing trenches, and establishing strong points and dugouts in preparation for a major allied offensive, later designated the Third Battle of Krithia, to commence on 4 June 1915. The Engineers main task was to follow the Manchester Regiment's main assault and secure the captured Turkish trenches. They were then to prepare strong points and dig out communication trenches in readiness for any Turkish counter-attack. Two Sections of Engineers, Nos. 3 & 4, were behind the 6th Manchesters, while No. 1 & 2 took up position behind the 8th battalion. Private Sheldon of 'C' company the 6th Manchester Regiment later recounted his experiences during the attack:

> I shall never forget the moment when we had to leave the shelter of the trenches. It is, indeed, terrible, the first step you take – right in the face of the most deadly fire and to realize that any moment you may be shot down; but if you are not hit, then you seem to gather courage and when you see on either side of you, men like yourself, it inspires you with a determination to press forward.

Sheldon was shot in the leg only a few yards from the British trenches. As they advanced, many Turkish snipers were missed and started shooting at the Manchesters from behind. At some point Captain Oswald Carver was hit in the back and fell. He was evacuated to 11th Casualty Clearing Station on 'W' Beach but died from his wounds three days later. On 2 July 1915 *The Stockport Advertiser* carried a moving tribute:

> The Scout movement has lost a very sincere well wisher and friend. Mr. Carver introduced the movement into Marple and gave it every assistance in his power. He seemed to realize the true spirit underlying it, not the popular one which I am glad to say is dying out, that it kept boys away from street corners, but the higher object, namely, that it gives an opportunity of applying their everyday life and games, the Christian principles they are taught in Church and School. Mr. Carver answered the call of duty immediately the War broke out and had not the opportunity of seeing the Troop since it was re-organized in August last. Now he has answered the higher call and we have lost his personal assistance.

Captain Oswald Carver is buried in the Lancashire Landings Cemetery, grave reference A.7.

His brother 2nd Lieutenant Basil Armitage Carver 6th Inniskilling Dragoons was killed in action on 21 August 1916. Also his cousin Geoffrey Hamilton Bagshaw 1st Royal Dragoons was killed in action 13 May 1915.

In 1927 Carver's widow married Bernard Montgomery later Field Marshal.

Lieutenant Alfred Georg Mickler
1912 Stockholm Olympics
Germany
Athletics
Reserve Infantry Regiment 203
Died 14 June 1915 aged 22

First German athlete to hold a single athletics world record

Alfred Georg Mickler was born 7 September 1892 in Charlottenburg, Charlottenburg-Wilmersdorf of Berlin. A gifted middle and long-distance runner he competed for Sports Club Charlottenburg. In 1911 and 1912 he was runner-up in the German 1,500 metre championship, a feat he duplicated in 1913. In the same year he also became the German champion in the 800 metres and set a world record in the 1,000 metres, making him the first German athlete to hold a world record in a single discipline. In 1914 he also competed for a season for Hungary, becoming the Hungarian champion, his personal best in the 3,000 metres being 9:19:2 and in the 1,500 metres 4:06:0.

Selected to run for Germany during the 1912 Stockholm Olympics in both the 1,500 metres and the 3,000 metres, he was eliminated from both competitions in the first rounds.

Mickler served as a lieutenant with the Reserve Infantry Regiment 203 during the war and was killed in action on 14 June 1915 in Tarnowski, Galicia.

German Infantry in 1915.

2nd Lieutenant George Eric Fairbairn
1908 London
Great Britain
Rowing Coxless Pairs
Silver Medal
10th Battalion Durham Light Infantry
Died 20 June 1915 aged 26

'Lost a Bronze Medal to gain a Silver'

George Eric Fairbairn (better known as Eric) was born on 18 August 1888 in Melbourne, Australia. He was the son of Thomas, a pastoralist concerned with the raising of livestock and animal husbandry, and Lena (née Simpson). They later moved to 9 Wilton St, Westminster, London.

Eric was educated at Geelong Anglican boarding school Corio Bay, before going to Eton College where he chose to become a 'Wet Bob' (rower). In October 1906 he went up to Jesus College Cambridge.

The Fairbairn family was already well known at Jesus College. Eric's uncle was Steven Fairbairn who is credited by many as being the man who turned the fortunes of the Jesus College boat and creating the 'Fairbairn style' of rowing. Steven Fairbairn, although a fine rower, was better known for his coaching. Basically Fairbairn wanted his crews to slide in their seats, which helped them use the power of their legs to much greater effect during the stroke. To this end he wanted longer slides fitted to the boats. He also wanted his oarsmen to concentrate on their oars and blade work and not how gracefully they moved in the boat. He called the advocates of the orthodox style the 'Pretty-Pretty Brigade' pointing out that crews never won medals and cups for style. Steven Fairbairn also took part in the Oxford-Cambridge Boat Race, rowing number five in 1882–83 and 1886–87.

It's also worth pointing out that Eric was not only a first class rower, but also a good Rugby player, turning out for Rosslyn Park FC. A popular character, a *Cock of the Roost* article gave us a small insight into the man: 'Like all geniuses, he has idiosyncrasies. He hates collars, takes no milk in his tea through fear of dead flies, and is a confirmed Peripatetic after bump-suppers.'

Eric quickly established himself in college rowing. He was head of the Lent bumps

1907, won the coxswainless fours, took part in the trials, and was finally selected to row number two in the 65th Boat Race held on 4 April 1908.

Cambridge went into the race as favourites, largely due to the fact that illness and injury swept through the Oxford crew. James Gillan, Oxford's number five, was banned from racing by his doctors. Influenza affected several members of the crew. A.G. Kirby still raced, despite not being fully fit, having suffered from a bout of jaundice.

Race day was cold with a strong head-wind but a good tide. Oxford won the toss and chose the Surrey side of the Thames, leaving the Middlesex side to Cambridge. Umpire Pitman got the race going at precisely 3.30 pm. Cambridge made the better start, out-rating Oxford by thirty-nine and a half to thirty-eight and began to pull ahead. The rough water also suited Cambridge's smoother, easier style and by the mile post they were clear. At Harrods Furniture Depository, Cambridge were a full two lengths ahead. Oxford spurted several times but the tactic failed; they were unable to close the gap and Cambridge were well ahead by Barnes Bridge. For the third time in a row Cambridge finally won the race, this time by two and a half lengths in a time of 19 minutes 20 seconds (the fastest time since the 1902 race). It took the overall record to 34–30 in Oxford's favour.

Eric had been a member of the winning crew in his very first Boat Race, which is more than his uncle Steven could achieve, Cambridge having been beaten by seven lengths in 1882.

Selected to row in the eight during the 1908 London Olympics, for reasons that were never really explained (maybe because of his Australian heritage) Eric lost his seat in the boat, replaced by fellow Jesus man and former Cambridge President, Henry Goldsmith. Eric remained as substitute. However the Cambridge eight were well beaten by the Belgians of the Royal Club Nautique de Gand [Ghent], twice winners of the Grand Challenge Cup at Henley. They did however pick up a bronze medal (fortunately the Leander crew saved the Empire's blushes by defeating the mighty Belgians in the final to win the gold).

However Eric would have his revenge. Teaming up with Philip Vernon (1886–1960) in the coxless pairs he went on to take a silver medal, beaten in the final by another British pair, John Fenning and Gordon Thomson. Eric must have gained a lot of satisfaction from that.

In 1909 Fairbairn captained the Jesus boat and was selected to row for Cambridge again in the Boat Race. However a week before the race Eric was forced to pull out due to illness. The Jesus boat also entered the Grand Challenge at Henley only to be beaten in the final by the Belgian eight, 'those pesky Men of Ghent'. They would have to wait until 1911 for another chance to take on the Belgians. He was back for the 69th Boat Race on 1 April 1911.

Oxford were the reigning champions having defeated Cambridge the year before by a convincing three and a half lengths. There was a particular buzz to this year's race due to the presence of Edward Prince of Wales and his brother Prince Albert who were to follow the race. To add to the excitement it was also the first race to be followed by an airplane, quite a rare sight in those days.

It was a clear day with a slight breeze and a strong tide. Oxford won the toss and selected the Middlesex side of the river giving Cambridge the Surrey side. The race began at 2.36 pm started by Umpire Pitman. Oxford set off at the faster rate. By the Craven Steps, Oxford were three-quarters of a length ahead, a lead they maintained to the mile post. By the Crab Tree pub Oxford were clear and by the time the Oxford boat reached Harrods Furniture Depository they were a further length ahead. At Hammersmith Bridge Oxford were two and a half lengths ahead and by the Chiswick Steps the Oxford crew were four lengths clear. Despite a late surge by Cambridge, Oxford maintained their lead winning by two and three-quarters lengths in a time of 18 minutes 29 seconds (the winning time was the fastest in Boat Race history). The overall record was now 37–30 in Oxford's favour. Eric had now won one and lost one. The disappointment of losing the Boat Race however was quickly put behind him as the greatest challenge of his rowing career loomed.

The following May 1911 the Jesus eight set out for what their coxswain, Conrad Skinner, called, 'The Belgian Expedition' rowing against the Belgian crew that had beaten them in 1909 in the Grand Challenge at Henley. Given the power of the Belgian eight the idea of a crew from a single college taking them on, never mind beating them, was greeted with a great deal of cynicism by the rowing world. *The Sportsman* wrote of the challenge, 'Once more it is necessary to point out that the Eight which has just left to row the Belgians is not a representative English crew. It is just Jesus College that is

going to race a combined Belgian crew, with the knowledge that the Belgians have won three of the last four occasions they have visited Henley – and when they were beaten it took one of the finest amateur eights, the Leander crew at the Olympic regatta. It is difficult to think that the Jesus men will win, but they carry with them the good wishes of their countrymen.'

However the crew did not lack experience or enthusiasm and contained six rowers that had been beaten by the Belgians in the 1909 Grand Challenge. They were itching for revenge. They were coached by the highly experienced Steve Fairbairn and Stanley Bruce (later Prime Minister of Australia). Thanks to the two coaches the Jesus eight started the race in great condition, able to produce between forty-three and forty-seven strokes per minute. On the day of the race, 25 May 1911, over 100,000 spectators lined the length of the Terdonck canal to see the race. Skinner later recounted his experience: 'Cheering broke out as the Belgian crew seized the lead on the first half dozen strokes, but then having set the boat moving in four quick but gradually lengthening strokes, we settled into our stride, and speedily drew level…we gave a 'ten' which let daylight in between our rudder and their bows, and with steady confidence this was increased to a lead of a length and a half before the bridge was reached. This huge structure marking the mile, witnessed the decisive struggle. Under cover of its shadow and hidden for perhaps a hundred feet from our opponents under our respective arches, we raised our stroke slightly and gave such a 'ten' that we leaped ahead…we both battled on to the finish, amid an uproar that was little short of deafening.'

Much to everyone's surprise the Jesus crew defeated the Belgians. The victory was hailed all over Cambridge and England: 'And these young fellows who had come down from Cambridge…to meet a picked Belgian crew just for the honour of English rowing…It was a thoroughly sportsmanlike piece of work on the part of the Jesus men. Their College may well be proud of them.'

Such was the excitement that a set of postcards was produced and over 170,000 copies were sold in a week. A march was also composed to the victory and thousands waited outside the banqueting hall just to glimpse their heros. Skinner later commented, 'No crew was ever feted as we were and many of us took shame at the poverty of England's welcome to Belgian crews at Henley in past times. Never will any member of the crew forget the amazing generosity of the Gantois, in fact of the Belgians as a nation.'

Later a poem was written to celebrate the Terdonck victory. The Fairbairns' part in the race was described:

> Ere fiercely upsprang,
> Eric the mighty;
> Red was his face
> And Blue was his raiment
> Kinsman was he
> To Steve the great trainer…

Of the Jesus crew that beat the Belgians that day four were not to survive the war. Lieutenant Hugh John Sladen Shields, RAMC (attached 1st battalion Irish Guards) died 25–26 October 1914. Lieutenant Henry Mills Goldsmith, Devonshire Regiment (attached 2nd battalion Lincolnshire Regiment) died 9 May 1915. Sub-Lieutenant Thomas Mervyn Crowe, Royal Naval Volunteer Reserve, Anson battalion Royal Naval Division. Eric Fairbairn, Durham Light Infantry, died 10 June 1915.

On 5 August 1914, a day after war was declared, Eric enlisted into the ranks of the Artists' Rifles, later, on 24 October 1914, receiving a commission as a second lieutenant into the 10th battalion, Durham Light Infantry. After training, on 22 May 1915 Eric travelled with his battalion to France. After only being at the front for a week, he was badly wounded by shrapnel from a rifle grenade. The War Diary for 20 June records: 'All companies returned from trenches early this morning… D. Coy reports 2/Lt Fairburn dangerously wounded.' Eric's wounds were serious and he died later the same day.

He is buried at Bailleul Communal Cemetery Extension, Nord, grave I.C. 135.

Lieutenant Colonel Amon Ritter von Gregurich
1900 Paris
Hungary
Fencer
Imperial and Royal Hussars
Died 28 June 1915 aged 48

The finest sportsman in Hungary

Amon Ritter von Gregurich was born on 26 May 1867 in Hietzing, Vienna. An outstanding all-round sportsman he was almost destined from birth to join the army. Between 1895 and 1897 he passed all his exams and trained under the Italian fencing master Luigi Barbasetti to become an expert with the sabre. He won the Hungarian AC (MAC, Hungarian Sports club) sabre championship in 1895, coming second in 1896.

Due to his success he was selected to fence for the Hungarian national team in the 1900 Olympics in Paris. Twenty-three competitors (ten from France) from seven countries took part in the individual men's sabre. Gregurich reached the final eight but just missed out on a medal – with four wins and three losses he came fourth. The French fencer Georges, Count de la Falaise took the gold, his team mate Leon Thiebaut the silver, and the Austrian Fritz Flesch the bronze.

During the war Lieutenant Colonel von Gregurich served with the Imperial and Royal Hussars and was killed in action on 28 June 1915 at Mukachevo, Zakarpattia, Ukraine.

Private Jakob 'Jacques' Person
1912 Stockholm
Germany
Athletics
2. Kompanie/Infanterie-Regiment Nr.96
15 July 1915 aged 26

Born in France, represented and died for Germany

Jakob Person was born on 1 May 1889 in Saverne, Bas-Rhin, France. Moving to Strasbourg with his family, he studied economics at Strasburg University and began training with and representing Sportverein Strassburg, specializing in the 400 and 800 metres. He competed well and was selected to run for Germany in both these events during the 1912 Stockholm Olympics.

The 800 metres competition was held from Saturday, 6 July to Monday, 8 July 1912. Forty-eight runners from sixteen nations took part in the event including all three of the medal winners from the 1908 Olympics. Unfortunately Person was knocked out in the heats. The gold went to the America runner, Ted Meredith in an Olympic and world record time of 1:51.9 (up until then the world record had been held by the Italian Emilio Lunghi which he set on 15 September 1909 in Montreal, Canada in a time of 1:52.1). The silver was taken by another American runner, Mel Sheppard in a time of 1:52.0 (Sheppard had won the gold medal in the 1908 Olympics in London. He also broke the world record). The bronze medal was taken by a third American Ira Davenport also in a time of 1:52.0.

Person's next event was the 400 metres held on 12–13 July 1912. Forty-nine runners from sixteen nations competed. Person ran well but was knocked out in the semi-finals. The gold was taken by the American Charles Reidpath in a time of 48.2, a new Olympic record; the silver was won by the German Hanns Braun in a time of 48.3, also breaking the Olympic record (Hanns was killed in action on 9 October 1918). The American Edward Lindberg took the bronze in a time of 48.4, equalling the Olympic record which had until then been held by the British runner Wyndham Halswelle, set in London on 22 July 1908.

Person served with the 2. Kompanie/Infanterie-Regiment Nr.96 during the war and was killed with them on 15 July 1915 in Vlaanderen, Belgium.

He was related to the well-known Berlin sports administrator Arthur Person (1926–93), who established and headed the German organization 'Youth training for the Olympics'.

Lieutenant Edward Gordon Williams
1908 London
Great Britain
Rowing (Coxed Eight)
Bronze Medal
2nd Battalion Grenadier Guards
Died 12 August 1915 aged 27

'The finest number four ever to sit in a boat'

Edward Gordon Williams was born on 20 July 1888 in Honiton, Devon, England. He was the son of Edward Gordon and Louise Davies Williams. He was educated at Eton before going up to Trinity Cambridge. Having excelled at rowing while at Eton he was a natural selection for his college and gained his blue. He took part in the annual Boat Race between Oxford and Cambridge on three occasions rowing number six in 1908 when Cambridge won by two and a half lengths in a time of 19 minutes and 20 seconds. In 1909 he rowed number five in the losing boat, Oxford taking the race by three and a half lengths in a time of 19 minutes and 50 seconds. And finally in 1910 he was once again on the losing crew, Oxford taking the honours by three and a half lengths but in a slower time of 20 minutes and 14 seconds. In 1909, partnered by Banner Johnstone (1882–1964), he also won the Silver Goblets at Henley Royal Regatta.

In 1908 he was selected to row in the coxed eight during the Olympic Games held in London. Rowing number four for the Cambridge University Boat Club they were defeated by the Belgian crew largely because of poor training and bad preparation. However they still took the bronze medal sharing it with the Canadians.

The crew consisted of:

1. Bow. Frank Harold Jerwood, Jesus (1885–1971)
2. Eric Walter Powell, Third Trinity (1886–1933, died mountain climbing)
3. Oswald Armitage Carver, First Trinity (1887–1915)
4. Edward Gordon Williams, Third Trinity (1888–1915)
5. Henry Mills Goldsmith, Jesus (1885–1915)
6. Harold Edward Kitching, Trinity Hall (1885–1980)
7. John Sotherden Burn, First Trinity (1884–1958)

8. Stroke. Douglas Cecil Rees Stuart, Trinity Hall (1885–1969)
9. Cox. Richard Frederick Rrobert Pochin Boyle, Trinity Hall (1888–1953)

Williams was appointed as a colonial administrator in North-Western Rhodesia, however at the outbreak of the war he returned to England and took a commission in the 2nd battalion Grenadier Guards (*London Gazette* 1 January 1915). He was accidentally killed near Bethune on 12 August 1915.

He is buried in St Venant Communal Cemetery, French Civilian Plot.

Ensign Rudolf Watzl
1906 Athens
Austria
Wrestling
1 Gold 1 Bronze
Austria Hungarian Army
Died 15 August 1915 aged 33

Despite his inexperience he took a gold and silver medal at his first Olympics

Rudolf Watzl was born on 14 April 1882 in Vienna, Austria-Hungary. He began wrestling in 1904 aged 24, training and representing First Vienna Sports Club (*Ersten Wiener Ringsportclub*) fighting lightweight. In 1906 and with little experience he was selected to take part in the wrestling, taking part in the men's lightweight Greco Roman G and men's all-around Greco Roman B competitions during the 1906 Olympics in Athens.

Greco-Roman wrestling was contested at the first modern Olympic Games in 1896 and has been included in every Olympics since 1908. The competitions were conducted according to the rules of Greco-Roman wrestling. There was no time limit to the fights. The two wrestlers are scored on their performance in three two-minute periods, which can be terminated by a pin (or fall). Greco-Roman wrestling forbids holds below the waist; this is the major difference between Greco-Roman and other forms of wrestling in the Olympics.

Watzl first took part in the men's lightweight Greco-Roman event. This was a single-elimination tournament in the early rounds, concluding in a three-way round robin for the medals. The event took place at the Panathenaic Stadium in Athens between 25 and 26 April 1906. Rudolf Watzl took the gold medal; the Danish wrestler Carl Carlsen took the silver and the Hungarian Ferenc Holubán the bronze. Watzl next took part in the men's all-around Greco-Roman event. The Dane Søren Jensen took the gold, the Finnish wrestler Verner Weckman the silver, with Rudolf Watzl taking the bronze.

During the First World War Watzl served with the Austrian-Hungarian army. He was taken ill during the counter-offensive that secured the fortress of Przemysl captured by the Russian Army on 22 March 1915 with the loss of 119,000 Austrian-Hungarian soldiers taken prisoner. He was diagnosed with typhoid and died on 15 August 1915.

Lieutenant Edmond Georges Richard Wallace
1900 Paris
France
Fencing
89ᵉ Régiment d'Infanterie
Died 18 August 1915 aged 38

Brother fencers both reached the Olympics

Edmond Wallace was born on 4 October 1876 in Saint-Maur-des-Fosses, Val-de-Marne, France. Together with his brother Richard, Edmond became one of the finest fencers in France specializing in the épée. He was selected together with his brother Richard to represent France in the individual épée at the 1900 Olympics to be held in their own capital Paris. The

individual épée was the most popular event during the 1900 Olympics. One hundred and four competitors from nine nations took part. It required four rounds of round-robin elimination pools, with three semi-finals advancing the top three from each pool to a final pool of nine fencers.

Edmond reached the final of the épée. In the final, each fencer had either five or six bouts. Competing in six events Edmond lost four and won two, eventually coming sixth. Although the French, with their strong tradition in fencing were favourites to take all the medals, it was the American (Cuban) Ramon Fonst who, after defeating the French fencer Louis Perrée took the gold. Although he represented the US he was brought up and trained in France. His victory in the épée made him the first Latin American ever to take a medal at the Olympic Games. He would go on to win the event again in the 1904 Olympics held in St Louis USA. Remarkably he also took part in the 1924 Olympics, held once again in Paris. The two French fencers Louis Perrée and Léon Sée took the silver and bronze.

Edmond Wallace was commissioned into the 89ᵉ Régiment d'Infanterie in 1897 and served with them during the First World War. He was killed in action during the battle of the Butte de Vauquois on 28 February 1915.

Brigadier General Paul Aloysius Kenna VC DSO
1912 Stockholm
Great Britain
Equestrian
General Staff Commanding 3rd Mounted
Brigade/21st (Empress of India) Lancers
Died 30 August 1915 aged 53

'A credit to his school, regiment and country'

Paul Aloysius Kenna was born on 16 August 1862 in Everton, Liverpool. He was the second son of Thomas Kenna, a wealthy stockbroker of Liverpool who was descended from a family of minor gentry from County Meath, Ireland. Kenna was educated at Stonyhurst College where he was remembered as 'a cheery, vigorous boy, abounding with energy, and a strenuous player of all the games'. After leaving school he continued his education at St Francis Xavier College, Liverpool. However since a boy at school he had decided to make his career in the army. Entering the Royal Military College at Sandhurst he served two years with the militia and was initially commissioned into the 2nd West India Regiment. He was gazetted into the 21st Lancers in 1889, taking part with them in the Khartoum Expedition in 1898. It was at the Battle of Omdurman (also described as the 'Battle of Khartoum') in this campaign, that Captain Kenna won the VC by an exploit the details of which we give later. In the last South African War he served on the staff and commanded a column, being mentioned in despatches and receiving the DSO. He commanded mounted troops in the Somaliland expedition in 1902–04, and was mentioned in despatches. He was made ADC to the King and Brevet Colonel in 1906. He transferred to the 21st Hussars in 1889, which later became the 21st Lancers (Empress of India). In 1905 he was Brigade Major of the 1st Cavalry Brigade at Aldershot and the following year took command of 21st Lancers. In 1911 he took command of the Notts and Derby (Yeomanry) Mounted Brigade and was promoted to Brigadier in August 1914.

During this time he served with the Nile expedition (1898) and in the Boer War (1899–1902), as well as serving in East Africa. During the battle of Khartoum (2 September 1898) Kenna was to win Britain's highest award for bravery, the Victoria Cross. An extract from the *London Gazette*, dated 15 November 1898, reads,

At the Battle of Khartoum, on 2nd September 1898, Captain P.A. Kenna assisted Major Crole Wyndham, of the same regiment, by taking him on his horse, behind the saddle (Major Wyndham's horse having been killed in the charge), thus enabling him to reach a place of safety; and after the charge of the 21st Lancers, Captain Kenna returned to assist Lieutenant de Montmorency, who was endeavoring to recover the body of second Lieutenant R.G. Grenfell.

A slightly more detailed account of the action appeared in *With Kitchener to Khartoum* by Stevens:

Lieut. de Montmorency missed his Troop-Sergeant, and rode back among the slashes to look for him. There he found the hacked body of Lieut. Grenfell. He dismounted, and put it on his horse, not seeing in his heat that life had drained out long since by a dozen channels. The horse bolted under the slackened muscles, and De Montmorency was left alone with his revolver and 3,000 screaming fiends. Capt. Kenna and Corpl. Swarbrick rode out, caught his horse, and brought it back; the three answered the fire of the 3,000 at fifty yards, and got quietly back to their own line untouched.'

The *Liverpool Daily Post* expanded on the award still further:

VICTORIA CROSSES WON BY STONYHURST STUDENTS.

Capt. Paul Aloysius Kenna, V.C., another old Stonyhurst boy, also succeeds in winning the much-coveted honour by a not less plucky performance at the Battle of Khartoum. Indeed, Capt. Kenna's claims to the distinction are founded on more than one brilliant exploit. In the early part of the charge of the 21st Lancers, which was the sharpest piece of fighting during the day, Major Crole Wyndham's horse was shot under him right in the middle of the Dervishes, but just carried him through their lines and then fell. Capt. Kenna, who was riding a little in advance, seeing Major Wyndham's danger, turned, waited for him, and took him up behind his saddle. They had galloped but a short distance when the horse, under the unaccustomed weight, plunged, reared, and threw off both officers. However, Capt. Kenna was soon upon his horse again, and observing Lieut. de Montmorency riding back to seek his Troop-Sergeant among the Dervishes, he rode back along with Corpl. Swarbrick to his aid. De Montmorency had just found the body of Lieut. Grenfell, whom he supposed to be still alive. Whilst he was endeavouring to place Grenfell's body on his own horse, the animal bolted, and he was left alone with his revolver some fifty yards from 3,000 Dervishes. It was at this stage that Kenna returned, and along with Swarbrick, caught De Montmorency's horse, when all three answered the Dervishes' fire with their revolvers, and then retreated to their own line untouched. Only a couple of years ago Capt. Kenna showed similar prompt courage by jumping into the Liffey in Dublin and saving a drowning woman's life.

Kenna next took part in the Boer War in 1899–1902. Initially holding a staff appointment he was later placed in command of a column. He took part in the relief of Kimberley including operations at Paardeberg; actions at Poplar Grove, Dreifontein, Karee Siding, Vet River, and Zand River in the Transvaal, including actions near Johannesburg, Pretoria and Diamond Hill; in the Transvaal, East of Pretoria, including actions at Reit River and Belfort; in Cape Colony, South of Orange River, including actions at Colesberg; in the Transvaal and Orange River Colony; and in the operations on the Zululand frontiers of Natal where he was mentioned in despatches, received a brevet of major, and was made a DSO.

Major Kenna next saw action in East Africa, where he took part in the operations in Somaliland, 1902–04. Once again he was at first on the staff as Special Service Officer being present at the action of Tidballi. He later commanded mounted troops, and was mentioned in despatches twice during the campaign. He also received the brevet of Lieutenant Colonel.

During an active career Kenna found the time to marry twice, firstly to Lady Cecil Bertie, daughter of the 7th Earl of Abingdon and then Angela Mary, daughter of Herbert Hibbert. They had one daughter, Kathleen (who died as recently as 1998).

An outstanding horseman he excelled at hunting, polo and steeplechasing and rode in several military competitions. As a jockey he won approximately 300 races in both flat and steeplechase racing. As a result he was selected as part of the British Olympic equestrian team at both show jumping and three-day eventing for the 1912 games to be held in Stockholm. His Olympic performances were not memorable, a fact he blamed on the haphazard preparation of the British team. He came 27th in the individual show jumping and was unplaced in both the three-day event individual and team.

On the outbreak of the Great War he was for some months in command of a brigade near Dover. In August 1915, he became Temporary Brigadier General Commanding Notts and Derby Brigade (4th Mounted Brigade), 2nd Mounted Division, Mediterranean Expeditionary Force. He travelled with them first to Egypt and then Suvla Bay to take part in the Gallipoli Campaign.

It was Kenna's habit frequently to visit the advanced trenches of his brigade. At 8 pm on 29 August 1915 during one of these inspections at Chocolate Hill, he was severely wounded by a Turkish sniper, the bullet passing through his arm and into his stomach. He was carried to the beach for treatment at 31st Field Ambulance but he died the following day from his wounds. A couple of letters sent home later describe his death in more detail:

From 2nd Lieutenant Alan Brodrick, 1st County of London Yeomanry, 4th Mounted Brigade, 2nd Mounted Division :

31 August, 1915

The object of this letter, written in a dug-out in Gallipoli, is to tell you the sad news of General Kenna's death. He was shot by a sniper last night in the trench on our right. The bullet passed through his arm, smashing it, and then through his stomach, making a terrible wound. He died in hospital a few hours later. Had it not been for his desire of going right up to the forward trench, to cheer up everyone and have a yarn with the men, he would be alive now. He commanded the Notts, and Derby Brigade in this Division, and was very popular. Also as senior Brigadier he was in command of the Division the first time we went into action.

A letter from Corporal John Forsyth, RE, an old Wimbledon College boy, gives more precise details:

No doubt by this time you will have heard of the death of Brigadier-General Kenna, V.C. I was there when he was hit, and helped to ease him by bathing his head. I heard him say something about Agnus Dei, so I asked him if he wished for one. He said he had one, but would like to have a crucifix. At the moment I forgot about my rosary, so I gave him the medal, which he eagerly took. I took them back before I left, as my identity disc was on the string. He died about four hours later. The two hours I spent with him I shall always remember, and it was grand to see the comfort and relief these simple objects of piety gave his mind.

He is buried in Lala Baba Cemetery, grave reference II. A. 1. His VC is on display in the Queens Royal Lancers and Nottinghamshire Yeomanry Museum in Thorsby Park, Nottinghamshire. Well worth a visit.

Offizier Stellvertretter (NCO) Friedrich (Fritz) Bartholomae
1912 Stockholm
Germany
Rowing
Bronze Medal
3. Kompanie/Garde-Reserve-Schützen-Bataillon
Died 12 September 1915 aged 28

'Won his Olympic Bronze with his brother Willie'

Fritz Bartholomae was born on 29 October 1886 in Krefeld, Nordrhein-Westfalen, Germany. Fritz and his brother Willi were both talented rowers and both competed for Berlin-Spindlersfeld fields rowing club, winning the German championship in 1910 and coming third in 1911 beaten by the Stettin and the Berlin Rowing Club of 1876

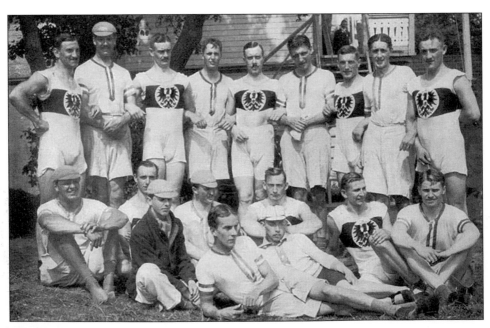

Bartholomae can be seen here standing, third from the left.

into third place. In 1912 Bartholomae joined the Berlin RV 1876 winning the German championship that year.

In 1912 he was selected to row in the eight at the Stockholm Olympic Games. Rowing on the Djurgårdsbrunnsviken in Stockholm, Berlin RV of 1876 beat the Hungarian eight in the first round. In the second round they defeated anther German eight, Sports Borussia. However in the semi-final Bartholomae's boat was defeated by the British Leander club (who went on to take the gold medal). Since only three boats reached the semi-finals, the Germans took the bronze. The German eight consisted of Otto Liebing, Max Broske, Fritz Bartholomae, Willi Bartholomae, Werner Dehn, Rudolf Reichelt, Hans Mathiae, Kurt Runge and Max Vetter.

Fritz Bartholomae was killed in action on 12 September 1915 while his regiment were stationed at Pixtern (Kurland). The regimental history outlines the following:

In February 1915 the Garde-Reserve-Schützen-Bataillon found itself on the Courland theatre of the war. It marched in the ranks of the 8th Army all the war to the Duna and up to the autumn of 1915 participated in the difficult, but victorious offensive fighting. At Borkowo and Drobin, along the Dubissa and at Schaulen, the battalion deployed for the assault, and with the fighting at Popeljani, Bausk, on the Njemeneck, and at Lennewaden during July and August the advance came to an end. The Army had reached the Duna sector. The battalion then occupied permanent/fortified positions along the Duna.

Lieutenant Arthur Norman Victor Harcourt Ommundsen
1908 London; 1912 Stockholm
Great Britain
Shooting
Two Silver Medals
Honorable Artillery Company
Died 19 September 1915 aged 37

'The Greatest shot in Britain'

Arthur Norman Victor Harcourt Ommundsen was born on 23 November 1898 in Alloa, Clackmannanshire. He was the son of Adolph and Margaret Ommundsen. His father was a Norwegian shipping agent and his mother a native Scot. Educated in Edinburgh he became one of the country's finest shots. After completing his education he worked as a law clerk before enlisting into the ranks of the 4th battalion Royal Scots (later transferring to the 5th battalion). While still a corporal, Ommundsen won the King's Prize in 1901 with 304 points. Promoted to sergeant he was also runner-up in 1906 with 94 points and 1913 with 92 points. He was also five times winner of the Service

Lieutenant Arthur Harcourt being piped as victor of the tournament.

Rifle Championship between 1905 and 1913 and won the Bisley Grand Aggregate three times being runner-up twice between 1900 and 1912.

Selected for the team event in the 1908 London Olympics he won a silver medal in the team military rifle event. In 1912 he was once again selected to represent Great Britain in the Olympics this time in Stockholm and once more taking a silver medal in the team military rifle event, and also managed seventh place in the 600 metre free rifle event. He went on to write, in partnership with E.H. Robinson, *Rifles and Ammunition*, which was one of the most comprehensive text books of the day on rifle shooting. He was also an analytic and inventive soul, and was responsible, in conjunction with E.J.D. Newitt (King's Prize winner 1923) for the design of the Remington Negative-Angle Battle Sight. This sight permitted

Lieutenant Arthur Harcourt in the champion's chair being held aloft and piped through the crowd.

aiming a fixed distance below the target, and was intended to 'enlarge the danger zone under skirmishing conditions' to enhance the chance of a hit. Shortly before the outbreak of the war he found time to marry his long-time girlfriend, Beatrice Alice Ommundsen, and the couple moved to, 192 Portsdown Rd, Maida Vale.

Shortly after the outbreak of the war in November 1914 Ommundsen was commissioned 2nd lieutenant into the Honorable Artillery Company, being further promoted to lieutenant in June 1915. For a time he acted as a sniper, and although not as successful as Britain's number one sniper Pegahmagabow, who claimed to have picked off 378 Germans using an open sight, it is likely that Ommundsen scored around a dozen kills. Ommundsen was killed in action on 19 September 1915 during the Battle of Ypres. A shell landed at the entrance of No.4 Company HQ which killed not only Lieutenant Ommundsen but also Captain Hayden, Lieutenant Bazin, and Lieutenant Leeds.

A letter home from a brother officer describes what happen:

One of the four officers mentioned above was Lieut. Ommundsen, who was my bombing officer. His death was most unfortunate, as he had just formed the Grenadier Section, and it was our first time in action as a separate unit. What Mr. Ommundsen did not know about bombs and rifles was not worth knowing. He was considered the world's best shot, having won the King's prize at Bisley on several occasions. One of his feats of firing is rather interesting. With his sights ranged at 1,000 yards, he fired from 1,000 yards to 100 yards and hit the bull every time.

He is buried in Brandhoek Military Cemetary, grave reference I. D. 3.

Sous-Lieutenant Renon Georges Boussière
1912 Stockholm
France
Marathon
403ᵉ French Infantry
Died 25 September 1915 aged 33

The finest runner in France

Renon Boussière was born on 31 August 1882 (although mystery surrounds his date of birth and parentage) in Amfreville-sous-les-Monts, France. A keen long-distance runner, he represented the Quevillais sports club based in Rouen. He won the Normandy marathon in 1903, covering the 36 km in just over two hours. He was also, for a time in 1909, the French marathon record holder with a time of 1:52.30. As French champion he was selected to run for France in the marathon in the 1912 Olympic games to be held in Stockholm.

It was the first occasion that the marathon was run as an out-and-back race. It was held on Sunday, 14 July 1912. The runners had to cover a distance of 40.2 kilometres and 68 runners from 19 nations competed. The race commenced in the Olympic stadium; from there the competitors made their way to the town of Sollentuna, where they turned and headed back to the Olympic stadium. The conditions for the race were hot, some estimates giving the temperature as having been 32°C (89.6°F) in the shade – and the runners were not in the shade. Largely due to the weather conditions, the Olympics had their first tragedy. Portuguese marathon runner Francisco Lázaro collapsed from the heat and was rushed to Seraphim Hospital. He never recovered consciousness and died the following morning. It was the first recorded death in the Olympic Games' long history. The race was eventually won by the South African Ken McArthur who took the gold in a time of 2:36:54.8. Another South African, Chris Gitsham, came second, winning the silver in a time of 2:37:52.0. The American runner Gaston Strobino came third in a time of 2:38:42.4. Renon Boissière came thirteenth in a time of 2:51:06.6. In addition to the gold medal, Kennedy McArthur was awarded the Challenge Trophy for the marathon race that had been donated in 1908 by the King of Greece. The runners who finished between 4th and 28th were also awarded diplomas of merit.

During the First World War, Boussière served as a sous-lieutenant with the 403ᵉ French Infantry. He was reported missing during the battle of Ville-Sur Tourbe, Marne, Northern France, on 25 September 1915. His body was never recovered or identified and he is commemorated on Le Petit-Quevilly memorial.

Private 2nd Class Michel Léon Marie Soalhat
1906 Athens
France
Athletics
315ᵉ Infantry Regiments
Died 25 September 1915 aged 39

Champion of France

Michel Léon Marie Soalhat was born on 17 November 1875 in Clermont-Ferrand, Puy-de-Dôme, France. Soalhat was a gifted and determined runner and champion of France. He ran for several clubs including Nogent and Racing Club de France who he competed for from 1896 onwards. He was champion of France and French record holder in just about every race on the calendar. In the 800 metres he was champion in 1895 and 1896 and then again in 1904 and 1905. In the 1,500 metres he was champion in 1894 and 1895 and again in 1904 and 1905, steeplechase champion in 1895 and 1896, and cross-country champion in 1896 and 1897. He also set French records in the 800 metres with a time of 2.03.6 in 1895 and again in 1896 with a time of 2.01.0. In 1896 he also set the French 1,000 metre record with a time of 2.38.0, the 1,500 metres in 1895 with a time of 4.16.4, and again in 1904 with a time of 4.08.2.

He was selected to run for the French team at the 1906 Olympics held in Athens in both the 800 and 1,500 metres. He failed to reach the final in either event. The 800 metres was won by the defending champion and favourite Paul Pilgrim from the United States, Jim Lightbody also of the United States taking the silver, and the British runner Wyndham Halswelle receiving the bronze. Halswelle was killed in action in March 1915.

In 1896 he enlisted into the French Army serving with the 317 Infantry Regiment. He left the army in 1898 but remained on the reserve. As a territorial reservist he was recalled to the colours in August 1914 serving with the 315 infantry regiment as a second class private. He was killed in action at St Hilaire le Grande, Marne on 1 October 1915 during the second Battle of Champagne.

His body was never recovered or identified and he is commemorated on the war memorial at Martine Forest.

Captain Ferdinand Marie Ismael de Lesseps
1908 London
France
Fencing
3ᵉ Regiment de Chasseurs d'Africa
Died 30 September 1915 aged 43

One of seventeen children, two of whom were to die in the war

Ferdinand Marie Ismael de Lesseps was born in Paris on 27 November 1871 into a very distinguished French family. He was the son of Ferdinand Marie, Vicomte de Lesseps (1805–94), a diplomat who was responsible for the building of the Suez Canal. The Vicomte fathered seventeen children with two wives – a man of great energy clearly. Ismael's mother was Louise Helène Autard de Bragard (1848–1909).

Ismael decided to make his career in the army and was commissioned into 3ᵉ Regiment de Chasseurs, eventually rising to the rank of captain. During this time he might have served in Madagascar and would certainly have served in Morocco. He married Marie Gabrielle Louise La Fontaine e Solare. They had three children together.

De Lesseps is seen here seated on the left.

A keen fencer specializing in the sabre, he trained under the watchful eye of the fencing master Marc Perroden. Perroden went on to win a silver medal for France in the 1920 Olympic games in Antwerp (on YouTube there is a British Pathé film of him giving a fencing demonstration). Ismael was selected to represent France in the fencing competition, taking part in the men's individual sabre during the 1908 London Olympics. The event was held between 17 and 24 July 1908 at the fencing ground just outside the White City stadium. He failed to win a medal being knocked out in the first round (pool seven) and finishing below his brother Bertrand, Count de Lesseps (killed in action 28 August 1918). The gold medal was taken by the Hungarian fencer Jenő Fuchs (it was his first gold medal in this event. Fuchs would eventually win four Olympic gold medals in sabre fencing: 1908 individual and team, and 1912 individual and team). The silver was won by another Hungarian fencer Béla Zulawszky (killed in action 24 October 1914) and the bronze by the Bohemian fencer Vilém Goppold z Lobsdorfu, Sr.

On 21 January 1913, de Lesseps was made a member of the Legion d'Honneur for his services to France.

He was mobilized with his regiment on 5 August 1914 and was involved in the heavy fighting and the eventual retreat from the Marne during 1914, going into the trenches in 1915. He was killed in action on 30 September 1915 in Vigny, Val-d'Oise, France.

De Lesseps (left) at fencing practice.

Lieutenant Heinrich Schneidereit
1906 Athens
Germany
Tug-of-War/One Hand Lift/Two Hand Lift
One Gold, two Bronze
Artillery
Died 30 September 1915 aged 30

'The German Wonder boy'

Heinrich Schneidereit was born on 23 December 1884 in Cologne, Nordrhein-Westfalen, Germany. From youth he had a keen interest in health, fitness and strength and participated in a variety of athletics. However it was weightlifting in which he finally specialized. In 1900 at the tender age of 16 he joined his first weightlifting club, Kölner Athleten Club 1882. A committed athlete he made rapid progress and in 1903 competed in the world championships in Paris. The competition took place on 5 October 1913 at the Moulin Rouge. Eighteen competitors from five countries took part. There was only one weight class. Heinrich lifted 513.5 kg, which was 6 kg more than his nearest rival, the Swiss strong man Francois Lancaud, who only managed 507.5 kg. However the judges still awarded the gold to Lancaud marking him higher than Heinrich for technical execution disciplines. This knocked the enraged Heinrich into the silver medal position. Because of his youth and his remarkable abilities the German press nicknamed him 'the German Wonder Boy'.

In 1906 he was selected as part of the German team to take part in the Olympic Games in Athens. He won a gold medal in the tug-of-war, defeating the much fancied Greek team. He also went on to take two bronze medals, the one-handed lift 73.75 kg, and the two-handed lift 129.5 kg.

The year 1906 turned out to be a good one for Heinrich. The ninth world championships were held in Lille, France on 18 March 1906. Thirty-three men from four nations took part in the competitions. Heinrich took the gold medal in the 80-plus kg defeating the Swiss lifter Emile Besson and another French weightlifter Gustave Falleur. He won the European championship in Milan and then in 1907 came second in the world championships in Frankfurt Germany, defeated by fellow German Heinrich Rondi.

On 30 August 1908 while competing in Aachen, Germany, he broke the world record in the one-arm lift by lifting 90.8 kg. In 1911 the world championship was held in Stuttgart. On this occasion Heinrich took bronze behind the Austrian Josef Grafi who won the gold and his old rival Heinrich Rondo who took the silver.

His final major success came in 1914 during the Baltic Games in Malmo when he took the gold in the heavyweight division (he failed to compete in the 1908 or 1912 Olympic Games because no weightlifting event had been organized for either of the games).

After his weightlifting career was over Heinrich began to study business administration, however the war interrupted his studies. He took a commission into the German army becoming a lieutenant in the artillery. He was killed in action on 30 September 1915 at Thionville, Moselle, France, and buried together with his comrades in a mass grave.

Sergeant Major Joseph Louis Alphonse Caulle
1912 Stockholm
France
Athletics (800 metres)
41st Colonial Infantry Regiment
Died 1 October 1915 aged 30

A Champion of France

Joseph Louis Alphonse Caulle was born on 3 May 1885 in Bosc-le-Hard, Seine Maritime, France. A resident of Paris and a gifted runner, he competed for Metropolitan Club, Colombes. He became champion of France in the 800 metres in 1909. He was selected to take part in the 800 metres at the Olympic Games of 1912 held in Stockholm. Forty-eight runners from sixteen nations competed. The competition was held between Saturday, 6 July 1912, and Monday, 8 July 1912. Caulle however was eliminated in the first round and failed to win a medal. The medals were all taken by Americans. Ted Meredith (1891–1957) took the gold in a time of 1.51.9, Mel (Peerless Mel) Sheppard (1883–1942) who had won the gold during the 1908 Olympics took the silver in a time of 1.52.0 and Ira Davenport (1887–1941) the bronze in a time of 1.52.0.

During the war Caulle served with the 41st Colonial Infantry Regiment and was killed in action on 1 October 1915 in Souchez, Pas-de-Calais. He was later buried at Vimy. He is also commemorated on the Saint-Victor-l'Abbaye war memorial designed by Francois Pompon.

Lieutenant Béla von Las-Torres
1908 London; 1912 Stockholm
Hungary
Swimming
Silver Medal
KuK Luftfahrtruppen (Austrian Air Force)
Died 12 October 1915 aged 25

'As famous for not turning up for a race as he was for competing'

Béla von Las-Torres was born on 20 April 1890 in Budapest, Hungary. He was of Spanish noble descent, the family finding themselves in Austria due to the War of the Spanish Succession. His father Julius Las Torres owned a china shop in Budapest. A gifted freestyle swimmer he swam for both Budapest BEAC and the ICC. At the tender age of 18 he found himself competing for Hungary in the 1908 London Olympics. He took part in two competitions, the 400 metre freestyle, being knocked out at the semi-final stage, and the 4×200 metres freestyle swimming relay, in which the Hungarian team came in second taking the silver medal.

During his swimming career Las-Torres won eighteen Hungarian championships. In 1909 he won the saltwater championship in Abbazia against the much-fancied 1906 Olympic champion Otto Scheff, in 1910 he won the 1,500 freestyle in Germany championships, and on 5 July 1912 he took the 400 metre freestyle world record while swimming in Budapest in a time of 5.28.4.

In 1912 he was invited once again to take part on the Olympic Games, this time being held in Stockholm. Strongly fancied for a medal he finished fifth in the 400 metre freestyle. Oddly, although he qualified for the 1,500 metre final he failed to arrive for the race and it took place without him. He also failed, together with the rest of the Hungarian team, to turn up for the 4×200 metre relay where he was due to race fourth. Why this occurred twice I have not been able to discover. He also lost his 400 metre world record to the Canadian George Hodgson who swam a time of 5.24.4 at the 1912 games.

During the First World War Las-Torres served as a lieutenant at the Kuk Lufttfahrtuppen (air force) base. During this time he was decorated with the Signum Laudis (Military Merit Medal (Austria) for outstanding achievements in war). Taken ill he was rushed to the fortress hospital of Meljina, a district of Castelnuovo in Dalmatia, where he died of appendicitis on 12 October 1915. He was later buried in the local military cemetery.

On 12 December 1982 the Hungarians named a street after their swimming hero, Las-Torres Béla utca, in Budapest XXIII. He was also included in the Hungarian swimming hall of fame.

Einjährig-Freiwilliger Lieutenant Alfred Staats
1912 Stockholm
Germany
Gymnastics
8. Kompanie/Infanterie-Regiment Nr. 82
Died 22 October 1915 aged 23

Paid for all his military service

Alfred Heinrich Karl Richard Staats, born on 2 November 1891 in Hondelage, Braunschweig, Niedersachsen, Germany, became a keen gymnast and represented the Allgemeiner Akademischer Turnerbund Sports Club in Leipzig. Interestingly Staats did his national service as an Einjährig-Freiwilliger. Basically this meant that the recruit served as a one-year volunteer. The conscript agrees to pay his own costs for the procurement of equipment, food and clothing, in return for spending a shorter-than-usual term on military service. It also gave better opportunities to receive a commission

German athletes at the 1912 Olympic games.

in the reserve of officers. He was selected to take part in the gymnastics events during the 1912 Stockholm Olympics. He competed in the men's team all-around and the men's team all-around, free system.

His first event was the men's team all-around, free system. The event took place on 10 July 1912 at the Stockholm Olympic Stadium. It was the first time this event was held; it was competed for one more time during the 1920 Olympics in Antwerp, after that it was discontinued. The rules were simple: One team per nation, 16–40 gymnasts per team, all performing simultaneously. There was a time limit of one hour including the march in and march out. The Olympic committee provided the fixed apparatus. The teams were judged on execution of the exercises, the composition of the programme, and the posture and attention of the team. Five judges marked the teams between one and twenty-five points. Norway took the gold with 22.85 points, Finland the silver with 21.85 points and Denmark the bronze with 21.25 points. Germany came fourth with 16.85 points.

His second event, on the following day, was the men's team all-around. Once again it was the first time this event had been competed for in the Olympic games (it was used one more time in 1920 in Antwerp then discontinued). Each nation was allowed one team consisting of between 16 and 40 gymnasts performing simultaneously. The time allowed was one hour including march in and march out. Fixed apparatus was provided for each team, consisting of four horizontal bars, four parallel bars, four pommelled horses, and four Roman rings. Teams had to provide their own hand apparatus for the free-standing disciplines. Competitors could score up to twelve points per apparatus, twelve points for free-standing exercises and up to ten points for free exercises. Five judges could score up to 58 points per competitor. The Italians took the gold with 53.15 points, Hungary the silver with 45.45 points and Great Britain the bronze with 36.90 points. Germany came fifth with 32.40 points.

During the war Staats, serving as a lieutenant with the 8. Kompanie/Infanterie-Regiment Nr.82, was killed in action on 22 October 1915 in Kolky, Volyn, Ukraine.

Of the eighteen members of the German Olympic gymnastics team in 1912, four were to be killed in the Great War: Alfred Staats, Walter Jesinghaus, Wilhelm Brülle and Hans Sorge (see chapters within book).

Sergeant Dragutin Tomašević
1912 Stockholm
Serbia
Marathon
18th Infantry Regiment
Died October 1915 aged 24

'The runner with two hearts'

Dragutin Tomašević was born on 20 April 1890 in the village of Bistrica near Petrovac, Serbia. He was the eldest son of Milos Sedmoslanoj, a trader. At the age of 15 he was sent to Belgrade to be educated. While there he demonstrated a gift for both athletics and gymnastics becoming a member of the famous Sokol Society, 'Dušan the Mighty'. He also competed for both OFK Beograd and Beograd (SRB). Specializing in the marathon, he won the Obrenovac marathon in Belgrade on ten occasions. In 1909 the local train company challenged him to a race over forty miles between Požarevac and Petrovac. He beat the train and was waiting for it at the station, to the amazement of the train driver and company executives.

He won the right to participate in the 1912 Stockholm Olympics by winning the 33 km Obrenovac–Košutnjak marathon in May 1911 against forty other competitors. He was the first person from the Kingdom of Serbia (together with the sprinter Dusan Milosevic) to ever take part in the Olympic Games. At his official farewell he was presented with a bun and a wicker bag as a blessing to properly represent the young Kingdom of Serbia. At the opening ceremony of the Olympic Games in Stockholm, Dragutin Tomašević carried the Serbian flag.

Sixty-eight runners from nineteen countries took part in the marathon, which was run over a distance of 40.2 kilometres. Dragutin finished well down the field in 37th position in a time of 2 hours 47 minutes, much to many people's surprise, especially the Serbians. Rumours about cheating soon followed. Had he had been poisoned by a beautiful Swedish woman to stop him winning the race? Had he been pushed into a ditch and held there until it was too late to win the race? As he came in battered and bruised it seems more likely that he fell or was pushed and injured, explaining his condition. The gold was taken by the South African (of Irish decent) Ken McArthur in a time of 2:36:54.8, the silver by another South African, Christian Gitsham, in a time of 2:37:52.0 and the bronze by the American Gaston Strobino in 2:38:42.4.

After returning from the Olympics, Dragutin began his preparations for the next Olympics to be held in 1916. Unfortunately war was declared and put paid to any hopes of glory he might have had. He went into the army serving with the 18th Infantry Regiment, being promoted to sergeant during the Great War. He was seriously wounded during an attack at Drum Hill near Pozarevac. Several of his men crawled out into no man's land and dragged him back into cover. He was evacuated from the front but his wounds were too serious and he died in the village of Rasanac in October 1915. He was returned home and buried in his native village of Bistrica in the family tomb, along with their sporting trophies. On his grave it says,

He is buried with his mother and his courage.

An interesting story came out after his death. The doctor who carried out a post-mortem on his body declared that Dragutin had two hearts. A second and smaller one was found on the right hand side of his body. I have no idea if this is true or just a myth surrounding one of Serbia's greatest sporting heros.

His place of birth is now a museum in his memory. There is also an annual marathon run in his name at Petrovac and a street was named after him in Belgrade.

Lieutenant Lajos Gönczy
1900 Paris; 1904 St Louis USA; 1906 Athens
Hungary
Athletics
Bronze (1900) Silver (1906)
46th Honved Infantry Brigade
Died 4 December 1915 aged 34

'One of the few that competed in three separate Olympics'

Lajos Gönczy (Grön) was born on 24 February 1881 in Szeged, Csongrád, Hungary. He was educated in his home town at the Piarist High School. It was while there that he developed his talent for athletics, specializing in the high jump, pole vault and distance running, winning a number of cups and tournaments. After leaving school in 1899 he went up to Pázmány Péter University to read law. While there he joined the Budapest University Athletics Club (BEAC). He held four Hungarian high jump national records, jumping 172 cm in 1900, 179 cm in 1901, 181 cm in 1902 and finally 182 cm in 1904.

He was not only a lover of sports but also of life and made many friends and spent many nights in local restaurants drinking Gönczy spiccert (a sort of soda), and acquired the nickname 'Spicceres' which stuck with him for the rest of his life.

In 1900 at the age of 19 he was one of seventeen Hungarians selected to compete in the Paris Olympics. Not the best organized Olympics, with even Parisians either not knowing it was happening or showing little interest, Gönczy managed to win a bronze medal in the high jump, clearing 175 centimetres. He was selected to represent Hungary again in the 1904 Olympics in St Louis. The Hungarian team only consisted of four athletes. This time Gönczy only managed fourth in the high jump, just missing out on a medal, and fifth in the men's standing high jump.

Returning to Hungary he became the Hungarian high jump champion in both 1904 and 1905, breaking the Hungarian high jump record in 1904 with a jump of 182 centimetres. In 1906 he was selected to represent the Hungarian team for a third time, in Athens. This time Gönczy jumped 175 centimetres taking the silver medal. He came fifth in the men's standing high jump. This was to be his last Olympic Games; he eventually retired from athletics in 1910. Returning to Szeged he became a magistrate and in 1913 married Olga Heller.

The Extinguished Flame

At the outbreak of the First World War Gönczy was mobilized and at the end of June 1915 sent to the Italian front defending a position near the village of Marcottini where he was involved in some of the heaviest fighting on the front.

On 30 November 1915 Gönczy together with his battalion was positioned in the village of San Martino in the north-western corner of Monte San Michele. On 3 December 1915, during the first battle of Galician, Gönczy's battalion was subjected to an artillery barrage from Italian troops as a precursor to an all-out assault. Lieutenant Gönczy's dugout received a direct hit killing him and two other officers instantly (the Italian attack was later beaten back).

He was buried in grave number 1168 in the 17th division cemetery in the Vallone valley. During the 1930s the graveyard was emptied to make way for a development. To date no one has any idea where the remains of the Hungarian soldiers buried there, including those of Gönczy, were taken.

Captain Edmund William Bury
1908 London
Great Britain
Racquets
Silver Medal
11 Battalion King's Royal Rifle Corps
Died 5 December 1915 aged 31

'Not the greatest of players, but the most determined'

Edmond William Bury was born on 4 November 1884 in Kensington, London. He was the son of Henry Entwistle and Angela Mary Bury. He was educated at Eton before going up to Trinity Cambridge. While at Trinity he was a double racquets blue in 1904 and 1905. He was a great forehand court player with the ability to escape from seemingly impossible positions. He played in the Amateur Championship on several occasions but was never quite good enough to become champion.

The silver medal won by Bury in 1908.

His skills were considered good enough however to make him part of the London Olympic racquets team in 1908. His singles competition was a bit of a disaster. He received a bye in the first round before scratching from his second round match against Henry Brougham. However, playing together with Cecil Brown he won a silver medal in the doubles losing the gold medal place to Vane Pennell and John Jacob Astor 1–4.

After university Bury qualified as a solicitor, working for his father's company. He also met and married Ida Carrick and they had one son.

At the outbreak of the war he took a commission into the 11th battalion King's Royal Rifle Corps and landed in France with them. He was killed in action on 5 December 1915 near Fleurbaix. He is buried in Rue-Petillon Military Cemetery, Fleurbaix, grave reference I.H.78.

His brother Harold Bury had been killed in action eleven months earlier. We can only imagine what his parents must have gone through.

His son David lost his life during the Second World War whilst flying with 111 Squadron RAF and is also buried in France.

Georg Baumann
1912 Stockholm
Russia
Greco-Roman wrestling
Died 1915 aged 23

'The unlucky wrestler'

Georg Baumann was born on 1 September 1892 in St Petersburg Russia to Estonian parents. Considered by many to be the most gifted wrestler of his time he began his sporting career in St Petersburg at the Sanitas, St Petersburg. He specialized in Greco-Roman wrestling as a lightweight. Greco-Roman wrestling has been contested since the first modern Olympics in 1896 and has been part of every Olympic Games since 1908. Basically two wrestlers of similar weight are scored for their performance in two three-minute periods, which can be terminated early by a pin down or fall. It also forbids holds below the waist which is the major difference between Greco-Roman wrestling and freestyle wrestling, the other Olympic wrestling event.

Georg was selected to take part in the 1912 Olympic Games in Stockholm with two other Estonian Greco-Roman wrestlers, August Kippasto (1887–1973) and Oskar Kaplur (1889–1962). Unfortunately he was knocked out in the early stages by losing to both Finnish wrestlers, Emil Vare in the 37th minute who went on to take the gold, and Johan Salonen who he lost to in only four minutes. Baumann was in fact a little unlucky. Having bulked up before the voyage to Sweden, intending to eat nothing on board the ship taking them to Sweden in an attempt to avoid seasickness from which he suffered badly, he found himself on arrival assigned to a different weight class in which he struggled to compete.

Returning to Russia and continuing with his training it was the following year, 1913, that was to see him reach his peak in the sport. Taking part in the world championship in the lightweight division he defeated all comers to take the gold medal in Breslau. He also took the gold medal in the Russian championships and was awarded the title of Best Amateur Wrestler of the Baltic States.

In 1914 Baumann joined the Russian army and was sent to the front. All that is known is that he was killed sometime in 1915.

1916

Second Lieutenant (formally Squadron Sergeant Major) Hugh Durant RVM
1912 Stockholm
Great Britain
Shooting/Modern Pentathlon
Two Bronze Medals
9th (Queens Royal) Lancers
Died 20 January 1916 aged 38

'One of the Finest Shots in the Army'

Hugh Durant was born on 23 February 1877 in Brixton, the son of James Henry and Clara Durant, of 115 Sutton Court, Chiswick. After leaving school he was apprenticed as an engineer before enlisting into the ranks of the 9th Queens Own Lancers on 7 January 1897. He served with his regiment during the South African (Boer) War and was awarded the Queen's South Africa medal 1899–1902 with seven bars, Belmont, Modder River, Relief of Kimberley, Driefontein, Johannesburg, Diamond Hill, Wittebergen and King's South Africa medal with two bars, S.A.01 and S.A.02. A crack shot, he won the revolver championship in South Africa and then in Bisley in 1911.

He was selected to represent the military revolver team in the 1912 Olympic Games in Stockholm. He won a bronze medal in the 30 metre team event with a score of 1,107 and a further bronze in the 50 metre team event scoring 1804. In the 50 metre individual pistol event he finished 20th. A fine all-round athlete he also took part in the first ever modern pentathlon event coming 18th. Also in 1912 he was awarded the Royal Victorian Medal (*London Gazette* September 1912). He was also promoted to squadron sergeant major. His list of shooting awards is impressive. He won the Whitehead Challenge medal in 1911, 1912, 1913 and 1914, the Whitehead Challenge silver medal in 1912 and 1913, the NRA silver medal for revolver for 1912 and 1914, the NRA bronze medal for revolver for 1909, the ARA Revolver gold medal for 1911, came second in the Army Champion SSM Hollins Cup in 1909, won the TRA 50-yard revolver cup medal for 1910, and the NRA revolver medal for 1913.

Travelling to France with his regiment he was seriously wounded at the Lancer's famous charge at Moncel on 7 September 1914 in the final 'lance on lance' action of the First World War in which Lieutenant Colonel David Campbell led a charge of two troops of B Squadron and overthrew a squadron of the Germans' 1st Guard Dragoons. He was commissioned into his regiment on 16 December 1914. Returning to the 9th Lancers after recuperating from his wounds he was both mentioned in despatches and received the (French) Medaille Militaire in April 1915. He was killed instantly on 20 January 1916 when a two-inch mortar shell fired from Guildford trench by a detachment of the 62nd Trench Mortar Battery under his command prematurely exploded immediately after firing. He had served over seventeen years with the Lancers.

He was buried in Vermelles British Cemetery, grave reference II. N. 1.

Although several records note that he was decorated with the Distinguished Conduct Medal (DCM) for bravery, including the Commonwealth War Graves, I can find no record of his being awarded this decoration and believe there has been some confusion between the DCM and RVM.

His Royal Victorian Medal together with his two bronze Olympic medals and military medals were sold in 1910 for over £7,000 (note, no DCM).

Second Lieutenant Arthur William Wilde
1908 London
Great Britain
Shooting
1st Battalion Hampshire Regiment
Died 21 January 1916 aged 37

'He loved shooting'

Wilde is seen here, furthest on the right.

Arthur William Wilde was born in Paris in 1883, the son of Thomas Wilde, gentleman. Returning to England he resided in Putney before moving to East Sheen, Surrey. On 10 March 1906 he married Gladys Gertrude Belcher in St John the Evangelist, Putney, the daughter of Alexander Belcher, a solicitors' clerk. They had one son, Eric Arthur, born in 1907. He began his professional life as a commercial traveller before becoming a fine art dealer. On 3 February 1900 he enlisted into the ranks of the 68 company of 19 battalion Imperial Yeomanry becoming 13303 Private (later Corporal) Arthur Wilde. He served in the South African War in 1899 (the Boer War) and was awarded the Queen's South Africa Medal with clasps for Cape Colony and Transvaal.

He spent most of his leisure time sports shooting and was on the committee of the Ham and Petersham Miniature Rifle Club serving on the committee until 1915. During that time he won the Throne Cup for shooting in 1914 (the Royal Toilet Soap Challenge Cup presented by Edward Cook and Co Ltd, the Soap Specialists) and the Walker Cup for shooting in 1914 (this had been presented in 1906 by Mr J. Walker who was a vice president of the club). He was selected to shoot in the 1908 Olympic Games in London. He was unplaced in the small-bore rifle prone 50 and 100 yards, 6th in the small-bore rifle disappearing target 25 yards, and unplaced in the small-bore moving target 25 yards.

At the beginning of the war he enlisted into the ranks of the 1/9 battalion London Regiment (Queen Victoria's Rifles) as Private 2886, later being promoted to sergeant. He travelled to France with them landing in Le Havre on 5 November 1914 and was quickly in action. He was commissioned on 25 April 1915 into the 1st battalion the Hampshire Regiment and joined them in France. He was killed with the battalion on 21 January 1916. The battalion war diary has a basic outline as to his fate:

20 January 1916. Battalion relieved 1st East Lancs in the Hamel Trenches.

21 January 1916. Quiet day. In the evening 2Lt. A W Wilde was posting sentries on the gates of the Mill in the Marsh when a fracas with the enemy occurred. All got away except 2 Lt Wilde and Pte Chapman who have not since been seen. Patrols sent out immediately could see no sign of them. Two Sergeants were slightly wounded but got away alright.

Enquiries were made but no trace was ever discovered and it was assumed that he had been killed in action on that day.

The annual report of the Ham and Petersham Miniature Rifle Club for the year ended 1915 states, 'Every member heard, with sincere sorrow that Second Lieutenant A W Wilde shortly after obtaining his commission, was reported missing, so far nothing has been heard of him, but it is sincerely hoped that he may yet turn up.' They were to be disappointed.

Arthur William Wilde is commemorated on the Thiepval Memorial to the missing, pier and face 7 C and 7 B. Administration (with will) London 23 May to Gladys Gertrude Wilde, widow, effects £2,302.

2749 Private Geoffrey Horsman Coles
1908 London
Great Britain
Shooting
Bronze Medal
24th Battalion Royal Fusiliers
Died 27 January 1916 aged 44

'A born officer that joined the ranks'

Geoffrey Horsman Coles was born on 13 March 1871 in Hastings, East Sussex. He was the son of Timothy and Amelia Coles of St Helen's Ore, Hastings and 76 Westbourne Terrace, London. He was educated at Mr Malan's school at Wimbledon before going up to Winchester College (Chernocke House) being one of six brothers that were educated there. In 1889 he left Winchester to study practical engineering at Manchester, working subsequently at University College London, and at the Great Western Railway Works at Swindon. He gave up engineering in 1895 and resided for many years at Sennen, Cornwall.

A fine shot, he was selected as part of the shooting team to take part in the 1908 Olympic Games in London. He came eleventh in the men's individual free pistol 50 yards, but managed to pick up a bronze medal in the men's free pistol 50 yards team.

In January 1915 he enlisted as a private in the 24th (Sportsmen's) Battalion Royal Fusiliers who had been formed in London on 20 November 1914. In March 1915 the battalion moved to Hornchurch and then in June 1915 it came under the command of 99th Brigade, 33rd Division. Coles landed at Boulogne in November 1915 with his battalion, then on 13 December 1915 the battalion transferred to 5th Brigade in 2nd Division. Private Coles was killed by an exploding rifle grenade on 27 January 1916 while on outpost duty at Festubert.

He is buried in Brown's Road Military Cemetery Festubert, grave reference I. G. 17. He is also commemorated in Winchester School Cloisters, outer H3; a plaque is dedicated to him in St Buryan's Church in Cornwall (see photograph); and his name is on the war memorial in Sennen, Cornwall.

Lieutenant Albert Aristide Jenicot
1908 London
France
Football
165ᵉ French Infantry
Died 22 February 1916 aged 31

One of France's finest footballers

Albert Jenicot was born on 15 February 1885 in Lille, France. A gifted football player he played for the French club RC Roubaix. In 1908 he was selected to represent France at football in the London Olympics. It was the first Olympic games that national teams had played against each other. Up until then it had been club sides that played against each other. Eight teams entered (including two from France, France A and France B.

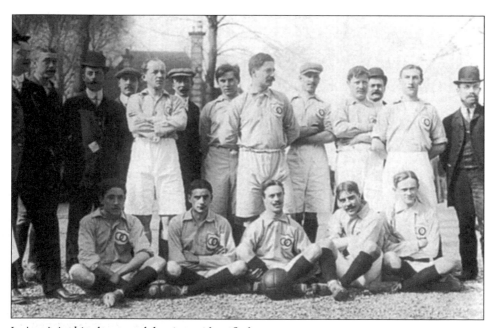

Jenicot is in this photograph but is not identified.

Jenicot played for France B) although Hungary withdrew due to the Bosnian crisis and Bosnia withdrew after losing their FIFA membership. On 19 October 1908 France B lost to Denmark 9–0. France A, who were due to play Bosnia, had a pass due to their non-attendance. On 22 October 1908 France A played Denmark losing the match by a record 17–1. Denmark's Sophus 'Krølben' Nielsen scored a record ten goals in the match, Vilhelm Wolfhagen four, August Lindgren two and Nils Middelboe one. France managed a consolation goal in the sixteenth minute scored by Emile Sartorius. Great Britain went on to win the gold defeating Denmark in the final 2–0. Denmark won the silver and the Netherlands the bronze after defeating Sweden 2–0.

Jenicot won three caps for France in total, against Switzerland, Belgium and Denmark.

Jenicot served as a lieutenant with the 165ᵉ French Infantry during the war and was killed in action on 22 February 1916 at Vacherauville, Mause, France during the First Battle of Verdun. Five members of the French 1908 Olympic football team were to die during the war.

Private Walter Jesinghaus
1912 Stockholm
Germany
Gymnastics
10th Company, 267Nr Reserve of Infantry
Died 22 February 1916 aged 31

Only just failed to win a medal

Walter Jesinghaus was born on 10 October 1887 in Dusseldorf, Nordrhein-Westfalen, Germany. A keen athlete and gymnast, he competed for the Allgemeiner Akademischer Turnerbund Leipzig. In 1912 he was selected to compete for Germany in the Stockholm Olympics. He competed in two events, the men's team all-around and the men's team all-around free style.

The first event, the men's team all-around, free style was held on 10 July 1912 at the Stockholm Olympic Stadium, Stockholm. Germany came in fourth with 16.85 points (see Alfred Staats, died 22 October 1915).

His second event the, men's team all-around was held on the 11 July 1912 at the same venue. Once again each team was made up of between 16 and 40 gymnasts. Germany came fifth with 32.40 points (again see Alfred Staats, died 22 October 1915).

During the First World War Jesinghaus served with the 10th Company, 267Nr Reserve of Infantry. He was killed in action on 22 February 1916.

Captain Alan Patterson
1908 London; 1912 Stockholm
Great Britain
Athletics
71st Brigade Royal Artillery
Died 14 March 1916 aged 30

'A champion in everything he did'

Alan Patterson was born on 12 March 1886 in Deal, Kent. He was the son of the Rev Robert Patterson MA and Esther Beatrice (née Marshall). He had two sisters, Beatrice and Margaret, and three brothers, Robert, John and Leonard. He was educated at Charterhouse School (Bodeites House). An outstanding athlete at school he carried his talent into the army. He went to the Royal Military Academy at Woolwich after which he was commissioned into the Royal Field Artillery. Stationed in Sheffield, he ran with the Sheffield Harriers for several years. He became the Army quarter-mile champion in both 1908 and 1909. In 1909 he added the half-mile champion title, and became the amateur quarter-mile champion. He also won the 440 yards at the 1909 AAA championship in an exciting run-off after he had dead-heated with the well-known runner Lionel Reed (who also took part in the 1908 Olympics). Patterson also came fourth in the AAA 440 yards in 1910 and in the 880 yards in 1912. During this time he met and married Nan Patterson and they moved to 30 Clarence Rd, Walmer, Kent. He was posted to both South Africa and Madras, India, returning to England to take part in the war.

He was selected to run for Great Britain in the 1908 Olympic Games in London. Running in the 400 metres he took second place in his preliminary heat with a time of 50.6 seconds to the eventual winner John Atlee's 50.4 seconds. This loss stopped Patterson advancing to the semi-finals. He was selected to run in the 1912 Stockholm Olympics in both the 400 and 800 metres but didn't advance beyond the heats in either event.

Captain Alan Patterson was killed in action while serving with the 71st Brigade, Royal Artillery on 14 March 1916. A later account of his death explained what happened. Walking from his gun pit to his mess in Flanders a stray shell exploded close to him and a piece of shrapnel struck him in the head killing him instantly. His CO later wrote to his wife pointing out that he had recommended Alan for a DSO twice, once after the battle of Loos, and again shortly after his death.

A brother officer wrote, 'We were all awfully fond of him.'

His sergeant also took the trouble to write: 'He was liked and respected by all…we would follow Captain Patterson anywhere, as he took such good care of his men and never exposed them to unnecessary danger…A real good one.' Captain Paterson died two days after his 30th birthday.

He is buried in the Fosse 7 Military Cemetery, (Quality Street) Mazingarbe, Pas-de-Calais, grave ref: II. G. 2.

Gunner Karl Braunsteiner
1912 Stockholm
Austria
Football
Austrian Artillery
Died 19 April 1916 aged 24

Considered the finest Austrian footballer of his day

Karl Braunsteiner was born on 27 October 1891 in Vienna. Considered one of the finest footballers and defenders of his time he played successfully for the Wiener Sports Club (WSC). The club was established in 1883 and is one of Vienna's oldest athletic and footballing clubs.

He was selected to be part of the Austrian football squad to take part in the 1908 Olympics to be held in London. The 1908 Olympics were the first time that national sides played against each other; previous to that it had been selected club sides. Eight teams entered, including two from France (France A and France B). Hungary withdrew from the games due to the Bosnian crisis and Bosnia withdrew after losing their FIFA membership.

Eleven European nations entered the competition. It was played between 29 June and 5 July 1912 at three different stadia: Tranebergs Idrottsplats, Rasunda Idrottsplats and Olympiastadion. Austria started well beating Germany 5–1 on 29 June 1912. The following day, 30 June, they were beaten by the Netherlands 3–1 in the quarter final, knocking them out of the main competition. Playing in the 'consolation quarter-final' they defeated Norway 1–0, then Italy 5–1, but lost in the consolation final 3–0 to Hungary. Great Britain took the gold, Denmark the silver and the Netherlands the bronze. Braunsteiner played for Austria on eight occasions, five of which were during the Olympic games.

At the outbreak of the war Braunsteiner joined the Austrian Artillery as a gunner and was posted to Poland. He was taken prisoner of war and shipped to Tashkent in Uzbekistan where he died from typhoid fever on 19 April 1916. I have been unable to find a record of his burial place.

Captain Guido Romano
1908 London; 1912 Stockholm
Italy
Gymnastics
Gold Medal (1912)
Italian Infantry
Died 18 June 1916 aged 28

'The perfect physical specimen'

Guido Romano was born on 31 January 1888 in Modena, Italy. Very little seems to be known about him other than he was an outstanding gymnast who represented Italy in both the 1908 London Olympics and the 1912 Stockholm Olympics. In 1908 he came nineteenth in the individual gymnastics event, and in 1912 he improved his place, coming ninth. Then he went on to be part of the Italian team that took the gold medal in the team event beating both Hungary and Great Britain.

Serving with the Italian Infantry during World War One he was killed in action on the plateau of Asiago near Vicenza on 18 June 1916 during the Battle of Asiago.

The Guido Romano public swimming pool in the Via Ampere in Milan was later dedicated to him.

Captain Maurice Auguste Raoul-Duval
1900 Paris
France
Polo
Bronze
66ème French Infantry
Died 5 May 1916 aged 50

The handsomest man in France

Maurice Auguste Raoul-Duval was born on 27 April 1866 in Le Pecq, Yvelines, France. He was the son of Fernand Raoul-Duval, a civil engineer, and Henriette Marie Dassier. Despite coming from a wealthy Parisian family he was sent to England for his education studying at King's College Cambridge. Described as a 'tall good looking Frenchman, who had lost a fortune and was trying to regain it', he married into the British aristocracy by attaching himself to Fanny Lawrence Venables-Vernon, daughter of the 7th Baron Vernon.

A keen and energetic polo player, he belonged to both the Bagatelle Polo Club de Paris and the Compiègne Polo Club team. Selected to play for France in the 1900 Olympic games in Paris he represented both of his polo clubs. The matches were held on 28 May, 31 May, and 2 June 1912. Twenty players from four nations – France (two teams), Great Britain, Mexico and the United States of America – took part in the competition. The teams were also made up of mixed nations. The Bagatelle Polo Club de Paris included the British player Frederick Freke. Compiègne Polo Club was knocked out in the quarter finals by Foxhunters Hurlingham, a mixed British and American team, 10–0. Duval's second team, Bagatelle Polo Club de Paris, was knocked out in the semi-finals, once again by the Foxhunters Hurlingham, 6–4. Foxhunters Hurlingham went on to take the gold, BLO Polo Club Rugby the silver, with Duval's club Bagatelle Polo Club de Paris taking the bronze.

During the First World War Duval served as a captain with the 66ème French Infantry and was killed in action on 5 May 1916 at Verdun.

Captain John Robert Somers-Smith MC
1908 London
Great Britain
Rowing (coxless four)
Gold Medal
1/ 5th London Regiment (London Rifle Brigade)
Died 1 July 1916 aged 28

'One of the bravest men I ever saw'

John Robert Somers-Smith was born on 15 December 1887 in Walton-on-Thames, Surrey. He was the son of Robert Vernon Somers-Smith and his wife Gertrude. Somers-Smith's father, also an old Etonian, had been an athlete of note while at Oxford, running against Cambridge in 1868 and 1869 and being the AAA's half-mile champion on two occasions.

John became 'captain of the boats' at Eton and he rowed for Magdalen College Oxford. He did not row in the university boat although his brother Richard did, rowing for Oxford in the Boat Race twice, losing in 1904 and defeating Cambridge in 1905. Instead of rowing in the eight John chose to concentrate on the coxless fours. He won the Stewards' Challenge Cup and the Visitors' Challenge Cup at Henley Regatta in both 1907 and 1908.

As a result of his several successes he was selected to row in the coxless fours during the 1908 Olympics in London, together with Collier Cudmore (1885–1971), Angus Gillan (1885–1971) and Duncan Mackinnon (1887–1917); Somers-Smith rowed stroke. Defeating another British Leander crew as well as crews from Canada and the Netherlands Somers-Smith's coxless four took the gold medal. In both 1910 and 1911 as a member of the Leander Club Somers-Smith went on to win the Grand Challenge Cup twice. On leaving Oxford he practised as a lawyer.

At the outbreak of the First World War Somers-Smith took a commission into the 5th London Regiment (London Rifle Brigade). Promoted to captain he won the Military Cross (MC) for bravery and was killed in action on 1 July 1916 (the first day of the battle of the Somme) during the attack by the 56th London Division at Gommecourt.

His body was never recovered or identified and he is commemorated on the Thiepval Memorial to the missing, pier and face 9 D.

Duncan Mackinnon, who had rowed with Somers-Smith and won the gold in 1908, was killed in action serving with the Scots Guards on 9 October 1917.

John's brother Richard was killed in action on 30 June 1915, aged 31, serving with the King's Royal Rifle Corps.

Second Lieutenant Alfred Edward Flaxman
1908 London
Great Britain
Men's Standing High Jump, Men's Discus, Men's
Discus Greek Style, Javelin Throw Free Style
1/6 Battalion South Staffordshire Regiment
Died 1 July 1916 (First Day of the Somme) aged
36

'The Army's pocket athlete'

Alfred Edward Flaxman was born on 1 October 1879 in Wombwell, South Yorkshire, the youngest son of Alfred Edward, the rector of St Mary's Church, Wombwell, and Harriet Jecks Flaxman. The family lived at The Rectory, 10 Summer Lane (now a car park). Flaxman's mother died in the autumn of 1880, shortly after the birth of Alfred's younger brother and only sibling Samuel. In 1901 his father became the rector of Grundisburgh and the family moved to Suffolk.

In 1911, Alfred, a gifted artist and musician, went to London to study violin at the Royal Academy of Music while at the same time beginning to develop an athletic career. Although modest in stature, under the guidance of the German athlete and trainer Eugen Sandow (1867–1925), known as the 'father of modern bodybuilding', he developed a fine strong physique. He featured in the AAA hammer throw for ten years between 1905 and 1914, winning in 1910. He won the AAA pole vault in 1909, when oddly he was the only competitor, as well as being placed in the first six in both the shot and discus at the championships. He was also a fine boxer and gymnast. In 1908 he was selected to take part in the 1908 London Olympics. He competed in the discus, Greek discus, free style javelin and standing high jump (some records also say pole vault but I can find no evidence of this). Although he competed hard he failed to win a medal.

Taking a commission as a second lieutenant with the 1/6th South Staffordshire regiment on 18 June 1915, he arrived in France and was given command of a battalion of bombers. There was good reason for this. During his time training at the 'Bull Ring' at Étaples, when he first arrived in France, he caused consternation by hurling a bomb well over seventy-five yards. A pocket Hercules, he only stood 5'9" tall and weighed 10 stone.

The Extinguished Flame

On 1 July 1916, during the first day of the Somme, 1/6 Battalion formed part of the 137th Brigade 46th (North Midland) Division, and were detailed as part of the ill-fated diversionary attack at Gommecourt on the most northern section of the attacking front. The attack was made under the cover of smoke and although the South Staffs reached the enemy wire, they discovered it was largely intact. Caught out in the open, the German machine gunners and bombers made short work of them. The few that managed to get into the German trenches were quickly killed or driven back. The second and third waves were caught in a fierce barrage, and machine gun crossfire from the 'Z' salient to the north of the attack, and battalion casualties amounted to 305 killed and wounded. Flaxman, who was part of the first wave and had command of a company of bombers, was caught up on the wire as he tried to push through and was killed by German machine gun fire. His brother, Captain Samuel Flaxman, who had studied medicine and qualified as a doctor and was serving with the 1/2nd North Midland Field Ambulance RAMC, searched for his brother's remains, but they were never found.

His commanding officer, Lieutenant Colonel F.A.M. Webster, described Flaxman: 'He could bend a horseshoe or rip a half pack of playing cards in half... A simple gentleman, the best of sportsmen and a very gallant soldier.'

Flaxman is commemorated on the Thiepval memorial, pier and face 7 B.

He is largely forgotten in his home town of Wombwell, the only remaining sign of his family being the crumbling grave of his parents in Wombwell cemetery. The stone is inscribed:

> Their elder son 2nd Lieut Alfred Edward Flaxman
> Amateur Champion Hammer Thrower & Pole Jumper
> Born October 1st 1879 Killed in action July 1st 1916
> and whose grave is not known
> Loving and beloved

Captain Béla Békessy
1912 Stockholm
Hungary
Fencing
2nd Hussars Regiment
Died 6 July 1916 aged 40

Hungary's Finest Fencer

Béla Százados Békessy was born on 16 November 1875 in Debrecen, Haydú-Bihar, Hungary. A career soldier, he became one of Hungary's greatest fencers, competing for the Hungarian Athletic Club (MAC). He studied under the great fencing master László Borsody (d.1941), who is recognized as being the primary creator of the modern Hungarian style of sabre fencing that led Hungary to a half-century of superiority and gold medals at the World Championships and Olympics. He also spent time with the Italian master-fencing instructor, Talo Santelli (1866–1945) who was considered to be the 'father of modern sabre fencing'. Békessy concentrated on both the foil and the sabre. He won numerous Hungarian titles between 1902 and 1907 and was the Hungarian champion in both 1905 and 1906 (he also won the Hungarian dressage championship in Budapest in 1907).

In 1912 he was selected as part of Hungary's fencing team to take part in the Olympic games being held in Stockholm. He took part in the sabre, épée and foil. The foil event took place between 6 and 8 July 1912 at the Östermalm Sporting Grounds, Stockholm. Békessy came a commendable seventh. The gold was taken by the Italian fencer Nedo Nadi (1894–1940). Nadi was considered the most versatile fencer in history, uniquely winning an Olympic title with each of the three weapons at the same games. The silver was won by another Italian, Pietro Speciale, and the bronze by the Austrian Richard Verderber. Békessy's next event was the men's individual épée. It was his best event but he failed to proceed beyond the heats. The gold was taken by the Belgian fencer Paul Anspach, the silver by the Danish fencer Ivan Osiier and the bronze by another Belgian fencer Philippe de Beaulieu. Békessy's final and best event was the sabre. This time Hungary won all three medals. The gold was taken by Jenő Fuchs, Békessy took the silver, and Ervin Mészáros the bronze.

Mobilized during the First World War the 2nd Hussars were used on the Russian front behind enemy lines to attack and harry the Russian forces in quick commando-style attacks. On one occasion they attacked a large formation of Russian troops acting as a rearguard. They captured over 200 Russian prisoners, a quantity of important secret papers, and war materials including a mobile bakery. For his actions on this day he was awarded the Hungarian Iron Crown for bravery. Békessy was killed in action during a similar attack on 6 July 1914 in Volyn-Podilsk Upland, Ukraine. An annual fencing competition is held in his memory every year in Hungary.

L/7489 Company Sergeant Major William Philo
1908 London
Great Britain
Boxing (Middleweight)
Bronze Medal
8th Battalion Royal Fusiliers
Died 7 July 1916 aged 36

'Born into poverty, went on to win an Olympic Medal'

William Philo was born on 17 February 1882 in Islington, London. He was baptized at St Silas, Pentonville on 23 December 1885 together with his brother James and sister Jane. He was the son of Robert Philo, a butcher, and his wife Margaret who died in 1890. At some point William's father was convicted of child neglect and served a short term of imprisonment.

On leaving school he joined the army as a boy soldier (almost certainly underage) and took part in the South African war of 1899. While in the army he boxed middleweight and did well. In 1908 he was selected to box middleweight at the 1908 London Olympics. In the first round Philo beat fellow British boxer Arthur Murdoch after a hard fought match. He received a bye in the second round only to be knocked out by Reginald Baker the New Zealander in the semi-final (Baker lost the final to the British Boxer Johnny Douglas). However Philo still walked away with an Olympic bronze medal. He went on to box for the Gainsford Amateur Boxing Club.

He left the army in 1908 and became an engineer's assistant residing at 206a Cassland Rd, Hackney. On 26 December 1908 he married Ellen Margaret Coleman and they had two daughters. Unfortunately she was very unhappy about his boxing so he reluctantly gave it up.

During the first war he served with the 8th battalion Royal Fusiliers rising to the rank of company sergeant major. He was posted missing at Albert during the battle of the Somme on 7 July 1916.

The Extinguished Flame

The Royal Fusiliers in the Great War by H.C. O'Neill pages 116–7, explains the action in some detail: 'Ovillers.— On the 7th (July 1916) two other Fusilier battalions were also engaged in the battle. The 8th and 9th battalions of the 36th Brigade, with the 7th Sussex between them, made another attempt to capture Ovillers, and few more costly actions were fought in the whole of the battle of the Somme. The 8th battalion was on the right, and the plan was to take Ovillers from the S.W. flank. The bombardment began at 4.30 a.m., and at 8.26 the two leading companies, A and D, crawled over the parapet and lay out in the open. The weather was bad; and though no rain fell during the night, the fumes of the gas shells were blanketed into the hollows of the ground, and formed a death-trap for many who fell wounded. Lieut.-Colonel Annesley, waving his stick, led the attack as the barrage lifted, and the men leaped forward into a withering machine-gun fire. The Prussian Guards who held these battered positions were worthy foemen, and though the first and second trenches were captured, the cost was very terrible. Annesley, a most gallant officer, was early hit in the wrist. Later he was wounded in the ankle; but he still kept on, and for a time the final objective was in the 8th's hands. Annesley was at length shot above the heart, and fell into a shell hole, where he lay till evening, when he was taken to Albert and died that night. Shortly after noon the Fusiliers were in Ovillers, and the brigade held about half of it on a north and south line. But every officer engaged was either killed, wounded or missing. Captain Featherstonehaugh, who had been wounded, but refused to leave, was killed. So also were Captains Chard and Franklin. Captain and Adjutant Robertson-Walker was never heard of again, and Second Lieutenant Procter was killed; 17 other officers were wounded. The battalion had gone into action 800 strong; they mustered 160 at night, but held on until relieved on the following day.'

William Philo's body was never recovered or identified and he is commemorated on the Thiepval Memorial, pier and face 8 C 9 A and 16 A.

Sous Lieutenant Pierre Charles Henri Six
1908 London
France
Football
329th French Infantry
Died 7 July 1916 aged 28

One of the five French Olympic footballers killed in the war

Pierre Charles Henri Six was born on 18 January 1888 in Le Havre. He was a fine footballer, playing full-back for Olympique Lillois. He played for France in the 1908 Olympics in London in which the France B team lost to Denmark 9–0 and the France A team lost to Denmark 17–1 (see Albert Jenicot, died 22 February 1916).

Six was killed in action at Estrées-Mons, Somme on 7 July 1916.

Sergeant Josef Rieder
1912 Stockholm
Germany
Cyclist
4th Kompanie, Infanterie-Leib-Regiment
Died 13 July 1916 aged 22

Germany's Strongest Cyclist

Josef Rieder was born on 26 December 1893 in Munich. A keen cyclist he represented V.-KI. Germania, München. He was selected to cycle for Germany in the 1912 Olympic games in Stockholm. He took part in the men's road race, team and men's road race, individual. Both events took place on 7 July 1912 at the Stockholm Olympic Stadium.

One hundred and twenty-three riders started the race, setting off at two-minute intervals with the last rider pedalling off at 7 am. The South African Rudolph Lewis took the gold in a time of 10:42:39.0. The British rider Freddie Grubb took the silver in a time of 10:51:24.2 and Carl Schutte the American rider the bronze in a time of 10:52:38.8. Rieder came well down the field in a time of 12:12:32.4 mainly due to a series of mishaps such as punctures and falls.

His next event was the men's road race, team. It covered a distance of 196 miles and there were twelve riders per team with the top four finishers from each team counting towards the teams' overall score. Sweden took the gold in a time of 44:35:33.6. Great Britain took the silver in a time of 44:44:39.4. The bronze went to the USA in a time of 44:47:55.5. Rieder's team came sixth in a time of 46:35:16.1.

He was killed on 13 July 1916 at Verdun.

Corporal Hermann Bosch
1912 Stockholm
Germany
Football
6 Battery (reserve) 58Nr Field Artillery
Died 16 July 1916 aged 25

The hardest defender in Germany

Hermann Bosch was born on 10 March 1891 in Öhningen, Baden-Wurttemberg, Germany. A gifted footballer, he played for Karlsruher FV. In 1912 he was selected to be part of the German football team to take part in the Olympic games in Stockholm. Eleven European teams took part in the tournament. The footballing event took place between 29 June and 5 July 1912 (see also Karl Braunsteiner, died 19 April 1916).

Germany lost their first match to Austria 5–1 eliminating them from the main competition. In the consolation tournament Germany beat Russia in the first round 16–0 with the German player Gottfried Fuchs scoring a remarkable ten goals. In the semi-final they lost to Hungary 3–1, ending their Olympics. Great Britain beat Denmark in the final 4–2 taking the gold.

During the First World War Hermann Bosch served as a corporal with 6 Battery (reserve) 58Nr Field Artillery. He died of wounds on 15 November 1916 (although this date seems to vary depending on source) in Braşov, Romania.

Medical Assistant & Major Maurice Salomez
1900 Paris
France
Athletics
246e Infantry Regiment
Died 7 August 1916 aged 36

Killed while helping others

Maurice Fernand Salomez was born on 10 April 1880 in Paris. A keen athlete and runner he competed for the Racing Club de France. He was selected to compete for France in the 800 metres in the 1900 Olympic Games being held in Paris.

The event was held between 14 and 16 July 1900 at the Bois de Boulogne, a large public park located along the western edge of the 16th district of Paris. Eighteen athletes from seven nations competed. There were three heats in the first round with the top two runners from each heat advancing to the final. Unfortunately Salomez came fourth in his heat, beaten by the American David Hall in a new Olympic record time of 1:59.0 (the previous record of 2:10.0 was held by the British runner Edwin Flack, which he set on 6 April 1896 during the Athens Olympics). British runner Alfred Tysoe, in a time of 1:59.4 (also beating the Olympic record), took second place, knocking Salomez out of the competition.

Despite his disappointing result Salomez went on to come second in the French National Championships in 1901.

He was killed while serving as a medical assistant and major with a field hospital on 7 August 1916 in Ville-sur-Cousances, Meuse. He is commemorated on a plaque outside the Town Hall in Neuilly-sur-Seine.

Captain John Yate Robinson MC
1908 London
Great Britain
Hockey
Gold Medal
Adjutant 7th (Service) Battalion Prince of Wales
Own (North Staffordshire Regiment)
Died 23 August 1916 aged 31

'and all the brothers were valiant'

John Yate Robinson was born on 6 August 1885 in Catford, Lewisham, the second (of seven sons) and twin son (his twin brother being Lawrence) of the Reverend Edward Cecil Robinson (late vicar of Hanbury, Staffordshire) and Edith Isabella of 'Chadsmore', Orchard Rd, Malvern. He was educated at Radley where he was in the first cricket eleven and the football eleven. On leaving Malvern he went up to Merton College Oxford to read history, later receiving his MA. While at Oxford he got his blue for hockey, playing for the university side from 1905, captaining the side in 1909 and later in 1912. During his first three matches against Cambridge, John's twin brother Lawrence was on the opposing team. Lawrence went on to captain Cambridge in 1908. A third brother, Hugh, also later captained Cambridge. John went on to play nine times for England between 1907 and 1911 and Lawrence was capped three times.

He was chosen to play hockey for England in the 1908 London Olympics, the only university blue in England's 1908 Olympic hockey team. In the first round Great Britain beat France 10–1. In the semi-finals they defeated Scotland 6–1 (having been 3–1 down at half time). In the final they defeated Ireland 8–1 winning the gold.

On leaving university he became a schoolmaster, first at Sherborne Prep School 1909–12, and later at St Peter's Court, Broadstairs 1912–14. At the outbreak of the war he joined the Officer Training Corps before being commissioned into the North Staffordshire Regiment. After training in England, John sailed with his battalion from Avonmouth in June 1915 to take part in the Gallipoli Campaign. After the peninsula was evacuated the battalion landed in Egypt on 26 January 1916. A month later the North Staffordshires arrived in Mesopotamia (modern day Iraq) as part of 39th Brigade, 13th Division. They were to be part of the campaign to relieve the besieged British garrison at Kut. Unfortunately before the British Army could reach it, the besieged garrison surrendered to Turkish forces in April 1916. John was promoted to captain and during the action at El Hannah was seriously wounded in the spine. He was mentioned in despatches and awarded the Military Cross (*London Gazette*, 2 February 1916). John was invalided home where he died from his wounds at Roehampton Hospital on 23 August 1916. He is buried at Great Malvern Cemetery, Worcestershire, grave reference 8. 4631.

Of John Robinson's six brothers, Captain Henry Ellis Robinson, RAMC attached 1/6 battalion Prince of Wales Own West Yorkshire Regiment, was killed on 25 April 1918, and Geoffrey Alan Robinson died 23 September 1916 (cause unknown). Edward Backhouse, Lawrence Milner, Hugh Methven, and Charles Stafford Gray Robinson, all survived the war.

Captain Robert Finden Davies
1912 Stockholm
Great Britain
Shooting
9th London Regiment (Queen Victoria Rifles)
Died 9 September 1916 aged 39

'One of the finest shots in England'

Robert Finden Davies was born on 10 December 1876 in London. He was the son of Frederick Herbert Davies, a member of the Stock Exchange. He was educated at Marlborough College and after leaving he became a prominent member of that famous shooting corps, the 1st Middlesex VRC serving in the South African war of 1899 where his company was attached to a battalion of the King's Royal Rifle Corps. He was awarded the South African medal with four clasps. Following in his father's footsteps he became a member of the Stock Exchange in 1898.

He was known for his ability with a rifle but it was much to everyone's surprise when he took the King's prize at Bisley in 1906. He reached the final stages of the King's Prize on four occasions and shot for England in 1910 and 1911 at Bisley. Davies was selected

Davies being carried in the champion's chair at Bisley.

to shoot for Great Britain in the 1912 Olympics in Stockholm, although he failed to win a medal. He participated in the men's military rifle, three positions, 300 metres, coming 39th, and men's military rifle, any position, 600 metres, coming 37th. A fine all round sportsman he occasionally turned out for the MCC at cricket.

The same year Captain Davies retired from the army with an honorary captaincy, however at the outbreak of the First World War he was recommissioned in to the 9th (Queen Victoria Rifles) London Regiment. After serving for two years on home duties he was sent to the front in 1916. He was killed at the head of his men on 9 September 1916 during the successful attack through Leuze Wood on Bouleaux Wood. On the same day, Charles Dickens' grandson Major Cedric Charles Dickens, serving with the 13th London (Kensingtons) Regiment, was also killed.

Captain Davies body was never recovered or identified and he is commemorated on the Thiepval Memorial, pier and face 9 C.

Corporal Quartermaster Justin Pierre Vialaret
1908 London
France
Football
16th French Infantry
Died 30 September 1916 aged 32

One of the five French footballers killed during the Great War

Justin Pierre Vialaret was born on 12 November 1883 in Millau, Aveyron. Playing midfield he represented CA Paris between 1908 and 1909. In 1908 he played for the French B team in the Olympic games held in London in which France B lost to Denmark 9–0 and France A lost to Denmark 17–1 (see Albert Jenicot, died 22 February 1916).

During the war Justin served with the 16th French Infantry rising to the rank of corporal quartermaster. He died of wounds received at Verdun while being evacuated to hospital at Marcelcave on 30 September 1916.

Vialaret is in this photograph but not identified.

Lieutenant René Victor Fenouillière
1908 London
France
Football
2nd Infantry Regiment
Died 4 November 1916 aged 34

Spain's first French footballer

René Victor Fenouillière was born on 22 October 1882 in Portbail, Manche, France. Fenouillière was a talented footballer and several clubs quickly recognized his abilities. He began his career with L'Union Sportive Avranches, Mont Saint Michel (founded in 1897). After studying in England, where he devoted himself entirely to rugby, he was picked up by the Spanish club RCD Espanyol, playing midfield between 1902 and 1903. His skills were quickly recognized and on 8 March 1903 the magazine *Los Deportes* wrote of him as 'a player with proven superiority over the rest'. Joining Barcelona FC on loan in 1903, he played for them on three occasions. His first game was against a team made up from the crew of the *Galliope*, an English ship anchored in the port of Barcelona; Barcelona won the match 1–0. His next match was against Salut on 28 May 1903; Barcelona won the game 3–2. His final match was against Mataroní which they won 8–2, with René scoring one of the goals. The match wasn't straightforward as Mataroní only had seven players, and Barcelona lined up with eight. Returning to Paris he joined Racing Club de France before transferring to Red Star Amical Club, Paris.

In 1908 he was selected to play for the French National football team in the Olympic games to be held in London. France entered two teams, France A and France B. He played for the A team. France B lost to Denmark 9–0 and France A lost to Denmark by a record 17–1 (see Albert Jenicot, died 22 February 1916).

Fenouillière played his final match in 1915 in a friendly between his old club US Avranches and allied soldiers. He joined the army at Granville, taking a commission into the 2nd French Infantry. He was wounded in combat in 1915 and after a period of recovery he rejoined his regiment. On 4 November 1916 he was shot in the head by a sniper and killed north of Rheims, Marne, France. He was later buried in the National Cemetery, Sillery, Marne.

**Lieutenant Commander Frederick Septimus Kelly
DSC
1908 London
Great Britain
Rowing
Gold Medal
Royal Naval Volunteer Reserve
(Hood Battalion Royal Naval Division)
Died 13 November 1916 aged 35**

Rupert Brooke's greatest friend

Frederick Septimus Kelly was born on 29 May 1881 at 47 Phillip Street, Sydney, Australia. He was the fourth son (the Kellys had six boys and one girl) of the Irish-born wool-broker Thomas Herbert Kelly and Mary Anne (née Dick), a local Sydney girl. He was educated at Sydney Grammar School before being sent to England to complete his schooling at Eton College (all five of his brothers went to Eton). While there he became a keen rower and stroked the school eight to victory in the Ladies Challenge Cup at Henley Royal Regatta in 1899.

After leaving Eton he went up to Balliol College Oxford. Music had always been Frederick's passion. He had memorized Mozart piano sonatas by the age of five and began composing at the same age. He was keen to leave Eton and attend a conservatoire, however his parents wouldn't hear of it and he remained at Eton. Kelly was awarded a Lewis Nettleship musical scholarship and became president of the university music club running the Sunday evening concerts at Balliol. He was also a protégé of Ernest Walker (1870–1949) the Indian-born English composer, pianist, organist, teacher and writer who was the director of music at Balliol from 1901 to 1925.

As if to make up the gap in his life of not being able to study music full time, he took up sports – football, cricket, and especially rowing. At Henley in 1902 he won the Diamond Challenge Sculls defeating the equally talented Raymond Etherington Smith in the final. He took part in the 1903 annual Oxford and Cambridge Boat Race rowing number four. It was to be Cambridge's day however as they took the honours by an impressive six lengths in 19 minutes and 33 seconds. In the same year he won the Diamond Sculls at Henley for a second time, this time beating Jack Beresford in the final. Jack Beresford won five medals at five Olympic Games in succession, an Olympic record in rowing which was not surpassed for sixty years until in 1996 Sir Steve Redgrave won his fifth Olympic medal at his fourth Olympic Games (four gold, one bronze). In 1905 he won the Diamond Sculls for a third time beating Harry Blackstaff in a time of 8 minutes 10 seconds, a record that stood for over thirty years.

Having obtained his BA (fourth-class honours in history) in 1903 (MA, 1912) he left Oxford but didn't give up rowing. He became a member of the Leander Club and was part of the Leander crew that won the Grand Challenge Cup at Henley on three occasions in 1903–05. They also took the Stewards' Challenge Cup in 1906. Selected to row number two in the Leander eight during the 1908 London Olympics, they defeated the favoured Belgian crew who had beaten the Cambridge crew in the semi-final by three lengths to take the gold medal. They said of Kelly after the race that 'his natural sense of poise and rhythm made his boat a live thing under him' and 'Many think [Kelly] the greatest amateur stylist of all time.'

Kelly's father died in 1901 and his mother a year later in 1902. Although greatly affected by their deaths he inherited a great deal of money which enabled him to pursue and develop his musical career. Kelly decided to make his home in England and bought Bisham Grange a large manor house on the banks of the River Thames in Berkshire where he lived with his sister Maisey. Although unmarried he did have several relationships, the most important of these being with the Hungarian violinist Jelly D'Aranyi, for whom he composed several works. However this relationship, like all the others, ended without marriage.

Kelly decided to study the piano and composition under the German composer and teacher Iwan Knorr (1853–1916) at the Hochschule Konservatorium in Frankfurt, a choice perhaps influenced by the attendance there of his friend and fellow Australian, Percy Grainger. In 1907 Kelly wrote in his diary, 'Oh to be a great player and a great composer.' After finishing his studies he became an adviser to the Classical Concert Society, championing modern composers.

At the outbreak of the First World War Kelly was commissioned into the Royal Naval Volunteer Reserve. He was initially posted to Drake battalion but was transferred to the Hood battalion serving with his friends the poet Rupert Brook and composer William Denis Browne. Together with others of an equally artistic bent, they became known as the Latin Club. Sailing aboard the *Grantully Castle* the small group of friends sailed towards the Dardanelles in the eastern Mediterranean. Brooke and Kelly grew close on the voyage to Gallipoli and spent a great deal of time together, talking late into the night about literature and music. On 22 April 1915, Kelly became aware that Rupert Brooke was dangerously ill and the following day his great friend died. Kelly composed an elegy dedicated to Brooke, as the poet lay dying nearby. Kelly never really recovered from the death of his friend. It was Kelly and Browne who sorted Brooke's belongings out after his death and it was Kelly who copied the contents of the poet's notebook.

Kelly was one of Brooke's pallbearers at his funeral, helping to bury him on the Greek Island of Skyros. The other bearers were all members of the Latin Club: Denis Browne, Arthur (Ock) Asquith (later Brigadier General, and son of the Prime Minister), Charles Lister, Patrick Shaw-Stewart (who at the age of 25 was a director of Barings Bank and wrote the poem 'Achilles in the Trench'), Bernard Freyberg (later General Lord Freyberg VC and Governor General of New Zealand), and 'Cleg' Kelly.

Although wounded twice during the Gallipoli campaign, Kelly survived, being promoted to lieutenant commander and being awarded a DSC for conspicuous gallantry during the evacuation in January 1916. While serving in Gallipoli and in the most appalling of conditions Kelly wrote musical scores while sitting in his tent.

Kelly was to lose his life not at Gallipoli but at Beaucourt-sur-l'Ancre in France when attacking a German machine gun post on 13 November 1916. On 2 May 1919 a memorial concert was held at the Wigmore Hall, London. Several of Kelly's piano compositions were played but the one that stood out and moved the audience most was his *Elegy for String Orchestra* written in memory of Rupert Brooke.

He is buried in Martinsart British Cemetery, grave reference I.H.25.

Kelly sculling on the Thames.

Private 2nd Class Léon Honoré Ponscarme, Jr.
1900 Paris
France
Cycling
315th Infantry Regiment
Died 24 November 1916 aged 37

Three hundred thousand men, but not enough
To break this township on a winding stream

Léon Honoré Ponscarme was born on 21 January 1879 in District 17, Paris. He was the son of Zechariah and Honoré Eugenie Loiseau. A keen cyclist he was selected to compete for the French Olympic team at the Paris Olympics in the men's sprint. The event was held at the Municipal Velodrome in Paris between 11 and 13 September 1900 over a thousand-metre distance. Ponscarme eventually finished sixteenth. Albert Taillandier the Italian took the gold, his team mate the Italian Fernand Sanz the silver and the American John Lake the bronze.

During the First World War Ponscarme served with the 315th Infantry Regiment. He was killed in action during the battle of Verdun on 24 November 1916. The battle of Verdun was fought between 21 February and 18 December 1916; approximately 375,000 French soldiers were killed during the battle. The German plan was to bleed the French army to death. They almost succeeded.

Ponscarme's name was later placed on a plaque by his parents in the church of Sainte-Marie des Batignolles in Paris.

1916

VERDUN

by Eden Phillpotts

Three hundred thousand men, but not enough
To break this township on a winding stream;
More yet must fall, and more, ere the red stuff
That built a nation's manhood may redeem
The Master's hopes and realize his dream.

They pave the way to Verdun; on their dust
The Hohenzollerns mount and, hand in hand,
Gaze haggard south; for yet another thrust
And higher hills must heap, ere they may stand
To feed their eyes upon the promised land.

One barrow, born of women, lifts them high,
Built up of many a thousand human dead.
Nursed on their mother's bosoms, now they lie—
A Golgotha, all shattered, torn and sped,
A mountain for these royal feet to tread.

A Golgotha, upon whose carrion clay
Justice of myriad men still in the womb
Shall heave two crosses; crucify and flay
Two memories accurs'd; then in the tomb
Of world-wide execration give them room.

Verdun! A clarion thy name shall ring
Adown the ages and the Nations see
Thy monuments of glory. Now we bring
Thank-offering and bend the reverent knee,
Thou star upon the crown of Liberty!

Commander Louis Marie Joseph le Beschu de Champsavin
1900 Paris
France
Equestrianism
Bronze
20e Regiment de Chasseurs
Died 20 December 1916 aged 49

One of the very bravest sons of France

Louis Marie Joseph le Beschu de Champsavin was born on 24 November 1867 in Asserac, Loire-Atlantique. His parents were Louis and Esther Poidevin of Larochelle. He married Amelie Clemence in 1894. Destined for a career in the army he was commissioned into a cavalry regiment, 20e Regiment de Chasseurs. A fine horseman he was selected to represent France in the 1900 Olympic games being held in Paris. Riding his horse Terpsichore he took part in two events, the mixed jumping individual and the mixed hacks and hunter combined.

The mixed jumping individual was held on 29 May 1900 in Breteuil Square, Paris. The competitors had to negotiate 22 jumps over an 850-metre course. The jumps included one double jump, one triple jump, and one water jump four metres wide. The gold was eventually taken by the Belgian rider Aime Haegeman riding Benton II, the silver by another Belgian rider Georges Van Der Poele on Windsor Squire, and finally the bronze by Louis de Champsavin on Terpsichore. His second event, the mixed hacks and hunter combined, took place on 31 May 1900, once again in Breteuil Square. In hacks and hunters the riders perform on the flat at a walk, trot, canter and hand gallop, and then jump two low fences. Scoring is based on the horse and riders' manners, gait, and conformation and their ability to jump the fences cleanly. This was the only time this event was staged at the Olympic games. It was won by the French rider Louis Napoléon Murat (the great-nephew of Emperor Napoléon I of France) on The General. The French rider Archenoul, on Retournelle, took the silver and Robert de Montesquiou-Fezensac took the bronze making it a one two and three for the French riding team. Unfortunately de Champsavin wasn't placed. Two women also competed in this competition, the Italian Elvira Guerra and France's Moulin (whose first name isn't known).

Champsavin riding during the Olympics.

During the war de Champsavin rose through the ranks to command the 20ᵉ Regiment de Chasseurs. He was awarded the Croix de Guerre with palms and mentioned in despatches twice for his bravery in the field. During the battle of Verdun he was put in command of Fort de Tavannes where he served for seven months between 20 April and 4 November 1916 during the height of the battle. Although the German offensive never quite reached the fort it was subjected to heavy shelling. Many of these shells were gas shells and de Champsavin was gassed on a number of occasions. Despite this, he refused to be evacuated and insisted on staying with his men. For his selfless behaviour during this time he was decorated with the Chevalier de la Légion d'Honneur. The gassing had destroyed his health and he eventually evacuated to hospital at Nantes where he died on 20 December 1916. He is buried in the French town of Guerande. He is also commemorated on the war memorial at Rennes.

Lieutenant Andrei Aleksandrovich Akimov
Андрей Александрович Акимов
1912 Stockholm
Russia
Football
Regiment not known
Died 1916 aged 25/26

One of the three Russian 1912 Olympic squad to have been killed

Andrei Aleksandrovich Akimov was born on 12 October 1890 in Gorodishchi, Vladimir, Russia. A talented and powerful footballer he played for Klub Sporta Orekhovo (OKS). This club has one of the most interesting histories of any club I have written about. It was established by two keen Blackburn Rovers fans Clement and Harry Charnock who came from Chorley in England. Both brothers were sent to Russia to advise on the cotton industry. Clement worked in a textile factory in Orekhovo-Zuevo, near Moscow. He decided to introduce the factory workers to football mainly because of his love of the game but also to divert them from drinking vodka. To help give the factory team an identity he brought blue and white Blackburn Rovers shirts back from England together with shorts and socks. However things didn't go well until Clement's brother Harry took over from him and galvanized the team in 1893. Harry also brought several players from England. The team was successful and became very popular. In 1909 a Moscow league was established and OKS became champions (playing with a number of British players) in both 1910 and 1914. Following the Russian Revolution in 1917 the brothers were forced to leave Russia. OKS Moscow was then taken over by the head of the Cheka, the Soviet Union's first secret police force, and renamed Dynamo Moscow. They still play in blue and white shirts.

Akimov was selected to play for the Russian national team in the 1912 Stockholm Olympics. Eleven European countries entered the competition (France and Belgium withdrew and Bohemia's entry was declined because they were not affiliated with FIFA) Austria, Denmark, Finland, Germany, Great Britain, Hungary, Italy, Netherlands, Norway, Russian Empire and Sweden. Russia received a bye in their first round match. Their second round match was played on 30 June 1912 in a hard-fought match in which Russia were defeated 2–1 by Finland and knocked out of the main competition. The

Russian goal was scored by striker Vasily Butusov, the only man to score a goal for Russia throughout the competition. Akimov was dropped for the next match, something he must have later been grateful for: playing in the consolation tournament on 1 July 1912 they were defeated 16–0 by Germany.

I have been unable to discover with whom he served during the First World War but did manage to find out that he was commissioned as a lieutenant. He was killed in action in 1916, the precise date is unknown.

(See also Nikolai Kynin, died 1916, and Grigori Mikhailovich Nikitin, died 1917).

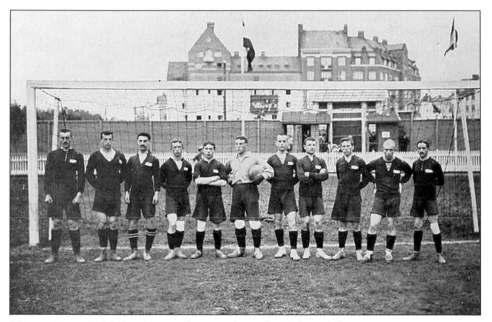

Akimov is seen in this Russian squad group photo, fourth from right.

Nikolai Dmitriyevich Kynin

Николай Дмитриевич Кынин

1912 Stockholm

Russia

Football

Regiment unknown

Died 1916 aged 21

One of the three Russian 1912 Olympic squad to have been killed

Nikolai Dmitriyevich Kynin was born in 1890 in Nikolskoye, Vladimir Oblast. A good footballer playing mid-field he first played for his home town team OKS Nikolskoye before playing for the Moscow-based side Klub Sporta Orekhovo.

Kynin was selected to play for the Russian national team in the 1912 Stockholm Olympics (see also Andrei Akimov, killed in 1916, and Grigori Mikhailovich Nikitin, died 1917).

I have been unable to discover whom he served with during the First World War or what rank he held. All I have been able to discover is that he was killed sometime in 1916.

Lieutenant Wilhelm Lützow
1912 Stockholm
Germany
Swimmer
Silver Medal
German Infantry
Died 1916 aged 22

A duellist and swimmer

William 'Willy' Lützow was born on 19 May 1892 in Esslingen am Neckar, Baden-Württemberg, Germany. He began swimming when he was five years old in 1896, later competing for the Magdeburg Swimming Club. He also became a member of the Stuttgart fraternity Ghibellinia where he almost certainly duelled.

He was selected to swim for Germany in the 200 and 400-metre breaststroke during the 1912 Olympics held in Stockholm. The events were held between 7 and 12 July 1912 with twenty-four swimmers from eleven nations taking part. The final of the 200 metres was a clean sweep for Germany with Lützow coming in second taking the silver in a time of 3:05.0. His fellow countryman Walter Bathe took the gold in a time of 3:05.0, a new Olympic record (beating the British swimmer Frederick Holman's Olympic record of 3:09.2 set in London on 18 July 1908). Paul Malisch, the third member of the German team, won the bronze in a time of 3:08.0. The British swimmer Paul Courtman came in a creditable fourth (Courtman was killed on 2 June 1917).

Lützow's next event was the 400-metre breaststroke. Although he swam his way into the final he was unable to finish. The race was eventually won by Walter Bathe in a new Olympic record time of 6:29.6. The Swedish swimmer Thor Henning (who had also broken the Olympic record earlier in the competition) came second winning the silver in a time of 6:35.6 and the British swimmer Percy Courtman the bronze in a time of 6:36.4.

'Willy' Lützow served as a lieutenant with the German infantry during the First World War and was killed in 1916.

1917

The Extinguished Flame

Sergeant (pilot) Marie Léon Flameng
1896 Athens
France
Cycling
Gold-Silver-Bronze
2nd Aviation Group
2 January 1917 aged 39

The entire stadium including the Greek Royal family gave him a
standing ovation at the end of the race

Marie Leon Flameng was born on 30 April 1877 in Paris. He was the son of Auguste Flameng and Clair Simon. He resided at 162 Boulevard Malesherbes in Paris. An outstanding athlete and cyclist he cycled for Vélocipédique Internationale. Flameng came to notice in France in 1895 when he cycled 3,000 kilometres across France in his own personal Tour de France (although he was never to be placed in the Tour).

At the tender age of 18 years he was selected to cycle for France in the 1896 Olympics being held in Athens. He took part in four events. The first event, the men's 100 kilometres, took place on 8 April 1896 in front of a crowd of 20,000 spectators including the Greek royal family. The event involved 300 laps of the stadium. With his friend and fellow Frenchman Paul Masson acting as his pacemaker and wearing a French flag wrapped around his leg he took the gold medal in a time of 3 hours 8 minutes and 19 seconds, this despite falling heavily shortly before the end of the race. The Greek rider Georgios Koletis took the silver. The entire stadium including the Greek Royal family gave Flameng a standing ovation at the end of the race. His other three events were all held on the same day, 11 April 1896. In the men's sprint Flameng came third gaining the bronze, his friend and fellow French cyclist Paul Masson taking the gold and the Greek rider Stamatios Nikolopoulos the silver. In the men's 333⅓ metres trial he failed to be placed, Paul Mason for France taking the gold, Stamatios Nikolopoulos the silver for Greece and the Austrian Adolf Schmal the bronze. In the 10,000 metres, Paul

Masson once again took the gold with Flameng winning the silver and Adolf Schmal the bronze. In total Flameng managed one gold, one silver and one bronze, quite an achievement for an 18-year-old.

He was conscripted into the French army in 1898 being attached to the eighth regiment of artillery. He transferred to the French flying corps in December 1914 and flew as an observer. On 12 January 1916 he obtained his licence as a pilot and transferred to the 2nd Aviation Group. On 21 June 1916 while on patrol over Verdun his plane was attacked. Flameng's observer was shot and killed and he was seriously wounded in the face. Despite his wounds he managed to get back to his own lines and land his aircraft. He was transferred to the military hospital at Vadelaincourt to recuperate. He was promoted to sergeant on 12 July 1916, returning to his squadron on 3 September. He took part in attacks on Thionville and Hayange Rombach. Flameng died on 2 January 1917 near Eve, Oise, when the engine on the aircraft he was test flying failed. He managed to jump from the plane but his parachute failed and he fell to his death. He was awarded the Croix de Guerre. He was buried in the municipal cemetery of Ermonville.

Flameng standing centre with his squadron Escadrille 25.

Captain Feliks Zenovich Leparsky
Феликс Зенович Лепарский
1912 Stockholm
Russia
Fencer
Russian Infantry
Died 10 January 1917 age 42

A fine fencer and a fine soldier

Feliks Zenovich Leparsky was born in 1875. He was a graduate of the Nizhny Novgorod Oblast. A fine and accomplished fencer he was selected to fence for Russia in the men's foil, individual, during the 1912 Olympics in Stockholm. Two styles of fencing were popular at the time, the French school and the Italian school. The French school insisted that the upper arm should be included in the touch, however the Olympic committee

Russian athletes at the 1912 Olympics opening ceremony.

disagreed with them so the French team refused to take part in the event leaving the competition open to the Italian fencers.

Unfortunately Leparsky was outclassed and finished well down the field. The gold medal went to the Italian fencer Nedo Nadi. Nadi was a remarkable fencer going on to win a further five golds in the 1920 Olympics in the foil (individual), foil (team), men's épée team, men's sabre individual, and men's sabre team. The silver went to another Italian fencer, Pietro Speciale (who also won a gold in the 1920 games). The bronze went to the Austrian Richard Verderber, who also won a silver in the men's sabre. (See also Hermann Plaskuda, died 21 March 1918).

During the War he served as a captain with the Russian Army and was killed on 10 January 1917 in a battle near Dobruja.

Captain Henry Sherard Osborn Ashington
1912 Stockholm
Great Britain
Athletics
(Long Jump, Standing Long Jump)
7th Battalion East Yorkshire Regiment
Died 31 January 1917 aged 25

'Even defeated the great C.P. Fry's record'

Henry Ashington was born on 25 September 1891 in Southport Lancashire. He was the son of Sherard Ashington (a solicitor) and Lydia, of West Hill House Harrow-on-the-Hill. He was educated at Harrow and King's College Cambridge. While at Harrow he was Head of House, won the cross country race, the quarter-mile, the half-mile and the mile in 1910. Going up to King's, he continued with his athletics winning the hurdles and long jump in 1912, and in 1913 the hurdles, the half-mile and the long jump, beating C.P. Fry's record by clearing 23 feet 5¾ inches. He set a further record by winning three events in the same year. In 1914 he won the high jump and the long jump, beating his own record with a jump of 23 feet and 6½ inches. Thus in Oxford and Cambridge sports he won seven events in three years, another record. He received his BA in 1910 and MA in 1914.

In 1912 he was selected for the British Olympic team to take part in the games in Stockholm. He finished tenth in the long jump and fourteenth in the standing long jump, failing to win a medal.

Shortly after the war broke out Captain Ashington was given a commission in the 7th East Yorkshire Regiment and went to the Belgian front early in 1915. He was wounded in the advance of July 1916 and was sent to the London Hospital. After some months of light duty he returned to the front in November 1916 and was promoted to captain. He was mentioned for a gallant action in the General's Divisional Orders on 27 December 1916. On 28 January he wrote the following letter about a suggestion that he should join the Intelligence Corps: 'I don't mind this life. I rather like it, and I like my present position very much indeed. Also I hate that spirit which is so prevalent of always hunting for cushy jobs – trying to get out of it at any price – it makes me want to stay here and see the thing through where I am.'

Three days later, on 31 January 1917, he was hit by a sniper as he was going round his posts and died the same night without recovering consciousness. His colonel wrote: 'It has been a nasty knock to every one of us, and personally I know that I have lost one of my best and bravest Officers... The men in his Company just worshipped him and would have followed him anywhere, and a sadder lot of men I never saw, when they knew he had been mortally hit.'

He is buried in Combles Communal Cemetery Extension, grave reference III. B. 25.

11187 Private Charles Alfred Vigurs
1908 London; 1912 Stockholm
Great Britain
Gymnastics
Bronze (1912)
11th Battalion Royal Warwickshire Regiment
Died 22 February 1917 aged 28

'If at first you don't succeed try, try again'

Charles Alfred Vigurs was born on 11 July 1888 in Birmingham. He was the son of Harry George and Emma Jane Vigurs of 186 Church Road, Yardley. One of the finest athletes in England, on the 'Horse' he was a member of the Birmingham Athletic Institute. He was in the team that won the Adams Shield International Teams Championship for three years in succession, although they lost to the Dunfermline Carnegie Gymnasium,

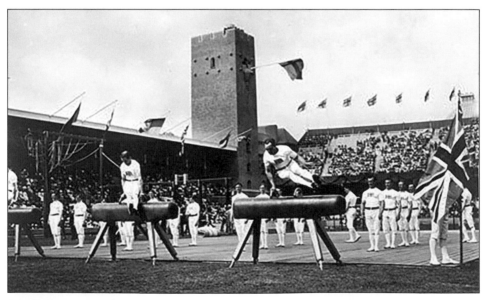

British Gymnasts at the 1912 Olympics.

the Scottish champions, in 1908, by 15½ points, Charles scoring 51½ points. In 1910 he was part of the team that went to Brussels to take part in an exhibition of athletics.

At the age of 19 he was selected to represent Great Britain in athletics at the 1908 Olympics. On this occasion he only managed to come eighth in the men's team all-around competition. However, invited to take part in the 1912 Olympics in Stockholm, he managed to win a bronze medal in the same event.

Shortly after the outbreak of the war he enlisted into the ranks of the 11th battalion Royal Warwickshire Regiment. The 11th battalion were formed in Warwick in September 1914. After training they landed in France on 30 July 1915. Charles Vigurs was killed by a shell near Grenay on 22 February 1917.

He is buried at Maroc British Cemetery, Grenay, grave reference I. N. 33.

Captain Alister Graham Kirby
1912 Stockholm
Great Britain
Rowing
Gold
5th Battalion London Regiment (London Rifle
Brigade)
Died 29 March 1917 aged 28

'Won the Boat Race after four attempts'

Alister Graham Kirby was born on 14 April 1886 in Brompton, West London. He was the son of Arthur Raymond Kirby, a Bencher of Lincolns Inn and his wife Gertrude Fleming. He was educated at Eton College before going up to Magdalen College Oxford.

Kirby is seen standing in the centre wearing a white cap.

He was selected to row in the Oxford boat against Cambridge on four occasions, losing the first three times. Despite this Oxford kept faith with him and he was once again selected to take part in the 1909 race. Now president of the Oxford Rowing Club he rowed number seven and was at last in the winning eight. Oxford defeated Cambridge by three and a half lengths in a time of 19 minutes and 50 seconds. He was the president of Vincent's Club in 1909 (the Vincent's Club is a sports club predominantly but not exclusively for Oxford blues founded in 1863 by the rower Walter Bradford Woodgate of Brasenose College Oxford).

Kirby became a prominent member of the Leander rowing club. Based in Remenham in Berkshire, the Leander Club was founded in 1818 and is one of the oldest rowing clubs in the world. He was selected as captain to lead the eight in the 1912 Stockholm Olympics. Together with Edgar Burgess, Sidney Swann, Leslie Wormwald, Ewart Horsfall, James Angus Gillan, Stanley Garton, Philip Fleming and Henry Wells they defeated the New College Oxford eight to take the gold medal, Germany picking up the bronze.

At the outbreak of the First World War Kirby was commissioned into the 5th battalion London Regiment (London Rifle Brigade). He was promoted to captain before becoming ill and dying on 29 March 1917. He is buried in Mazargues War Cemetery, Marseilles, grave reference III. A. 3.

Prince Tassilo Wilhelm Humbert Leopold Friedrich Karl of Prussia
Germany
1912 Stockholm
Equestrian
Bronze
Fliegerabteilung (Artillerie) 258
Died 6 April 1917 aged 24

'The German Prince who rode for his country and died for his country'

Prince Karl of Prussia was born on 6 April 1893 in Schloss Klein-Glienicke Potsdam, Berlin. He was the son of Prince Friedrich Leopold of Prussia and Princess Louise Sophie of Schleswig-Holstein-Sonderburg-Augustenburg. He was the grandson of Prince Frederick Charles of Prussia and the nephew of Kaiser Wilhelm I.

Prince Friedrich taking part in the show jumping competition during the 1912 Olympics.

Prince Karl was a good all-round sportsman. A fine rider and jumper, he also played football for SCC Berlin (founded in 1902) and was a keen track athlete, being coached by the famous American trainer Alvin Kraenzlein, who was the first man to win four individual gold medals at the Paris Olympics in 1900. He also took part in the *Stafetten-Wettlauf Potsdam-Berlin* several times and managed to achieve several 'German Officer Records'.

An accomplished rider he was selected to ride for the German equestrian team during the 1912 Olympic Games in Stockholm. He took part in both the individual and team events. He came eighteenth in the men's individual jumping. In the team event however, riding 'Gibson Boy', together with Sigismund Freyer, Wilhelm Count von Hohenau, and Ernst Deloch they scored 530 points and took the bronze medal behind France (silver, 538 points) and Sweden (gold, 545 points). He was the first athlete from the royal house of Hohenzollern to take part in the Olympic Games.

A passionate flyer during the war he commanded a German flying unit, FA (A) 258, an artillery observation unit equipped with two seats. He was awarded the Iron Cross both first and second class. Whenever he found the opportunity he also flew with Jasta 2 (better known as Jasta Boelcke after its first commander the legendary German ace Oswald Boelcke) a front line fighter unit flying the famous Albatros fighters. Flying in formation in an Albatros D1 with a distinctive skull and crossbones painted on the side on 21 March 1917 he became separated from his formation in cloud. He was attacked by

Prince Friedrich's crashed aircraft in the hands of the allies.

Lieutenant and Flight Commander Charles Edward Murray Pickthorn of 32 squadron Royal Flying Corps, flying a DH 2 single seater fighter. Pickthorn put bullets into the prince's engine and wounded him in the foot. The prince managed to bring his aircraft down under control and crash landed in no man's land. Crawling out of his plane he tried to make a run for his own lines but was shot and seriously wounded by Corporal B.D. James and 1217 Private Clare Henry Horace Hall (although some accounts also credit 1821 Company Sergeant Major Edward John Powell, 26 Battalion Australian Infantry). Later Lieutenant Pickthorn was awarded a Military Cross for this and other flying combats: 'For conspicuous gallantry and devotion to duty in attacking hostile aircraft, and in carrying out difficult reconnaissances. On one occasion, although wounded, he continued his combat and brought down a hostile machine. On two other occasions he brought down hostile machines in flames.'

The prince was admitted to hospital in Rouen on 3 April 1917 via No.30 Ambulance Train. Despite the best efforts of the surgeon he died on his 24th birthday, 6 April 1917. He was buried close to the hospital his grave marked by a simple wooden cross.

Herbert Haydon Wilson DSO
1908 London
Great Britain
Polo
Gold Medal
Royal Horse Guards
Died 11 April 1917 aged 42

'Life is a city of crooked streets; death is the market place where they all meet'

Herbert Haydon Wilson was born on 14 February 1875 in St Kilda, Victoria, Australia. He was the youngest son (having three brothers and three sisters) of Sir Samuel and Lady Wilson of Ercildoune, one of Australia's formidable sheep stations. Sir Samuel had moved to Australia with his brothers and made a fortune first in mining and then sheep farming. He moved back to England in 1881 and later became the MP for Portsmouth (1886–92) before returning to Australia in 1893. He was only there for a couple of years before coming home, dying in England in 1895 leaving fifteen million pounds.

Educated at Eton College, together with his three brothers, Herbert went up to New College Oxford in 1892. Shortly after leaving Oxford in 1895 he was commissioned into the Sherwood Rangers (Nottinghamshire Yeomanry) and served with the 3rd battalion. At the outbreak of the South African (Boer) War Herbert volunteered to serve overseas. He took part in operations in the Orange Free State, in the Transvaal west of Pretoria, at Venterskroom, in the Orange River Colony including actions at Lindley, and Rhenoster River. He was mentioned in despatches twice (*London Gazette*, 23 April and 10 September 1901) and later received the Queen's Medal with four clasps. He was also created a Companion of the Distinguished Service Order (DSO) (*London Gazette*, 23 April 1901) for his bravery in action: 'Herbert Haydon Wilson, Captain, 3rd battalion The Imperial Yeomanry. For gallantry in defence of posts in the Boer attack on Lichtenburg. Dated 6 March 1901.' He received the award from King Edward VII himself at Buckingham Palace on 25 July 1901. He became honorary captain in the Army in 1901.

The South African Campaign however also brought tragedy to the family. His brother Wilfred died of wounds serving with the 5 Imperial Yeomanry, and another brother, Clarence, was seriously wounded serving with the 8 Hussars on 25 December 1895 (he was so severely wounded that he was never considered fit enough to serve in the military again, which probably saved his life).

Considered one of the finest polo players in England he resided for many years at Ashby Folville. He was a member of the Hurlingham Committee, the governing body of the game. His polo triumphs were considerable and included the All-Ireland Open, the Ranelagh Open, the Social Clubs Cup, the Army Cup, the Roehampton Cup, the Public Schools' Cup and the Irish County Challenge. He played for England against America in 1909 (when England lost the cup) and was one of the members of Captain Hardress Lloyd's team, which attempted to regain the trophy in America two years later. He was one of the famous Roehampton team which won the Champion Cup at Hurlingham in 1905 and 1906, and the Open Cup at Ranelagh in four successive seasons (1904–1907), while he assisted England on three occasions (1908, 1909 and 1911) to gain victories over Ireland in the annual international match. In later years his summer residence was Lower Grove, Roehampton, adjacent to the polo ground. He was also well known with the Quorn, Cottesmore and Belvoir Hounds in Leicestershire.

Herbert Wilson is seen here on the far right with the Olympic team.

In 1908 he was selected to represent Britain at polo in the London Olympics. Despite being a committee member of the Hurlingham Club, Herbert Wilson played for the Roehampton Club – in fact his team defeated the Hurlingham club in round one. Defeating the Irish team in the final round, Roehampton went on to take the gold medal.

At the outbreak of the First World War he took a commission into the Royal Horse Guards, where his brother Lieutenant Colonel Gordon Chesney Wilson MVO was the CO. Having served in both France and Belgium he was killed in action near Arras on 11 April 1917 attempting to capture Monchy-le-Preux. Four regiments from the 3rd Cavalry Division supported the infantry attack. However they were met by a wall of machine gun and artillery fire. Over 600 cavalrymen became casualties and many more horses.

Captain Herbert Wilson is buried in Faubourg D'Amiens cemetery, Arras, grave reference V. A. 1. A short while after his death a memorial service was held for him at Christ Church, Down Street, Piccadilly.

His eldest brother Gordon was killed in action during the First Battle of Ypres on 6 November 1914. He also had an outstanding sporting record, and was one of two Eton boys that disarmed Roderick Maclean when he tried to assassinate Queen Victoria in 1882. Gordon later married Lady Sarah Churchill, sister of Randolph, son of Sir Winston. Of the four sons born to Sir Samuel Wilson, three were to be killed, one in the South African War, two in the First World War. The fourth was never to recover from his wounds but at least survived.

Second Lieutenant Gordon Reuben Alexander
1912 Stockholm
Great Britain
Fencing
2nd Battalion Royal Sussex Regiment attached
13th Battalion East Surrey Regiment
Died 24 April 1917 aged 31

'He died the death of a hero and deserved the VC'

Gordon Reuben Alexander was born in 1885 in Kensington, London, son of James and Florence Alexander of 52 Redcliffe Square. He was educated at Harrow before becoming a member of the Stock Exchange at his father's firm J.M. Alexander and Co in 1908.

A good and keen all-round sportsman, he was a member of the Corinthian Yacht Club, the Felixstowe and Coombe Golf Clubs, and the Sword Club. He won several trophies on the links and was Amateur Foils Champion of Great Britain. He was selected to take part in the 1912 Olympic Games to be held in Stockholm and competed in men's foil individual and men's épée individual. He was unplaced in both events.

Like so many other young men of the time, with the declaration of war he enlisted as soon as he could. Keen not to miss the big adventure and do their bit before it was all over – probably by Christmas. He enlisted into the ranks of the 10th (Stock Exchange) Battalion of the Royal Fusiliers in August 1914. Although offered a commission, he refused it but was quickly promoted to sergeant. He sailed to France with his battalion in June 1915. The following year in January 1916 he finally accepted a commission into the 10th East Surreys, and was then transferred to the 14th battalion Royal Sussex before finally being attached to the 13th East Surreys. He was killed in action on 24 April 1917 during an attack on Villers Plouich, north of Peronne.

His death was described later by a sergeant in his company in a letter to his father: 'Everything went very well in the attack, and we captured the first machine gun and many prisoners. After the objective was gained and the men were digging in under his supervision, one was badly hit and Lieutenant Alexander told a man to go to his assistance, but went himself instead as there was a lot of shelling, and while bandaging the man they were both killed by a heavy shell.'

The same sergeant relates how on one occasion when he went round the company for volunteers for a risky enterprise, the men volunteered 'too freely' on learning that Alexander was in charge. 'He happened to overhear some of it and told me afterwards that it was the greatest satisfaction he got out of the war—it paid him for everything.'

He continued: 'I am sure it would help you in your grief if you could hear how well the men speak of him. I was greeted with the words, "Sergeant, your old pal Alec is gone," and tears stood in eyes that were quite unused to them.'

A brother officer wrote to his father, 'It is with the keenest personal sorrow that I learn of the death of your son, whom we affectionately called "Togo". If it be any consolation to you, you may know that he died the death of a hero and deserved the VC. You will probably have learnt that he with a small party was in danger from a hostile machine-gun. He rushed at it, captured it, and accepted the surrender of the team. He then swung the gun round and fired on the enemy. He was supported by his men, but seeing one lying wounded in the open, he went out to fetch him. He reached his objective, but was immediately killed by shell-fire. It can truly be said of him that he gave his life for others. He was a man absolutely without fear, who commanded the affections and respect of his Company to such an extent that I think, without hesitation, every man would cheerfully have died for.'

The Padre of his battalion wrote to his father: 'We all loved him, and the camaraderie that existed between him and the other officers was really extraordinary. It was just like him to give his life in looking after one of his men.'

'He was a very gallant officer and liked by all,' wrote his commanding officer.

Second Lieutenant Alexander was mentioned in despatches 'for gallant and distinguished service in the Field' (*London Gazette*, 28 February 1918).

He is buried in Fifteen Ravine British Cemetery, Villers-Plouich. grave reference IV. I. 12.

Lieutenant Robert Branks 'Bobby' Powell
1908 London
Canada
Tennis
16/48th Battalion Canadian Infantry
Died 28 April 1917 aged 36

'Canada's Finest Tennis Player'

Robert Branks Powell was born on 11 April 1881 in Victoria, British Columbia. He was the son of Dr Israel and Mrs J. W. Powell, Victoria, British Columbia. Educated at the Victoria High School he later studied law and became a barrister. He served as the private secretary of Henri-Gustave Joly de Lotbinière, the seventh lieutenant governor of Quebec, from 1900 to 1904. A gifted tennis player he learned his trade on the family tennis courts.

He won a number of tennis tournaments early on in his career. He won the 1901 Western Canadian and Pacific Northwest in Tacoma singles competition. In 1903 he won the British Columbia tournament and then in 1904 the Oregon State title.

In 1904 Powell founded the North Pacific International Lawn Tennis Association, and continued to play competitive tennis winning titles in Washington, Oregon, France, Germany, Austria, and Monte Carlo. He reached the semi-final of the Wimbledon championship in 1908, finally losing to the eventual champion Arthur Gore in straight sets. He won the All England Plate at Wimbledon in 1909. In July 1908 Powell won the singles and doubles titles of the Scottish Championship, a victory that brought him finally to national prominence.

In 1908 he was selected to captain the Canadian tennis team in the 1908 London Olympic Games. He came joint ninth in the singles and seventh in the doubles together with his partner James Foulkes. During the Wimbledon championships in 1910 he reached the final of the men's doubles competition together with Kenneth Powell (killed in action 1915) losing in three sets to the eventual champions Major Josiah George Richie (1870–1955) and Anthony Wilding (killed in action 1915). In July 1910 Powell reached the final of the Surrey championship losing to his nemesis Major Josiah George Ritchie in four sets. In 1913 and 1914 he played in four Davis Cup ties for Canada.

On 1 September 1914, at the beginning of the First World War, Powell first served with the 50th Gordon Highlanders of Canada before being commissioned into the 48th battalion Canadian Infantry before transferring into the 16th battalion (Manitoba Regiment) and rising to the rank of lieutenant. Going to France with his regiment he wrote a moving letter to his parents:

Darling Mother, please don't worry and be anxious about me. If I fall, I should like you only to feel pride in the fact that I am trying to do my highest duty and never to mourn me. But I have confidence that God will help me to come through it. But the whole thing is hell.

He was killed while leading his platoon of fifty men in a charge in the battle of Vimy Ridge on 28 April 1917. All of Canada mourned.

He is buried in Écoivres Military Cemetery, Mont-St Éloi, grave reference VI. G. 22.

In 1993 he was inducted into the Canadian Tennis Hall of Fame, followed in 2000 by his induction into the USTA Pacific Northwest Hall of Fame.

56905 Sergeant Isaac Bentham
1912 Stockholm
Great Britain
Water Polo
Gold
'D' Battery, 83rd Brigade Royal Field Artillery
Died 15 May 1917 aged 30

One of the strongest swimmers in the country

Isaac Bentham was born on 27 October 1886 in Ince-in-Makerfield, Lancashire. He was the son of Isaac Bentham, a grocer and insurance agent, and Elizabeth Bennett of 48 Warrington Road, Wigan. He worked as both a grocer and in 1911 a tram conductor. On 12 December 1906 he married Alice Smith at St Mary's, Ince-in-Makerfield. The couple resided at 42 Warrington Road, Lower Ince, Wigan. They had two children Isaac and Florence.

Isaac Bentham, pictured here second from the left.

Bentham, a strong swimmer, had always been keen on water polo, playing forward. He was selected to represent Great Britain in the 1912 Olympic Games to be held in Stockholm. The rest of the team consisted of Charles Smith (1876–1951), George Cornet (1877–1952), Charles Bugbee (1887–1959), Arthur Hill (1888–?), George Wilkinson (1879–1946), and Paul Radmilovic (1886–1968). Interestingly Isaac Bentham and Arthur Hill were the only members of Britain's 1912 water polo team whose Olympic success was restricted to one gold medal. All the other team members won a second gold, either in 1908 or 1920. The British team defeated Belgium 7–5 and Sweden 6–3 before besting Austria 8–0 in the final to win the gold medal.

Isaac Bentham served as a sergeant (56905) with the RFA D/83rd Brigade during the First World War arriving in France on 26 July 1915. He was killed during the battle of Arras on 15 May 1917. He has no known grave and is commemorated on the Arras Memorial, Bay 1.

His swimming costume was later put on public display at Wigan baths and was to be seen there for many years. However when the baths closed the costume was lost.

Private 250755 Percy Courtman
1908 London; 1912 Stockholm
Great Britain
Swimmer (Breast Stroke)
Bronze (1912)
'D' Company 1/6th Battalion Manchester
Regiment
Died 2 June 1917 aged 29

A Bronze Medal and three World Records,
a champion of Manchester and England

Percy Courtman was born on 14 May 1888 at Chorlton-cum-Hardy, Greater Manchester. He was the son of James Courtman, an estates and insurance agent, and Percy Ann of 261 Stretford Rd, Manchester, and had three sisters and two brothers. Courtman attended William Hulme Grammar School between 1898 and 1903. A talented swimmer, he swam for the Old Trafford Swimming Club becoming their first champion, going on to win his first Amateur Swimming Association (ASA) championships in the 200 yards breaststroke on 16 September 1907 in Birmingham. His time was an impressive, for the time, 2:55.4.

Selected to swim for Britain in the 1908 London Olympics he didn't do well, not even getting through the heats of the 200 metre breaststroke race. Not a man to be put off easily he returned to Manchester and continued with his training. Employed by his father he trained in both the evenings and early mornings while working during the day. Selected once again to take part in the Olympic Games in 1912 this time in Stockholm, swimming in both the 200 metres and 400 metres breast stroke in the 100-metre-long course located in Stockholm harbour, he managed to take third place in the 400 metres taking the bronze medal, and come fourth in the 200 metres. It was one of the few successes in a poor Olympics for the British swimmers. Britain's only swimming gold was won by the women's 4×100 metre freestyle relay. This was the first Olympics in which women competed in swimming.

Returning to Manchester in some triumph Percy went on to become the Amateur Swimming Association champion for 200 yards breaststroke in five of the seven seasons between 1907 and 1913. He also set world records in the 400 metres in 1912, and the

500 metres breaststroke in the same year (now no longer recognized as swimming distances). Percy's most impressive achievement however came on 28 July 1914 when he gained the world record for 200 metre breaststroke at Garston Baths, Speke Road, Liverpool. His winning time was 2:56.6 making him the first swimmer to cover 200 metres in under three minutes. Courtman's record remained for eight years until it was finally beaten by the German swimmer Erich Ridemacher in 1922 in a time of 2:54.4.

We can only guess where Percy's swimming career would have led him, but the First World War intervened. Percy enlisted into the 6th (Hulme) Territorial Battalion, Manchester Regiment in 1914. Percy wasn't sent to France as he expected but to Gallipoli, sailing from Plymouth on 2 August 1915 aboard Cunard's *Franconia* as one of 200 replacements to fill the ranks of the 1st/6th battalion who had suffered heavy casualties on 6 August 1915 during the battle of the Vineyard. Percy arrived in Gallipoli on 18 August 1915. Remaining there for four months he finally left Gallipoli for Egypt on 20 January 1916 taking part in the Battle of Romani before chasing the Turkish army across the inhospitable Sinai desert.

From Egypt Percy and his battalion were posted to France arriving in March 1917. On 19 May 1917 the 1st/6th battalion moved to Havrincourt Wood, about 14 kilometres south west of the town of Cambrai, before being sent to reserve positions in June. They suffered a constant stream of casualties largely from German shelling. It was during one of these barrages that Percy was to lose his life, on 2 June 1917. Lance Corporal Stanley Cooke of D Company, 1/6 battalion, explained what happened in his diary entry for Saturday, 2 June 1917: 'Poor Percy blown to bits by one (a shell) about breakfast.'

Percy is buried in Neuville-Bourjonval British Cemetery, grave reference F. 20.

In a war where so many people became just numbers, the *Manchester Evening News* dated 11 June 1917 headlined Percy's death, such was the fame of the man: 'Percy Courtman Killed: A Famous Swimmer'. It also included a photograph of Percy.

The Percy Courtman Memorial Cup for the winner of the 200 metres breast stroke is awarded annually by the Old Trafford Swimming Club.

James Ernest Courtman, Percy's brother, was killed in action a few months later on 22 October 1917 serving with 'Z' Company 23 battalion Manchester Regiment. He is commemorated on the Tyne Cot Memorial.

Their names are remembered on the William Hulme Grammar School war memorial.

Captain Harold Ingleby Hawkins
1908 London
Great Britain
Shooting
Silver
2nd Battalion London Regiment
Died 16 June 1917 aged 30

From the ranks a natural officer

Harold Ingleby Hawkins was born on 22 July 1886 in Finchley, Greater London. He was the eldest son of Mr and Mrs Percy L. Hawkins of Durham Road, East Finchley. After leaving school in 1902 he joined the accounts department of the Northern Assurance Company Ltd (now known as Aviva). Later he was transferred to the accident department. A keen shooter he was a popular member of the insurance rifle club and captain and secretary of the Alexander Palace rifle club. He won several prizes at Bisley for rifle shooting and won high distinctions for miniature rifle shooting. He was also a member of the Queen's Westminster Rifles before the war. On 25 September 1915 he married Elizabeth Irene Morgan of St Brides, Stamford.

In 1908 he was selected to shoot for Britain in the Olympic Games in London. He took part in four events: the men's free rifle, three positions, 300 metres, team, in which he came 6th; the men's small-bore rifle, prone, 50 and 100 yards, coming 8th; the men's small-bore rifle, disappearing target, 25 yards, 2nd, silver medal; and the men's small-bore rifle, moving target, 25 yards, 19th.

At the outbreak of the First World War, and keen to do his bit, he enlisted into the ranks of the 15th London Regiment, being promoted to lance corporal. He was commissioned as a second lieutenant into the 2nd (City of London) London Regiment on 4 February 1915, being promoted to captain the following November. He travelled to France with his battalion in January 1917.

Captain Hawkins was reported missing after an attack on the German lines between Bullecourt and Croisilles on 16 June 1917. He was last seen wounded in an advance position after a German counter-attack and due to the urgency of the situation Captain Hawkins had to be left behind. It had been hoped that he had been taken prisoner of war, however as no news was heard from him it was assumed he had died from his wounds. His body was never recovered or identified and he is commemorated on the Arras Memorial, Bay 9.

740705 Cyclist Herbert Henry (Bert) Gayler
1912 Stockholm
Great Britain
Cycling
Silver Medal
25th London Regiment (Cyclists)
Died 23 June 1917 aged 35

'Peddled across England and India. Cycling was his life'

Herbert Henry Gayler was born on 3 December 1881 in Chislehurst, Kent (some records indicate he was born in Christchurch, Dorset, this is incorrect). He was the son of Henry Gayler, a coachman. His mother died when Herbert was still very young so his aunt Ellen Palmer, a dress maker living in Norfolk, came to look after Herbert and his brother Ernest. After leaving school Herbert became a barrister's clerk. Keen to better himself he attended Regent Street Polytechnic (forerunner of the University of Westminster) and by 1911 he was a clerk stenographer residing at 62 Langler Road, Willesden, with George and Harriett Tyler.

Herbert Gayler's burial place.

Cycling was always Gayler's passion and he rode for the Regent Street Polytechnic's Cycling Club, Westminster, winning several races. In the 1912 Olympic Games in Stockholm he was selected as part of the cycling team. He took part in two events, men's road race, single, where he came 30th and men's road race, team. The team came second overall and Gayler won a silver medal.

Enlisting in Fulham, Gayler served as a cyclist in the 25th London Regiment. In 1917 Gayler was sent together with his battalion to India as part of an expeditionary force to deal with a revolt amongst Mahsud tribesmen in Waziristan on what is now the Pakistan-Afghanistan border. He was killed by rifle fire during an ambush in a valley near Kotkai Bozi Khel on 23 June 1917. A letter home from a private in the 25th battalion describes the campaign and incident in a little more detail:

> On the 21st we went about picketing the hills for other troops to go out strafing. Our B Company met strong opposition on their hill & had to be reinforced before it was taken. They lost 1 killed & 3 wounded. 22nd we did the same as the 21st and we received slight opposition on my hill.
>
> On the 23rd we moved 6 miles up river leaving all tents and stores behind in camp with sufficient troops to protect them. There was strong opposition & the Nepalese earned themselves some praise for taking the heights round a very narrow gorge. We arrived at Hisu? Valley and of course sent pickets to the hills, one picket lost 2 killed & two wounded & we had to go out & help them up.

Gayler was buried where he fell and is commemorated on the Delhi Memorial (Indian Gate) face 23. There is also a memorial to Gayler in the Anglican Church in Jullundur.

Herbert's brother, Ernest William Gayler, 13th London Regiment, was seriously wounded and discharged 28 February 1918. He was awarded a Silver War Badge.

Captain Percival Talbot 'Percy' Molson MC
1904 St Louis America
Canada
Athletics
Princess Patricia's Canadian Light Infantry (Eastern Ontario Regiment)
Died 5 July 1917 aged 36

'The most honest sportsman ever to fly the Canadian flag'

Percival Talbot Molson was born on 14 August 1880 in Cacouna, Quebec. He was the son of John Thomas and Jennie Molson of Montreal and was part of one of Canada's most famous brewing families. At the age of 16 he became a member of the Montreal Victoria's hockey team that won the Stanley Cup championship in 1897. At McGill University, Montreal he became senior class president and played hockey (captaining the team), football, racquets, and tennis. He also competed in track and field events. So successful was he that he was named McGill University's 'best all-round athlete' three years in a row, a feat that has never been achieved since. During an American Athletics meet in 1900 he set a new world record in the long jump, going on to win the outdoor track and field long jump championship in the United States in 1903. In 1904 he won the 400 metres during the Canadian championship defeating the highly talented American Harry Hillman who went on to win three gold medals during the 1904 Olympic Games.

As a result of this victory he was selected to run in the 400 metres during the 1904 Olympic Games held in St Louis America. Highly fancied, he was unfortunately off form and finished well down the field, failing to win a medal.

On leaving university he became a solicitor in Montreal. He also became the youngest member ever appointed to the university's board of governors. He continued to play football, turning out for the Montreal Amateur Athletic Association, captaining the squad in 1903 and 1904. He was regarded as a sure-handed, brilliant running back and an exceptional kicker. He was a leading light in authorizing the construction of a new stadium in Macdonald Park, however the onset of the First World War delayed matters.

At the outbreak of War, Percy helped recruit students from McGill University into the ranks of Princess Patricia's Canadian Light Infantry. Over a thousand students enlisted, many going on to be commissioned. Percival Molson joined the 'Patricias' in France in October 1915 and was soon involved in the horrors of trench warfare. On 2 June 1916, in the Battle of Mount Sorrel, the Patricias occupied Sanctuary Wood. In the hard fighting that followed, No.1 Company was practically wiped out (it was here that the Canadian army was to suffer over 8,000 casualties). Although Lieutenant Molson survived, he was badly wounded. He was also awarded the Military Cross for his outstanding bravery for 'leading a desperate and successful resistance to German attacks'. Recovering from his wounds, he returned to his regiment. He was killed in action on 5 July 1917 at Avion, near Vimy Ridge after being hit by a shell fired from a German howitzer.

He is buried in Villers Station Cemetery, Villers-au-Bois, grave reference VIII. E. 1.

Percival left in his will $75,000 to McGill University to help towards the cost of the new sports stadium. On 25 October 1919 the stadium was official named the Percival Molson Memorial in honour of one of the university's finest students. In 1996, eighty years after Percy had been killed in action, he was finally inducted into the McGill University Sports Hall of Fame.

Sergeant Louis Octave Lapize
1908 London
France
Cyclist
Bronze
13th Regiment Artillery/French Flying Corps
Died 14 July 1917 aged 29

'Vous êtes des assassins! Oui, des assassins!'

Louis Octave Lapize was born on 24 October 1887 in Paris France. A fine and talented cyclist he cycled for several well-known clubs. In 1909 he cycled for Biguet-Dunlop 1010, in 1911 Alcyon-Dunlop, in 1913 La Française-Diamant and finally in 1914 La Française-Hutchinson.

He first came to notice in 1907 when he won the French road and cyclo-cross championships. In 1909–10 he won Paris-Roubaix and from 1911–13 he won the Paris-Brussels race. He was also French champion on the roads in 1910–13. He raced in the

Lapize greeted by his excited mother after a race.

The Extinguished Flame

Tour de France from 1909 to 1914. In his first Tour De France in 1909 he abandoned the race early due to the wintery conditions but not before he managed a Stage 2 second place behind Tour winner Francois Faber. Faber was the first foreigner to win the Tour de France in 1909 and his record of winning five consecutive stages stands to this day. Coming back in 1910, Lapize won the Tour taking four stages during that race. Riding for the Alcyon cycle club and going head to head with his old rival Faber he was fortunate that Faber, who was well ahead, collided with a dog at the foot of the Pyrenees. Faber also suffered several punctures in the final stage between Caen and Paris, which gave Lapize an unassailable lead. When asked about his victory he put it down to his cyclo-cross training which popularized that sport.

After his Tour success, he licensed his name not only to a line of bicycles (made by La Française) but also to accessories such as toe clips and straps.

Despite four more starts between 1911 and 1914 Lapize was never to repeat his 1910 victory, never fully completing another race, however he won stages in the 1912 and 1914 Tours.

Lapize is best remembered in cycling history for his comments to Tour de France officials Alphonse Steinès and Victor Breyer. In 1910 the race went for the first time into the high mountains, and as he pushed his bike up the Col d'Aubisque, completely exhausted he shouted out, 'You are murderers, yes, murderers!' The stage in question was 326 kilometres in length, featured 7 brutal climbs, and was raced on unsealed roads with single-gear bicycles, so maybe he had a point.

In 1908 he rode for the French cycling team in the London Olympics. He competed in the men's tandem sprint, 2,000 metres, the men's 20 kilometres, and the men's 100 kilometres in which he won a bronze medal.

During the First World War he first served with the 13th Regiment of Artillery before transferring into the French Flying Corps in 1915. Training as a pilot and being sent to the front in 1917 he served with the N504, the N203 and then the N90 in Toul.

He was mentioned in despatches and shot down a German plane in flames on 28 June 1917. However during a dog fight on 14 July 1917 his aircraft was hit by a burst of fire from one of the German planes and span to the ground out of control, crashing. Although pulled from his plane alive his injuries were too serious and he died at Toul hospital where he was buried at the military cemetery the same day. Later, on the request of his family, his remains were removed to Villiers-sur-Marne where in his memory a stage of the Tour de France is raced.

Lapize on the gruelling mountain climb.

Lieutenant Waldemar Tietgens
1900 Paris
Germany
Rowing (Coxed Four)
Gold Medal
Reserve-Feldartillerie-Regiment 49
Died 28 July 1917 aged 38

The first German boat ever to win a gold medal in the Olympics

Waldemar Tietgens was born on 26 March 1879 in Hamburg. On leaving school he became a merchant, but his passion was rowing. He rowed for the Germania Ruder Club, Der Hamburger (GRC). Founded in 1836 as *Der Hamburger Ruder Club*, the club is the fourth oldest rowing club in the world.

In 1900 he was selected to row in the Olympic Games to be held in Paris. He rowed in the coxed eight and the coxed four. The rowing events were held on the River Seine in Paris. The eight were unlucky to miss out on a medal, coming fourth. The coxed four however was to be a different story despite the race becoming the most controversial in rowing history. As a matter of course the winners of the heats, and the runner-up in heat three, which had four entrants, would become finalists. However a protest was lodge by the losers of heats two and three who pointed out, quite rightly, that they had posted faster times than the winners of heat one. To try to overcome this problem the rowing and Olympic officials tried to conduct another qualifying heat. However several of the crews were unable to be found and informed of this decision. In the end it was decided to allow the heat winners plus the three fastest losing boats to compete in the final, making it a six-boat final. The problem was that the course was only designed to allow a four-boat final. The heat winners were incensed by this and refused to take part.

The first final was held between the runner-up in heat two and the second- and third-place finishers in heat three. This seemed unsatisfactory, so a second final was contested among the heat winners. The winner of this final, *Cercle de l'Aviron Roubaix*, was invited to compete in the second final, but tempers were now very short and they refused to do so. In the end both finalists were considered to be Olympic championships. *Cercle de l'Aviron Roubaix* were gold medal finalists A, and the *Germania Ruder Club, Hamburg*, who defeated challenges from Amsterdam and Ludwigshafenern by a full boat length were gold medal finalists B. This made Tietgens and his crew the first German Olympic champions in rowing and the first German rowers ever to win a gold medal.

The German crew consisted of Gustav Goßler (1879–1940), Oskar Goßler (1875–1953), Walter Katzenstein (1878–1929), Waldemar Tietgens (1879–1917), and Carl Goßler (1885–1914) as cox.

During the First World War he served as a lieutenant with the Reserve Feldartillerie Regiment 49. He was killed in action on 28 July 1917 and was buried in Hooglede German Military Cemetery in West Flanders, Belgium.

Captain Noel Godfrey Chavasse VC & bar
1908 London
Great Britain
Athletics (400 metres)
Royal Army Medical Corps
Died 4 August 1917 aged 32

'One of only three men to win the VC twice'

Noel Chavasse was born on 9 November 1884 at 36 New Inn Hall Street, Oxford, England. Chavasse was one of identical twin boys (they had seven children in total) of the Rev Francis Chavasse, Bishop of Liverpool and founder of St Peter's College Oxford and Edith Jane, née Maude. Chavasse was educated at the Magdalen School, Oxford, and Liverpool College before going up to Trinity Oxford in 1904 to read medicine.

In 1907 and 1908 Chavasse ran for Oxford against Cambridge in both the 100 yards (where in 1907 he managed a dead heat with the celebrated Cambridge athlete Kenneth Macleod, considered by many as the greatest Scottish all-round athlete of his generation) and the 440 yards. He also played lacrosse against Cambridge in 1905 and 1906.

In 1907, Noel graduated with first class honours. Remaining at Oxford to continue with his studies, in 1908 Noel, together with his twin brother Christopher, was selected to run in the 400 metres at the 1908 London Olympics. Although Christopher finished second in his heat and Noel third, their times were not fast enough to take them any further in the competition and they were both eliminated.

Noel joined the Oxford University Officers' Training Corps medical unit in January 1909. On finishing his studies he returned to Liverpool for specialist training. He (on his second attempt) became a Fellow of the Royal College of Surgeons in May 1910. He began to work at the Rotunda Hospital, Dublin. In 1912 he passed his final medical examinations and was awarded the Derby Exhibition. He registered as a doctor with the General Medical Council and went to work at the Royal Southern Hospital in Liverpool before becoming house surgeon to his former tutor Robert Jones. He also managed to find time to get engaged to his cousin Frances, daughter of his uncle Sir Thomas Frederick Chavasse.

On 2 June 1913 Chavasse was commissioned as a lieutenant into the Royal Army Medical Corps and was attached to the 10th battalion King's (Liverpool) Regiment

(Liverpool Scottish), a territorial battalion, as a surgeon lieutenant. He continued to be attached to the King's Liverpool Regiment during the war, being promoted to the rank of captain (1 April 1915). In June 1915 at Hooge in Belgium Chavasse was awarded the Military Cross for gallantry (*London Gazette* 14 January 1916) and the following November was mentioned in despatches for his continuing gallant conduct.

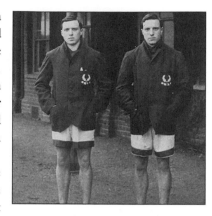

Chavasse was to become one of only three men to be awarded the Victoria Cross twice and the only one to achieve this during the First World War. His first award was made for his actions at Guillemont, France on 9 August 1916. His full citation (24 October 1916) read:

> *Captain Noel Godfrey Chavasse, M.C., M.B., Royal Army Medical Corps.*
>
> *For most conspicuous bravery and devotion to duty.*
>
> *During an attack he tended the wounded in the open all day, under heavy fire, frequently in view of the enemy. During the ensuing night he searched for wounded on the ground in front of the enemy's lines for four hours.*
>
> *Next day he took one stretcher-bearer to the advanced trenches, and under heavy shellfire carried an urgent case for 500 yards into safety, being wounded in the side by a shell splinter during the journey. The same night he took up a party of twenty volunteers, rescued three wounded men from a shell hole twenty-five yards from the enemy's trench, buried the bodies of two officers, and collected many identity discs, although fired on by bombs and machine guns.*
>
> *Altogether he saved the lives of some twenty badly wounded men, besides the ordinary cases which passed through his hands. His courage and self-sacrifice, were beyond praise.*

His second award came between the periods 31 July and 2 August 1917 at Wieltje, Belgium. His citation (14 September 1917) read:

> *His Majesty the KING has been graciously pleased to approve of the award of a Bar to the Victoria Cross to Capt. Noel Godfrey Chavasse, V.C., M.C., late R.A.M.C., attd. L'pool R.*
>
> *For most conspicuous bravery and devotion to duty when in action.*
>
> *Though severely wounded early in the action whilst carrying a wounded soldier to the Dressing Station, Capt. Chavasse refused to leave his post, and for two days not only continued to perform his duties, but in addition went out repeatedly under heavy fire to search for and attend to the wounded who were lying out.*
>
> *During these searches, although practically without food during this period, worn with fatigue and faint with his wound, he assisted to carry in a number of badly wounded men, over heavy and difficult ground.*

By his extraordinary energy and inspiring example, he was instrumental in rescuing many wounded who would have otherwise undoubtedly succumbed under the bad weather conditions.

This devoted and gallant officer subsequently died of his wounds.

Badly wounded, they did manage to get Chavasse back to a medical station where he was operated on but alas he died two days later.

Remarkably another double VC winner Lt-Col Martin-Leake VC and bar was involved after Chavasse had been badly wounded. He notes in his diary on 2 August 1917,

An ambulance came up tonight and in it was Captain Noel Chavasse VC RAMC of the Kings Liverpool battalion of 55 Division. His face was unrecognizable, all blacked from a shell burst very near and he seemed to be unconscious. As he had an abdominal wound besides, I did not take him out of the ambulance, which was sent on direct to 32 CCS (Casualty Clearing Station), where he will probably die.

He is buried in Brandhoek New Military Cemetery, grave reference III. B. 15. His grave has the unique feature of having two VCs carved into it.

He is also commemorated on the Chavasse family grave in Bromsgrove. In fact he is commemorated on no less then sixteen memorials – more than any other individual killed during the Great War.

His brother Aidan also died in the Great War, on 4 July 1917 serving as a lieutenant with the 17th battalion King's Liverpool Regiment, and is commemorated on the Ypres (Menin Gate) Memorial), panels 4 and 6.

His twin brother Richard went on to be the Bishop of Rochester.

Gladys, Noels fiancée, had applied for and been granted a marriage licence. While Noel was in France she took a job in a canteen in Paris so she was able to see him a little more often. Noel was killed shortly before they were due to marry. Gladys went on to be mentioned in despatches in 1945 for her actions during the battle of Monte Cassino, Italy. She was killed in an accident while crossing the road in France in 1962.

Noel Chavasse's medals were purchased by Lord Ashcroft from St Peters College Oxford to whom they had been left for the then record amount of £1.5 million. They are now displayed with dozens of other VCs at the Lord Ashcroft Gallery in the Imperial War Museum for all to see. A generous bequest to the nation and well worth a visit.

Sergeant Wilhelm Brülle
1912 Stockholm
Germany
Gymnastics
7th Infantry Regiment (Prussia)
Died 5 August 1917 aged 26

Second choice team that almost won a medal

Wilhelm Brülle was born on 17 February 1891 in Lippstadt, Nordrhein-Westfalen, Germany. A German gymnast, he was a member of Allgemeiner Akademischer Turnerbund, Leipzig, sports and gymnastics club and was selected to take part in the 1912 Stockholm Olympics. He competed in the men's team all-around, free system and the men's team all-around. Interestingly the Germans were unable to send their first team choice due to the German Gymnastic Association's refusal to send a team. Instead they were forced to send a mediocre university team from Leipzig, of which Brülle was part. Had the first team choice been the Deutsche Turnerschaft, it would almost certainly have won.

His first event, the men's team all-around, free system, took place on 10 July 1912 at the Stockholm Olympic Stadium. The gymnastic teams consisted of between 16 and 40 gymnasts. They had to perform their routines for up to an hour including the march in and march out. Five judges marked them on their performance. Norway finally took the gold with 22.85 points, Finland the silver with 21.85 points and Denmark the bronze with 21.25 points. Germany came fourth with 16.85 points. Interestingly, although between them the judges placed Norway first, the Finnish judge put Finland first and the Danish judge put Denmark first.

Brülle's second event was the men's team all-around. Once again teams of between 16 and 40 gymnasts performed for up to an hour including the march in and march out. The Olympic committee provided the fixed apparatus. Four horizontal bars, four parallel bars, four pommelled horses, and four Roman rings. Each team had to provide their own hand apparatus for the free-standing exercises. Five judges allocated points: Maximum points on each apparatus 12; Maximum points for free-standing exercises 12; and for free exercises 10. Maximum possible points 58. Italy took the gold with 53.15 points, Hungary the silver with 45.45 points and Great Britain the bronze with 36.90 points. Germany came fifth with 32.40.

During the First World War Brülle served as a sergeant with the 7th Infantry Regiment (Prussia) and was killed in action on 5 August 1917.

Captain James Patrick Roche MC
1908 London
Great Britain
Athletics
Royal Artillery
47th Trench Mortar Battery
Died 7 June 1917 aged 29

'An Roisteach Flaitheamhail, Fearamhail nar thug ariamh Eitheach'
(The generous and manly Roche who never uttered a falsehood)

James Patrick Roche was born in 1886 in Cork, Ireland. A native of Cahirciveen, Co Kerry, he was one of four sons born to Stephen and Elsie Roche, of Monasterevan, Co Kildare. He was educated at Blackrock College for boys (fifty-three Blackrock students were to die in the war) before going up to Queen's College, Cork to study law. He later became a barrister.

A gifted athlete, Roche ran for Knockrea Athletic Club. He won the 220 yards at the Gaelic AA Championships in 1906. He went on to compete in the Irish AAA Championships, coming first in both the 220 and 100 yard sprints in 1907 and the 100 yards again in 1908 and 1909. He also won the 110 yards for Ireland vs. Scotland three times between 1907–08 and 1910. Selected to take part in the 1908 London Olympics he competed in both the 100 yard and 200 yard sprints. In the 100-yard race Roche won his first round heat with a time of 11.4 seconds pushing him through to the semi-finals. However he only managed third in the semi with a time of 12.8 seconds and failed to qualify for the final. He did slightly better in the 200 yards reaching the semi-finals where he was edged out by fellow countryman George Albert Hawkins, who was also to die in the war a few months after Roche on 22 September 1917. Both runners were timed at 22.6 seconds.

During the First World War Roche was gazetted into the Royal Field Artillery (*London Gazette* 27 May 1915) being attached to 47th Trench Mortar Battery in support of 47th Brigade of the 16th (Irish) Division. In January 1917 Roche was decorated with the Military Cross (MC) for bravery in the field. In May 1917 Roche's battery went into action in support of the main attack near Wytschaete during the battle of Messines. It was here that he was killed on 7 June 1917. The circumstances of his death were reported later. Roche was in the Leinsters' dugout with several other officers including Lieutenant Colonel Thomas R.A. Stannus, the Adjutant Captain L.L. Acton, Captain J.A.J. Farrell, the battalion's acting second-in-command, two artillery liaison officers and four other-ranks when an artillery shell entered the dugout and exploded. Roche, the two artillery officers, and four other-ranks were killed outright. Lieutenant Colonel Stannus died later from his wounds and Captain Acton would never recover from the wounds he received that day.

Colonel Rowland Fielding, CO 6th Connaught Rangers later wrote: 'One of the wittiest raconteurs I have ever met, and as brave and ready a soldier as I have ever seen. As a brigade trench mortar officer, he was a genius. In conversation he was remarkable.'

Captain Roche is buried in Kemmel Chateau Military Cemetery, Grave X 87. His devastated parents had these words cut into his headstone in Gaelic:

> An Roisteach Flaitheamhail,
> Fearamhail nar thug ariamh Eitheach

Second Lieutenant Claude Murray Ross
1912 Stockholm
Australia
Athletics (400 metres hurdles)
Royal Flying Corps (45 Squadron)
Died 19 August 1917 aged 23

'He flew too close to the sun'

Claude Murray Ross was born on 13 May 1893 in Caulfield, Victoria, Australia. He was the son of Mrs Murray Ross, of 21 Hotham Grove, Elsternwick, Melbourne. A fine athlete he ran for the Malvern Harriers Athletics Club. He also trained as an engineer, giving his employment on enlistment as a travelling engineer.

Having competed successfully in numerous races he was selected as part of the Australian athletics team that took part in the 1912 Olympic Games in Stockholm. He was 18 years of age. He ran in the 400 metres hurdles but failed to qualify. The American Charles Reidpath took the gold, Hanns Braun the German runner the silver (killed in 1918), and another American Ed Lindberg the bronze.

During the First World War Ross enlisted into the Australian Field Artillery Brigade 2, Battery 6, as private 1154 later being promoted to wheeler sergeant. Sailing on HMAT *Shropshire A9* from Melbourne, Ross left Australia with the first contingent on 20 October 1914. He took part in the Gallipoli campaign being present at the landings in April 1915 and the evacuation the following December. After the evacuation of the Gallipoli peninsula he was posted to France and commissioned in January 1917 into 45 Squadron Royal Flying Corps.

On 19 August 1917, flying a Sopwith Strutter A8298 together with his observer Second Lieutenant J.O. Fowler near Zandvoorde, his aircraft was seen to break up in the air and crash to the ground killing both Ross and his observer.

His remains were never identified or recovered and he is commemorated on the Arras Memorial.

96501 Gunner George Albert Hawkins
1908 London
Great Britain
Athletics 200 metres
Royal Garrison Artillery (254th Siege Battery)
Died 20/22 September 1917 aged 33

'The first Britain to reach a sprint final'

George Albert Hawkins was born on 15 October 1883 in Tottenham, London. Hawkins was one of the finest sprinters Britain has ever produced. He was trained by the famous running coach Sam Mussabini who was to come to fame by training the 100 metre runner Harold Abrahams to gold in the 1924 Olympics, made famous by the Oscar winning film *Chariots of Fire*.

A surprise winner in the 1908 200 metre Olympic trails, he still failed to reach the final at the AAA championships. Despite this setback he was still selected to run in the 200 metres sprint in the 1908 London Olympics. Confounding all the 'experts' he reached the final coming fourth in a time of 22.9 seconds. He was beaten by the Canadian Robert Kerr who took the gold in 22.6 seconds, the American Robert Cloughen who won the silver, and the second American finalist Nate Cartmell who won the bronze. Had Hawkins run as well in the final as he had in the semi-final, winning that in 22.6 seconds, he might well have picked up the gold medal. However he still has the honour of being the first Britain to reach an Olympic sprint final. Later that year, running for the Polytechnic team, he helped set a British record in the 4×440 yard relay.

He married Violet Freeman and they had five children.

Hawkins served as a gunner with the 254th Siege Battery, Royal Garrison Artillery, during the First World War. He was killed in action on 20/22 September 1917 during the Third Battle of Ypres when a shell exploded in the doorway of a dugout while he was on outpost duty.

He is buried in Bard Cottage Cemetery, grave reference IV. H. 25.

99906 Gunner George Butterfield
1908 London
Great Britain
Athletics
Royal Garrison Artillery (230th Siege Battery)
Died 24 September 1917 aged 38

'He ran the world's fastest mile'

George Butterfield, known to his friends as Butt, was born in 1882 (some records say 1879) in Stockton-on-Tees. His parents were Alfred and Harriet Jane Butterfield of Myrtle Cottages in Whitfield. His father was a dairyman on a local farm, and his mother, the daughter of John Robertson, a shipwright, were both born in Dover. The family later moved to Archers Court Cottages. For a while he was the landlord at the Hole in the Wall public house in Darlington Market Place.

A gifted and determined runner, George Butterfield became a Darlington Harrier. After running in the International Cross-Country championship in 1906, George Butterfield won the Northern title at 440 yards and one mile that summer. He was the winner of the AAA mile title for three successive years between 1904 and 1906. In 1906 he broke the world mile record with his winning time of 4:18.6. He also did well at further distances. He finished second in the 1904 AAA ten mile run and later proved to be a first class half-miler. He also raced against a local greyhound and, according to reports, 'He didn't come second.'

Selected for the 1908 London Olympics, he took part in both the 800 and 1,500 metres. The 1,500 metre competition was considered to be one of the most exciting events of the Olympics. To add to the anticipation, the race took place during the opening week on 13 and 14 July. The British were favourite to take the gold especially with the powerful Butterfield among their ranks. However it wasn't to be other competitors that defeated him but the British officials and organizers. They insisted that only the winner of each heat should qualify for the final. This bizarre ruling meant that it came down to the luck of the draw as to whether a country's best medal hopes were pitted against one another in a first round heat. The draws were also held in secret, which didn't help build confidence, especially with the foreign teams like America. An example of this was demonstrated when Britain's Joe Deakin won his heat reaching the final in a time of 4:13.6, whereas Butterfield was knocked out of his heat coming second to the American running star Mel Sheppard despite his time of 4:11.8. Mel Sheppard went on to take the gold in a winning time of 4:05.0 – a new Olympic record.

In the 800 metres Butterfield came second in his semi-final heat in a time of 1:58.9. He was beaten by the Hungarian athlete and footballer Ödön Bodor but did manage to finish ahead of the American defending champion James Lightbody. Once again Butterfield did not advance to the final. It was a disappointing Olympics for Butterfield. Had the rules been a little fairer we can only speculate on what he might have achieved.

Butterfield joined the Royal Garrison Artillery in 1916 as a gunner and was attached to 230th Siege Battery. He was killed in action on 24 September 1917 when a German shell blew his legs off. He is buried in Birr Cross Roads Cemetery, grave reference III. A. 16.

Chiefly thanks to Ian Barnes of the Darlington Harriers, a plaque to Butterfield's memory was erected outside the Market Place pub in 2006.

His brother, 1409 Trooper Alfred John Butterfield, Household Battalion Household Cavalry, was killed in action only a few weeks before, on 3 May 1917.

Oberleutnant Bernhard von Gaza
1908 London
Germany
Rowing
Bronze Medal
185th Infantry Regiment
Died 25 September 1917 aged 36

'One of Germany's finest rowers'

Bernhard von Gaza was born on 6 May 1881 in Usedom, Mecklenburg-Vorpommern. He was the son of Bernhard Franz Philipp von Gaza (1829–1912) and Wilhelmine Karoline Holz (1859–1909). He had four brothers and one sister. One of Germany's finest rowers he competed for *Rudergesellschaft Wiking Berlin*. In 1907 he not only won the German single sculls championship but, together with Carl Ekkehard Ernst, he took the double sculls as well. A keen technician of the sport he wrote several books on the subject, *Rudersport (Skullen und Training)*, book No.17 in the series *Miniatur-Bibliothek für Sport und Spiel*, *Wanderfahrten im Rudder- und Paddelboot* book No.49, and *Rudersport (Riemenrudern und Training)* book No.59. By quoting from books and publications written by the British rowers W.B. Woodgate and R.C. Lehmann he also demonstrates how British rowing influenced him. Whether his views on sexual abstinence before events were also shared by British rowers we can only guess.

In 1908 he was selected to compete for Germany in the London Olympics. The competition was held on the Thames at Henley. Von Gaza won his first two races, against Erno Killer the Hungarian rower and the Canadian Lou Scholes. However he was beaten by the English rower Harry Blackstaffe who went on to the take the gold (Blackstaffe was a butcher from Islington). Another English rower, Alexander McCulloch, took the silver and von Gaza shared the bronze with the Hungarian sculler Karoly Levitzky.

He became the German champion in the single sculls again in 1907 and 1911, and in the double, with Carl Ekkehard Ernest, in 1907 and 1908, and with Wenzel Joesten in 1913. He also finished third at the European Championships in Ghent in the same year.

During the First World War he served as an Oberleutnant with the 185th Infantry Regiment. A brave soldier he was wounded in the left arm by a grenade early in 1915 and just over a year later in 1916 was awarded the Iron Cross for his leadership and bravery at the front. He went missing on 23 September 1917 defending his position against a British attack which went in at 7 am. Two German officers and 156 other ranks were captured during this action probably by the 12 battalion Kings Royal Rifle Corps. It is believed that one of these officers was von Gaza and he subsequently died in British hands.

He is buried in Dozinghem (British cemetery), block 16 row B grave 6.

Lieutenant Duncan Mackinnon
1908 London
Great Britain
Rowing
Gold
1st Battalion Scots Guards
Died 9 October 1917 aged 30

'Duncan Mackinnon was without doubt one of the
finest oars that ever rowed for Oxford'

Duncan Mackinnon was born on 29 September 1887 in Paddington, London. He was the third son of Duncan Mackinnon of Loup and Balinakill, Argyllshire who was for many years chairman of the British India Steam Navigation Company, and of Margaret Braid Macdonald his wife. He was educated at Rugby School entering in 1902 before going up to Magdalen College Oxford. While at Oxford he concentrated on his rowing. Rowing for Magdalen College in the coxless four he helped his college become Head of the River in 1910 and was part of the crew that won the Stewards' Challenge Cup and the Visitors' Challenge Cup at Henley Royal Regatta in both 1907 and 1908. Mackinnon was also in the winning crew that took the Grand Challenge Cup twice and in the Wyfold Challenge Cup once. He was only in the losing crew twice during all his Henley appearances – quite a record.

In 1908 the Magdalen crew was selected to represent Great Britain in the summer Olympics in London as part of the coxless fours. Mackinnon along with Collier Cudmore, John Somers-Smith and Angus Gillan defeated the Leander (also British) crew to win the gold medal, Canada taking the bronze together with the Netherlands.

In 1909 he was selected to row number five in the Oxford boat in the annual Boat Race, the Oxford crew taking the honours by three and a half lengths in a time of 19 minutes and 50 seconds. Made president of the Oxford University Boat Club in 1910, he was selected to row for Oxford once again in the same year, once again rowing number five in the winning boat, Oxford defeating Cambridge by three and a half lengths in a time of 20 minutes and 14 seconds. Mackinnon rowed number seven in 1911, once again being in the victorious boat, the Oxford boat crossing the line first by two and three quarter lengths, in a record time of 18 minutes and 29 seconds. Mackinnon was in the winning boat for three years in succession.

Between 1913 and 1914 he was in India, as a partner in Messrs Macneill and Co, and Messrs Mackinnon Mackenzie, Calcutta. During this time he also served as a lance corporal in the Calcutta Light Horse. At the outbreak of the First World War he returned to England and in March 1915 took a commission into the Royal North Devon Hussars. He served with them in Gallipoli seeing action in Suvla Bay before taking part in the evacuation of the peninsula in December 1915. He remained in Egypt until February before transferring into the Scots Guards and being posted to the front line in France on 1 August 1917. He was killed in action near Langemarck on 9 October 1917.

A brother officer late wrote, 'We have lost one who has endeared himself to all ranks and has proved himself a splendid and gallant soldier. We can ill afford to lose such an Officer. His Regiment honour his memory and realize his loss to it.'

Another wrote, 'Your son was a most splendid and gallant Officer, absolutely fearless, and one whom we can ill spare. I hope it may be some consolation to you to know how devoted all his brother Officers were to him.'

Still another wrote, 'We shall all miss your son dreadfully, as he was most extraordinarily popular and we were all devoted to him. All the men of his Company would have done anything for him. He was commanding his Company in the attack.'

Lieutenant Colonel Harcourt Gold OBE, President of the Oxford University Boat Club in 1899 wrote, 'Duncan Mackinnon was without doubt one of the finest oars that ever rowed for Oxford. His strength, stamina and will power were unsurpassed. It is probably no exaggeration to say that his strength of character and determination had an effect on the crews in which he rowed almost without parallel in the history of modern rowing.'

His remains were never discovered or identified and he is commemorated on the Tyne Cot Memorial, panel 10.

Mackinnon left a legacy of £80,000 to establish scholarships at Magdalen College.

His eldest brother, Captain W. Mackinnon, the London Scottish, was killed five months before him on 11 May 1917.

26765 Sergeant/Second Lieutenant Harry Crank
1908 London
Great Britain
Diving
1/2nd attached 17th Battalion Lancashire Fusiliers
Died 22 October 1917 aged 27

'Cock of the North'

Harry Crank was born in 1890 in Bolton, Greater Manchester. His father John Crank was a stonemason and later a caretaker. After leaving school he became a pastry cook residing at 22 Moor Lane, Bolton.

A well-known Bolton character swimmer and diver, he was selected to represent Great Britain in the 1908 London Olympics. He took part in the men's three-metre springboard (known as fancy diving). The diving competition is held from both the

Crank doing a demonstration dive at his local pool.

three-metre and one-metre boards. The competitors perform a running plain dive and a running forward somersault from the one-metre board, a one and a half somersault and a backward spring and forward dive from the three-metre board followed by three dives of the competitor's choice from the three-metre board. They are judged on style, difficulty and grace. He dived well but failed to win a medal. Germany took the gold (Albert Zurner), silver (Kurt Behrens) and bronze (Gottlob Walz) with the USA also taking a bronze (George Gaidzik).

During the First World War he served in the ranks firstly with the 4th battalion Lancashire Fusiliers and then with the 2nd battalion being promoted to sergeant. In 1915 he was commissioned as a second lieutenant (*London Gazette* 28 June 1915) and eventually posted to the 17th (service) battalion Lancashire Fusiliers.

Harry Crank was killed on 22 October 1917 in the action around the Houthulst Forest. The regimental history describes the action in some detail:

Monday 22nd October 1917 - Day 78
Houthulst Forest

35th Div. 105 Bde.

105 Bde attacked with 14th Bn, Gloustershire Regt and 16th Bn, Cheshire Regt. 15th Bn, Sherwood Foresters was in support and 15th Cheshires in reserve. The right of the 16th Cheshires advanced well and took its objective – Marechal Farm. The left was pinned down by MG fire from strongpoints in the wood north west of Colombo House. They dug in and consolidated. The 14th Glosters advanced to their first objective in the area of Panama House by 6.15 am despite strong opposition. On their way to the second objective they took two pillboxes and were in position by 6.45 am. At 4.40 pm the Germans attacked the left of the Cheshires and broke through. The Cheshires fell back to their original line but the Glosters hung on until the German attack was halted by artillery. The Glosters' right then fell back to form a defensive flank with the remaining Cheshires. Two platoons of 15th Sherwood Foresters came up in support. 104 Bde: The brigade attacked with 17th Bn, Lancashire Fusiliers and 23rd Bn, Manchester Regt. In support was 20th Bn, Lancashire Fusiliers and 17th Bn, Royal Scots was in reserve. The Mancs advanced to their first objective easily but ran into stiffer resistance on the way to the second. Eventually 50 men unsuccessfully attacked some pillboxes at Six Roads in conjunction with some 34th Div troops. The survivors then withdrew. 17th Lancs advanced quite well, bypassing Colombo House and arriving in their objective – Conter Drive at 6.45 am. A company of the 20th Lancs in support went adrift and wandered into Houthulst Forest but were driven back. At 8.30 am two more companies were sent forward to occupy a line running from 100 yards in front of Angle Point to 200 yards in front of Aden House.

The War Diary 17th battalion Lancashire Fusiliers, Appendix B page 2, describes Harry's death:

At 4.15 p.m. the 'S.O.S.' was sent up from the Front Line. This 'S.O.S.' was fired owing to a counter-attack developing upon the Cheshires on the left flank. The Cheshires appear to have lost most of their Officers and about 4.45 p.m. began falling back into Colombo House line. This rot was stopped by Capt. Heaps and the 'Y' Coy Officers, of whom 2/Lt. Crank was killed whilst running across to stop the retirement.

His body was never recovered or identified and he is commemorated on the Tyne Cot Memorial, panel 54 to 60 and 163A.

231462 Private Alexander Wuttunee Decoteau
1912 Stockholm
Canada
Athletics
49th Battalion Canadian Infantry
Died 30 October 1917 aged 28

'First Cree Canadian to become a Police Officer'

Alexander Wuttunee Decoteau was born on 19 November 1887 on the Red Pheasant Indian Reservation, near Battleford (Saskatchewan). He was the second son of five children born to Peter, an Indian department employee, and Mary Decoteau of Battleford. A Cree Canadian he attended the reservation day school. Then at the tender age of three his father was murdered and the family left without any means of support. As a result three of Mary's children were taken in by the nearby Battleford industrial school. Here Alexander excelled in soccer and athletics, being a fine middle distance runner. On leaving school he worked as a farm hand before moving to Edmonton, where he found employment as a blacksmith with his brother-in-law David Gilliland Latta. In 1909 he moved to Alberta where he became Canada's first Aboriginal-Canadian police officer when he joined the Edmonton force. He was also one of the first motorcycle policemen in the city. Alexander must have done well because he was promoted to desk sergeant in the South Side Police Station in 1914.

Between 1909 and 1917 Decoteau took part in numerous races, winning most. He ran for the Irish-Canadian Athletic Club and later for the Edmonton Police Association. Alexander's first competitive race was the mile run at Fort Saskatchewan on 24 May 1909. Much to everyone's surprise he came in second. Two months later, on 1 July, he managed to set a new western Canadian record of 27:45.2 in the five-mile Mayberry in Lloydminster. Still in form he went on to win the Hon C.W. Cross Challenge Cup Race in Edmonton. In 1910 he won a ten-mile race in Fort Saskatchewan smashing the rest of the field by eight minutes. Altogether he won the five-mile Hon C.W. Cross Challenge Cup five times and the ten-mile race at Fort Saskatchewan three times. His success got him a position in the Canadian Olympic team to take part in the Stockholm games. On 10 July 1912 he took part in the 5,000 metre final and much was expected of him. However he was not on the best of forms and only managed a poor eighth. He was awarded an Olympic Merit Diploma and participant's medal.

In September 1913 on returning to Canada he took part in the Orangemen's celebration in Edmonton. Returning to form he won the mile, breaking his own provincial record. Later that month he represented the Edmonton City Police Amateur Athletic Association at the Dominion track and field championships in Vancouver. In 1915 he won the Christmas Day race in Calgary for the second year in a row – and for an unprecedented third time.

With the outbreak of the First World War Alexander resigned from the police force and in 1916 enlisted as a private in the Canadian Expeditionary Force. He first served with the 202nd Infantry Battalion before being transferred to the 49th battalion. Arriving in England Alexander didn't stop running and was one of the Canadian army's star turns. After one successful race King George V who had been watching the race awarded him with his personal gold pocket watch as a prize.

Alexander was shot and killed by a sniper on 30 October 1917 during the battalion's advance through Passchendaele. The sniper that killed Alexander later looted his body stealing the watch King George V had presented to him. However his friends within the battalion managed to locate the sniper and kill him, retrieving Alexander's watch which was returned to his mother.

Alexander is buried in Passchendaele New British Cemetery, grave XI. A. 28.

Alexander Decoteau was inducted into the Edmonton Sports Hall of Fame in 1967, the Edmonton City Police Hall of Fame where many of his medals, cups, and photos are on display and the Saskatchewan Indian First Nations Sports Hall of Fame.

In 1985 a ceremony was performed in Edmonton to bring Alexander's spirit home. It was believed that as Alexander had not had a Cree burial, his spirit would wander the earth. A burial song to guide Decoteau's spirit home was performed by Red Pheasant band drummers and was followed by a chant of homage.

Lieutenant Ivan Laing MC
1908 London
Great Britain
Hockey
Bronze
2nd Battalion Coldstream Guards
Died 30 November 1917 aged 32

'Scored the very first goal in Olympic hockey'

Ivan Laing was born on 18 August 1885 in the family home of Springbank, the mill house situated above their Dickson and Laing's factory in Commercial Road, Hawick on the Scottish borders. He was the third son of John Turnbull Laing and Anna Drummond Laing of Ashleigh, Hawick, Roxburghshire. Ivan and his three brothers were all educated at the family home by a governess before going up to New College Eastbourne although Ivan also received additional schooling at Verviers in Belgium. A skilled all-round athlete he swam for Scotland and was a prolific try-scoring wing for Hawick rugby club. He also trialled for Scotland but was not selected. A fine hockey player he played for Teviotdale mixed hockey club together with all four of his brothers.

The 1908 Olympic Games were held in London and for the first time hockey was allowed as a competitive event. Scotland was asked to take part in their own right and eventually agreed to send a team. At first Laing wasn't selected, however due to a series of bizarre events he found himself representing his country. So the story goes, Laing was standing on the platform at Hawick station when the train carrying Scotland's hockey team to the games from Edinburgh to London pulled in. The team were a man down and seeing Laing standing there Dr Norman Stevenson, a well-known Scottish cricketer (Carlton Cricket Club and Scotland) who had played against Laing during his Rugby trial for Scotland, asked him if he would be willing to make up the numbers and join them. Laing agreed at once and became a member of the team.

Only six teams competed in the 1908 games, the four home unions with France and Germany. Travelling to London, Laing turned out for Scotland on 29 October 1908 at the White City in London against Germany, playing inside left. Scotland won 4–0, Laing scoring Scotland's first goal within the first two minutes of the match, the first goal ever scored in an Olympic hockey match. It was a great victory. However the following day Scotland were defeated by England 6–1 in the semi-finals. Laing and Scotland took the bronze medal.

At the outbreak of the First World War Laing initially enlisted into the ranks of the 1/28th London Regiment (Artist Rifles, forerunner of the SAS). He was commissioned into the 2nd battalion Coldstream Guards joining his elder brother Walter who was already a serving officer. The battalion were deployed to the Somme in 1916 and went into action on 15 September. The battalion's actions that day were later reported by a war correspondent:

> They had not gone more than 200 yards before they came under the enfilade fire of massed machine-guns. Men fell, but the lines were not broken. Gaps were made in the ranks, but they were closed up. The wounded did not call for help but cheered on those who swept past and on, shouting 'Go on, Lily Whites', which is the old name for the Coldstreamers. They went on at a hot pace with their bayonets lowered. Grey figures rose and fled. They were German soldiers, terror stricken by this rushing tide of men. The Guards went on. Then they were checked by two lines of trenches, wired and defended by machine-guns and bombers. They must be taken – and the guards took them.

For his actions on this day Laing was recommended for the Military Cross. His citation read:

> When he was the only officer left in his company he re-organized his men and rushed forward through a heavy barrage, and remained out, securing the front until ordered to withdraw.

On 30 November 1917 the Germans counter-attacked at Cambrai recapturing almost all the territory they had lost in 1916. They were eventually stopped by the intervention of British tanks and the Guards divisions. It was during this attack that Lieutenant Ivan Laing was killed. His brother Walter serving in the same battalion wrote a very difficult letter to another brother, Captain Maurice Laing, serving with the Royal Field Artillery. He wrote:

> I am sorry to have to send you bad news. Ivan was killed in our attack on November 30th, two days ago. When the Germans broke through, our people were just coming out after fighting at Bourlon. Ivan was in the line there and they were just back at Metz. He had got through all right.
>
> Then on the morning of the 30th they were ordered to retake Gouzeaucourt which they did, but Ivan was killed by a machine-gun just as he had reached our objective and died instantly having been shot in the head.
>
> As we did another attack yesterday and pushed the enemy back to Gounchen, they were able to send his body back, and today we had him buried in the cemetery on the left hand side of the road from Metz to Gouzeaucourt Wood. I had the Brigade Padre there and a cross will be erected tomorrow.

Almost 100 years later, Ivan's body remains in the same cemetery, Metz-en-Couture Communal Cemetery British Extension, grave reference II. D. 3.

Laing is still commemorated in an annual hockey match between the senior girls and boys of Hawick High School.

Grigori Mikhailovich Nikitin
Григорий Михайлович Никитин
1912 Stockholm
Russia
Football
Regiment Not Known
Died 1917 aged 28

One of the three members of the Russian 1912
Olympic football team to be killed in the war

Gori Mikhailovich Nikitin was born on 7 January 1889 in St Petersburg, Russia. A fast and talented striker he played for Sports St Petersburg. He was selected to represent Russia in the 1912 Olympic games to be held in Stockholm.

The Russians received a bye in their first round match. Nikitin wasn't selected to play in their next match against Finland. The match was played on 30 June 1912, with Russia being defeated 2–1 and knocked out of the main competition. Nikitin was however selected to play against the German side in the consolation tournament (something he might have later regretted) – on 1 July 1912 Russia were defeated 16–0 by Germany (see also Andrei Akimov, died 1916, and Nikolai Kynin, also died in 1916).

Not very much is known about Nikitin. I have been unable to establish which regiment he fought with or what rank he held. All we know for sure was that he was killed sometime in 1917 fighting for Russia.

1918

Johan Valdemar (Juho) Halme
1908 London 1912
Finland
Athletics
Journalist
Died 1 February 1918 aged 29

'Murdered by Red Guards'

Johan Valdemar Halme (Juho) was born on 24 May 1888 in Helsinki Finland. After finishing with his education he became a journalist in Helsinki. A gifted athlete he represented several Finnish sports clubs – Lisalmen Visa (founded in 1904), Helsinki Brisk, and Helsingin Kisa-Veikkoja (founded in 1909). Between 1907 and 1917 he won a total of six Finnish championships including the triple jump, the long jump, and the javelin as well as the pentathlon.

Selected for the Finnish team to take part in the 1908 London Olympics, he competed in the javelin throw, where he came sixth, the javelin throw free style, finishing ninth,

Finnish athletes during the opening ceremony at the 1912 Olympic games.

and the shot put and the triple jump in which he failed to get beyond the preliminary stages. In 1912 he was once again selected to represent Finland, travelling to Stockholm to take part in the games. This time he came fourth in the javelin throw, just missing out on a medal, ninth in the two-handed javelin throw and eleventh in the triple jump.

In 1913 he became only the second Finn to throw the javelin over 60 metres (the first being Julius Archipelago 1892–1969, who won both a gold and silver during the 1912 Olympics).

Juho Halme was executed on the steps of St Nicholas's Church (now Helsinki Cathedral) by Finnish Red Guards supported by the Bolsheviks on 1 February 1918 during the Finnish civil war. Over 36,000 Finns died during the war out of a population of three million. Mass executions and murders were committed by both sides during the civil war which lasted from January to 15 May 1918.

Major Reginald (Reggie) George Pridmore MC
1908 London
Great Britain
Hockey
Gold
Warwickshire Royal Field Artillery
'C' Battery 240th Brigade
Died 13 March 1918 aged 31

'A most gallant sportsman and comrade'

Reginald George Pridmore was born on 29 April 1886 in Edgbaston, Birmingham, the son of George William and Sarah Louisa Pridmore of Coventry. He was educated at the Elstow School Bedford (now closed) and Bedford Grammar School, where he was in the XI. On leaving school he became a stockbroker. He began playing hockey for the North Warwicks Hockey Club and Coventry, playing inside left, and he represented the English hockey team on nineteen occasions between 1908 and 1913. He also played first class cricket, turning out on fourteen occasions for Warwickshire.

During the 1908 Olympics in London he played for England at hockey and was their leading goal scorer, scoring hat-tricks against both France and Scotland. Reaching the final against Ireland, Pridmore scored four of England's eight goals in their 8–1 victory over their old adversaries to take the Olympic gold medal. His record stood for forty-four years, until in 1952 during the Helsinki Olympics Balbir Singh Sr, playing for India, scored five against the Netherlands during their 6–1 victory.

During the war Pridmore took a commission in the 4th South Midland Brigade, Royal Field Artillery (TF) in September 1914 before joining 241st Brigade in May 1916. An outstanding soldier Pridmore was awarded the Military Cross on the Somme in 1916 (*London Gazette*, 20 October 1916) for gallantry. His citation read:

> … *during operations as Forward Observing officer. He displayed great coolness under fire, notably on one occasion when his observation post was very heavily shelled, both he and his lookout man were partially buried but he carried on and sent in valuable reports.*

Between August 1917 and March 1918 he was the officer commanding D Battery 241st Brigade RFA and in March 1918 he transferred to C Battery 240th Brigade RFA, then based in Italy. He was killed in action on 13 March 1918 at the Piave River, Arcade (north of Venice) and is commemorated at the Giavera British Cemetery, Arcade, grave reference plot I row D grave 5. The inscription on his original wooden cross erected by his comrades read, 'A most Gallant Sportsman and Comrade'.

Olympic Field Hockey Champions (grass) 1908. Pridmore is seated, far left.

Hermann Plaskuda
1912 Stockholm
Germany
Fencer
German Army
Died 21 March 1918 aged 38

The German Fencing Champion

Hermann Plaskuda was born on 6 April 1879 in the mountainous region of Zobten, Wroclaw. A gifted and determined fencer he represented Deutsch-Italienischer Fechtclub, Berlin. Such was his skill with the sword that in 1912 he was selected as part of the German fencing team to take part in the 1912 Stockholm Olympics. He was entered for four events: men's sabre, team; men's épée, team; men's épée, individual; and men's foil, individual. There were two forms of fencing popular at the time: the Italian school and the French school. The French decided not to compete at the 1912 games so the Italian style was adopted.

The men's foil, individual took place on 6 July 1912 at the Östermalm Sporting Grounds, Stockholm. The famous Italian Fencer Nedo Nadi took the gold. His Italian team mate Pietro Speciale the silver and the Austrian fencer Richard Verderber, the bronze. Plaskuda finished well down the field. His next event was the men's épée, team, held on 9 and 10 July. Belgium took the gold, Great Britain the silver and the Netherlands the bronze. Germany came eighth. Plaskuda's next event was the men's épée, individual. The event took place between the 12 and 13 July 1912. The Belgian fencer Paul Anspach took the gold, Ivan Osilier from Denmark the silver and Philippe Le Hardy de Beaulieu, also Belgian, the bronze. Once again Plaskuda finished well down the field. His final event was the men's sabre, team. The event like the other three was held at the Östermalm Sporting Grounds, between the 14 and 15 July 1912. Hungary took the gold, Austria the silver and the Netherlands the bronze. The German team came seventh.

(See also Feliks Leparsky, died 10 January 1917).

On returning to Germany, Plaskuda became the German Fencing Association sabre champion in 1913. He fought in the German army during the First World War and was killed in action on 21 March 1918 in France.

Lieutenant Colonel Ronald Harcourt Sanderson
1908 London
Great Britain
Rowing
Gold
148th Brigade Royal Field Artillery
Died 17 April 1918 aged 41

'He was always cool, and one could invariably
place reliance on his sound judgment'

Ronald Harcourt Sanderson was born on 11 December 1876 in at The Vicarage, High Hurstwood, Uckfield, Sussex. He was the only son of the Rev Prebendary Edward and Mary Jane Sanderson, of The Rectory, Uckfield. He was educated at Harrow and Trinity College Cambridge.

Taking after his father the Reverend Canon E. Sanderson, who rowed number three in the Oxford and Cambridge Boat Race in 1862 (an Oxford victory by ten lengths in a time of 24 minutes and 34 seconds) Sanderson was selected to row number six during the 1899 Boat Race against Oxford. On this occasion however Cambridge took the honours by three and a quarter lengths in a time of 21 minutes and 4 seconds; it was Cambridge's first victory in ten years. He was selected to row once again in the 1900 Boat Race, once again rowing number six. One of the finest crews ever to take to the Cambridge boat they destroyed Oxford winning by twenty lengths in a time of 18 minutes and 45 seconds, equalling the Boat Race record established by Oxford in 1893. He also rowed in the Head of the River Boat for three years, won the University Fours and the Lower Double Sculls twice, as well as the Colquhoun Sculls.

In the 1908 Olympics held in London he was selected to row for the Leander eight, rowing in his usual seat, number six. Defeating crews from Canada (*Toronto Argonaut*) and Hungary (*Pannonia/Magyar*) and going on to defeat the Belgian boat (*Royal Club Nautique de Grand*) in the final, the Leander crew took the gold medal.

In 1900 he obtained his BA before going on to take a commission in the Royal Horse Artillery the following May. He served as a second lieutenant during the South African War and was promoted to lieutenant on 8 March 1902. He married in August 1916

Norah Dorothy the eldest daughter of Warwick and Frances Butler of Linden Lodge, Dorchester. They had one son.

Promoted to captain at the outbreak of the First World War he disembarked to France on 7 August 1914 with the 3rd Royal Horse Artillery Brigade. He took part in the Retreat from Mons and was involved in the heavy fighting through to the end of 1914. He was mentioned in despatches in October 1914 and received the Legion of Honour for distinction in the operations of 21–30 August 1914. His citation read:

> In the fight at Petit Morin when all the other Officers of the Battery were killed or wounded he succeeded in bringing the Battery safely out of action.

In January 1915 he was recalled home to train a new Battery, which he took out to the front in May of that year. In May 1916 he was appointed to command D (RHA) Battery and served with it till June 1917 when he again returned home to organize a command depot of some six thousand men. Promoted to Lieutenant Colonel he returned to the front in March 1918 and was given command of a brigade. He was killed, almost instantaneously, by the bursting of a shell while trying to find the headquarters of a neighbouring battery.

Brigadier General White, RA, later wrote:

> We have had some stirring times since the offensive began, and Sandy did splendidly and was the greatest help and comfort to me. He was always cool, and one could invariably place reliance on his sound judgment. I should most certainly have recommended him for a D.S.O., and I think it is safe to say he would have got it.

He is buried in Lijssenthoek Military Cemetery, grave reference XXXVII. G. 3. There is a memorial brass in Ripon Cathedral to the brave colonel.

Lieutenant Kurt Bretting
1912 Stockholm
Germany
Swimming
Reserve of Infantry
Died 30 May 1918 aged 25

World Record Holder of 100 metres Freestyle Swimming

Kurt Bretting was born on 6 June 1892 in Magdeburg, Sachsen-Anhalt, Germany. A good swimmer, he developed his talent while swimming for the SC Hellas Magdeburg swimming club, becoming the club's freestyle champion in 1910. He was also the first German to adopt the front crawl (the first person to adopt this style being the Australian swimmer Cecil Healy who also died during the war on 29 August 1918). Bretting was the German 100 metre freestyle champion in 1910, 1911 and 1913. He was also the 100 metre freestyle world record holder, beating American swimmer Charles Daniels' record of 1:02.8 on 6 April 1912 with a time of 1:02.4 (Duke Kahanamoku beat this world record later the same year.

In 1912 he was selected to represent the German swimming team in the 1912 Olympics to be held in Stockholm. His first event was the men's 100 metre freestyle, held between 6 and 12 July at the Swimming Stadium, Djurgården Bay, Stockholm. Although Bretting swam well he eventually finished fourth, just missing out on a medal. The American swimmer Duke Kahanamoku took the gold, the Australian swimmer Cecil Patrick Healy the silver, and another American Ken Huszagh the bronze. Bretting's next event was the men's 4×400 metre freestyle relay. Once again he was unlucky, with the German team coming fourth once again. Australia took the gold in a new world record time of 10:11.6, almost nine seconds ahead of the Americans who took the silver; Great Britain took the bronze.

During the First World War, Bretting served as a lieutenant with the German infantry and was killed in action on 30 May 1918 at Merville, France.

Lieutenant István Mudin
1906 Athens; 1908 London
Hungary
Pentathlon and Greek Style Discus
Silver and Bronze
101 Infantry Reserve
Died 22 July 1918 aged 36

'And all the brothers were valiant'

István Mudin was born 16 October 1881 in Ketegyhaza Bekes, Hungary. He was one of six children born to Albert Mudin, a French hat maker, who had moved to Hungary on marriage, and Róza Hécsel. He was one of six children, having two sisters and three brothers. Only his brother, Imre, and himself survived into adulthood. He was educated at the local elementary school where he began to play sports and later represented both Athletic Club Arad and the Hungarian Athletic Club (along with his brother Imre). He later obtained a teaching qualification in Budapest and became a teacher and later headmaster at a rural school in Lippai. He specialized in the shot put, javelin and discus, breaking several Hungarian records.

Selected to compete for Hungary in the 1906 Intercalated games in Athens, he won two medals. He took the silver in the men's pentathlon and the bronze in the discus throw, Greek Style. He also took part in the standing long jump, men's shot put, men's discus, and men's javelin throw, free style. Two years later in 1908 he was once again selected to take part in the Olympics in London. This time he was the Hungarian team's flagbearer for the games. Alas he failed to win another medal, his best position being seventh in the discus throw, Greek Style.

In 1915 he was commissioned into the 101st Infantry reserve. A good and brave soldier he was decorated with the silver medal for bravery, first class in 1915, the bronze medal with swords in 1917, the silver medal with swords in 1917 and the Military Cross of Merit III Class in 1918. He was killed in action on 22 July 1918.

His brother Imre also an Olympian (1908–1912) was killed in action on 23 October 1918.

The sports hall at Ketegyhaze was named in honour of the two brothers in 2008.

32540 Second Lieutenant Albert Edward MacKay Rowland
1908 London
New Zealand
Walking
'H' Coy 3rd New Zealand Rifle Brigade
Attached New Zealand Cyclist Battalion
Died 23 July 1918 aged 32

The First New Zealander to compete in the Olympics

Albert Edward Rowland was born on 26 October 1885 in Christchurch, Canterbury, New Zealand. He was the son of Edward Anthony and Anne Evlyn Rowland. An optician and jeweller by trade, Albert won both the New Zealand three mile and one mile walking races in 1906 and 1907 and qualified for the 1908 London Olympics. It helped that he was working in London at the time; the Games had been originally awarded to Rome, but after Italy was plunged into financial crisis following the eruption of Mount Vesuvius in 1906 the fourth modern Olympic Games was relocated to London.

Albert Rowland took part in both the men's 3,500 metre walk and the men's ten mile walk. Albert Rowland, Harry Kerr (also a walker) and Henry St Aubyn Murray (110m hurdles) made history as the first three New Zealanders ever to compete at an Olympic Games. Fijian-born New Zealander Victor Lindberg competed in the 1900 games in Paris as part of the water polo team, but he did this under the British flag. At this time the New Zealand team competed under the Australian banner, an 'anomaly' that would continue until 1920 when New Zealand finally competed as an independent nation at the Antwerp Games. Rowland managed to finish fifth in the 3,500 metre walk in a time of 16:07.0 behind teammate and fellow New Zealander Harry Kerr who won the bronze medal – the first time a New Zealander had won an Olympic medal in the Games. Rowland then went on to finish fifth in the heats of the ten mile walk, failing to progress to the final.

Rowland remained in London after the Olympics, walking for the Herne Hill Harriers Club in South London. Eventually returning to New Zealand, he established the Wellington Scottish Athletic Club in 1915. He married Agnes Ludlow Rowland of Wellington, New Zealand.

During the war Rowland served as a private and then sergeant with H Company 3rd New Zealand Rifle Brigade. He was later commissioned as a second lieutenant and became attached to the New Zealand Cycling Battalion. He must have had quite a sense of humour and literary aspirations because while serving as a sergeant he became involved as a sub-editor with the military, slightly satirical magazine *The Waitemata Wobbler*.

Rowland was killed in action by machine gun fire during an assault on the village of Marfaux near Reims during the second battle of the Marne on 23 July 1918. He was one of 18,000 New Zealanders to be killed in the conflict – a large number for such a small country.

He is buried in Marfaux British Cemetery, grave reference I. A. 14.

In 1996 Harry Kerr the first man to win an Olympic medal for New Zealand was indicted into the New Zealand Sports Hall of Fame. Perhaps consideration could also now be given to Albert Rowland.

Second Lieutenant Ernest James Keeley
1912 Stockholm
South Africa
Shooting
4th Regiment South African Infantry
Died 23 July 1918 aged 28

One of the finest shots in South Africa

Ernest James Keeley was born on 26 May 1890 in Pretoria, South Africa. He was the son of Jane Mansfield of PO Gezina, Pretoria. A fine and accurate shot who took part in competitions at Bicester, he was selected to shoot for South Africa in the 1912 Olympics. His first event was the men's military rifle team, 200, 400, 500 and 600 metres. The event took place at the Kaknäs, Djurgården, Stockholm (where all the shooting events took place) on 29 June 1912. Keeley just missed out on a medal, coming fourth. The United States took the gold, Great Britain the silver and Sweden the bronze. His second event was the men's military rifle, three positions, 300 metres individual, which took place on 1 July 1912. Keeley came thirteenth. The Hungarian, Sandor Prokopp, took the gold, Carl Osburn from the United States took the silver and Embret Skogen from Norway the bronze. This was followed by the men's free rifle, three positions, (individual) 300 metres. Keeley came fifty-sixth. The gold was taken by the French shooter Paul Colas and the two Swedish shooters Lars Jorgen Madsen and Niels Larsen took the silver and bronze. Keeley's final event was the men's free rifle, three positions, 300 metre, team. Once again Keeley just missed out on a medal, coming sixth. The Swedish team took the gold with Norway winning the silver and Denmark the bronze. Keeley continued shooting at Bisley right up to a year before his death.

At the outbreak of the First World War Keeley first enlisted into the Northern Mounted Rifles, Cycle and Motor Corps, becoming a corporal. Always in the thick of the action, he was wounded at Delville Wood on 17 July 1916 and then again at Arras on 9 April 1917. Joining the 4th South African Infantry (South African Scottish) he was commissioned as a second lieutenant. He was killed in action on 23 July 1918 at Vlaanderen, Belgium. John Buchan in his *The History of the South African Forces in France* describes his death in a little more detail:

The capture of Metreen was a good example of a perfectly planned and perfectly executed minor action. The captured material consisted of 1 field gun 13 trench mortars 30 machine guns of which the Composite Battalions share was 10 trench mortars, and 23 machine guns. Between 200 and 300 prisoners fell to the brigade. The casualties of the Composite Battalion were 130 of whom 27 were killed and 2 died of wounds. Besides Captain Scheepers, Second Lieutenants Mackie, Anderson, Douglas, Male and Keeley fell and Lieutenant Mackay was wounded.

His body was never discovered or identified and he is commemorated on the Ploegsteert Memorial, panel 11. He also has a commemoration stone in Rebecca Street Cemetery in Pretoria.

Captain Henry Maitland Macintosh
1912 Stockholm
Great Britain
Athletics
Gold
1/8 Battalion Argyll and Sutherland Highlanders
Died 26 July 1918 aged 26

'If at first you don't succeed...'

Henry Maitland Macintosh was born on 10 June 1892 in Kelso, Roxburghshire, Scotland. He was the son of the Rev William Macintosh and Annie Smith Macintosh, of St Paul's Rectory, Kinross. He was educated at Glenalmond College Perth before going up to Corpus Christi College Cambridge.

An outstanding athlete he was selected to run for Great Britain in the 1912 Olympic Games to be held in Stockholm. He was chosen to run in the 100 metres, 200 metres, and the 4×400 metre relay team. He was in many ways lucky to be selected. Prior to the games Macintosh had had a poor domestic season. He was beaten by his old rival Duncan Macmillan in the 100 yards, came last in the AAA championships and failed to run in the 220 yards.

He did little better in the Olympics. He was eliminated in the first round of the 100 metres, and failed to finish in the semi-final of the 200 metres. He had only one last chance of glory the 4×400 metres where he was to run second. It looked as though the British team had been knocked out in the semi-final then they came second behind America. However the United States were disqualified for an infringement in passing the baton and the British team went through. In the final the German team, favourites for the gold medal, made the same mistake and the British four took the honours. With the German disqualification only the gold and silver medal were awarded and no bronze, making it the only athletics event ever to be awarded two medals. The British four were David Jacobs, Henry Macintosh, Willie Applegarth and Victor d'Arcy. In 1913, Macintosh served as president of the Cambridge University Athletics Club. During that time he won the Scottish title and managed to equal the British 100 yards record of 9.8 seconds while running in Vienna. He ran his last race in 1914, the 100 yards against the old enemy Oxford.

The Extinguished Flame

On leaving Cambridge, Macintosh became an assistant district commissioner in South Africa. At the outbreak of the First World War he returned to England and took a commission into the 1/8 Battalion Argyll and Sutherland Highlanders. He was promoted to captain before dying of wounds received in action during the Second Battle of the Somme on 26 July 1918.

He is buried in the Senlis French National Cemetery, grave reference I. C. 21.

British 4X400 metre gold winning relay team. Macintosh is on the far right of the photograph.

Sergeant/Lieutenant Hans Eberhard Sorge
1912 Stockholm
Germany
Gymnastics
4th Company 180th Infantry Regiment & 120th Infantry Regiment
Died 6 August 1918 aged 26

Unlucky not to win a medal

Hans Sorge was born on 27 May 1892 in Braunlage, Niedersachsen, Germany. A natural athlete he competed for Allgemeiner Akademischer Turnerbund gymnastics club, Leipzig. He was selected as part of the German gymnastics team to take part in the 1912 Olympic Games in Stockholm. He took part in the men's team all-around and the men's team all-around, free style.

In the men's team all-around free style Hans Sorge and his team were unlucky not to win a medal, coming fourth with 16.85 points. His next event was the men's team all-around. The German team managed fifth with 32.40 points. (See Alfred Staats, died 22 October 1915).

During the First World War Sorge first served as a sergeant with the 4th Company 180th Infantry Regiment and was wounded. He was then commissioned as a

A soldier of the 180th Infantry.

lieutenant with the 120th Infantry Regiment and was wounded again. He was finally killed on 6 August 1918 in Bray-sur-Somme, France.

Lieutenant Colonel Thomas Head Raddall DSO
1908 London
Great Britain
Shooting
8th Battalion Canadian Infantry (Manitoba Regiment)
Died 9 August 1918 aged 40

He was smiling as he kissed us all goodbye, but his eyes were full of tears, like ours. I can still see the trap trotting away, the driver flicking his whip and the man in khaki dabbing at his eyes with a handkerchief. Three years later, almost to the day, he was lying dead on the battlefield of Amiens

Thomas Head Raddall was born on 9 December 1876 in Farnborough, Hampshire. On leaving school he became a clerk but it wasn't a life he enjoyed. On 18 October 1892 he enlisted as a boy soldier with the Royal Marines at Gosport. He was promoted to private in 1894, corporal 1898 and sergeant in 1901. A crack shot he was transferred as a military instructor to the Hythe Musketry School in 1909. He also took part in a number of shooting competitions at Bisley between 1905 and 1911 becoming a well-known figure at the event. In 1913, Raddall and his family transferred to Halifax, Nova Scotia in order to take up a training position in the Canadian Militia. During this time he met and married Ellen Gifford.

An expert shot, Randall was selected to take part in the 1908 Olympic Games, to be held in London, as part of the shooting team. He took part in the men's free rifle, three positions (standing, kneeling, prone) 300 metres team. The team came sixth.

He served as a quartermaster sergeant with the Canadian Militia until the outbreak of the First World War in 1914. On 22 September 1914 Raddall was commissioned into the 8th battalion, Canadian Infantry (Manitoba Regiment) at Valcartier, Quebec, becoming a lieutenant. Going to France with his battalion he was wounded during the Second Battle of Ypres and returned to Nova Scotia during the summer of 1915 to recover. Offered a training position in Canada he refused it and insisted on returning to the front to be with his battalion and his men. He was back in the front line by August 1915. Writing about Raddall's return to the front, his son, the well-known Canadian

230

writer of the same name, remembered feeling that 'instinct told him that this was the last time he would see his family'.

On 6 December 1917 the Raddall family were lucky to survive the infamous Halifax Explosion in his home town, when the SS *Mont-Blanc*, a French cargo ship laden with explosives, collided with the SS *Imo* and blew up in Halifax Harbour. Over 2,000 people were killed and a further 9,000 injured.

Whilst serving as a major, Raddall was awarded the Distinguished Service Order for bravery and outstanding service (*London Gazette* 3 June 1918). Promoted to lieutenant colonel, Raddall became the commanding officer of the Manitoba Regiment on 20 April 1918. Unfortunately only four months after he had assumed command of the regiment he was killed in action by machine gun fire during the battle of Amiens on 9 August 1918 near Meharicourt, on the Somme.

In his last letter home to his son, Raddall wrote: 'strive to make a name for yourself.' Thomas Head Raddall (1903–94) took him at his word. Remembering his last request he went on to become one of Canada's most celebrated authors, specializing in historic fiction. He was made a member of the Order of Canada in 1971. He also wrote a very moving poem to his father.

Colonel Raddall is buried in Manitoba Cemetery, Caix, grave reference A. 4.

Orderley Frederick Overend Kitching
1908 London
Great Britain
Athletics
British Red Cross Society, Field Ambulance Unit
Died 11 August 1918 aged 32

'A conscientious objector who served his country and died for it'

Frederick Overend Kitching was born on 7 (some records have 4) July 1886 in Cockerton, County Durham. He was one of seven children born to John and Annie Elizabeth Kitching of Branksome Hall, near Darlington. A deeply religious family they were members of the Society of Friends (the Quakers). Frederick was the grandson of Alfred Kitching, the man who founded the Whessoe Engineering Company which in 1845 built the Derwent locomotive designed by the great Timothy Hackworth.

After leaving school Kitching became a solicitor and moved to Oaklands, Kingston Hill, Surrey.

Always a first class athlete he competed for the London Athletics Club. He specialized in the standing broad jump (only an Olympic event until 1912). The competitors had to jump as far as they could from a standing start. Both feet had to be on the ground or they were disqualified. He also specialized in the javelin being the first Briton to exceed 120 feet, 130 feet, and 140 feet. He eventually achieved a personal best of 143 feet 3 inches (43.6 metres).

He was selected to take part in the 1908 Olympic Games in London. He competed in the standing broad jump (one of the six jumping events) but was unplaced among seventeen competitors.

As a Quaker, Frederick appealed for absolute exemption from military duties during World War One. Although he was granted his exemption it was on the understanding that he joined the Friends Ambulance Unit (FAU). He joined the FAU in April 1916, going to the front in July 1916. He was first posted to the driving school to learn how to drive ambulances, although most of his service he worked as an orderly and occasionally helped on local farms. On 11 August 1918 Frederick was killed during a German air raid on the Hotel Pyl in Dunkirk, then the HQ of the FAU.

He is buried in Dunkirk Town Cemetery, grave reference IV. C. 11.

He is also commemorated on the War Memorial Hospital plaque, Hollyhurst Road, Darlington.

Captain Bertrand Marie de Lesseps
1908 London
France
Fencing
20e Battalion de Chasseurs
Died 28 August 1918 aged 43

'Never far from his brother's side'

Bertrand de Lesseps, brother of Olympic fencer Ismael de Lesseps who died on 30 September 1915, was born on 3 February 1875 in Paris.

Bertrand was a keen aviator and pioneer pilot, something he did together with his brothers. He received his official French flying certificate in 1910 and flew many hours as a pilot. He met and married Marguerite Sara Favre and they had one son who they named Bertrand after his father. It was said of the Lesseps brothers that they were never too far away from each other, as close as brothers could be. The brothers all looked very much the same too and were difficult to tell apart.

A keen fencer specializing in the sabre he was selected together with his brother Ismael to represent France in the London 1908 Olympic games. He took part in both the men's sabre, team, and the men's sabre, individual. In the men's sabre, team, which was held just outside White City Stadium, London between 21 and 24 July 1912, he was unlucky to miss out on a medal, the French team coming fourth behind Hungary who took the gold. Italy took the silver and Bohemia the bronze. In the men's individual sabre he failed to reach the final but did finish ahead of his brother Ismael. The gold went to the famous Hungarian fencer Jenő Fuchs who would go on to win four gold medals, two in the 1908 Olympics for the individual and team sabre and two in 1912 for the same events (he was also a champion bobsledder and rower). The silver was taken by another Hungarian fencer Béla Zulawszky (died 24 October 1914). The bronze went to the Bohemian fencer Vilém Goppold z Lobsdorfu, stopping a Hungarian clean sweep.

During the First World War Bertrand served with the 20ᵉ Battalion de Chasseurs becoming a captain. He was killed at the head of his men on 28 August 1918 while on a reconnoitring mission near Cauvigny, Oise, France.

Keeping up their keen interest in flying, another of the Lesseps brothers, Jacques, flew for the 2nd Bombing Group of the French Service as a captain and pilot. He went on to win the American Distinguished Service Cross (foreign award) for his bravery on 15 August 1918 a few days before his brother was killed. His citation read:

'The Distinguished Service Cross is presented to Jacques B. M. De Lesseps, Captain, French Army, for extraordinary heroism in action at Conflans and Audun le Roman, August 15, 1918. Captain De Lesseps made three successful bombing raids in one night, two in Connans and one on Audun le Roman, causing great damage. Despite the heavy anti-aircraft fire, he flew at an extremely low altitude and besides his successful raids, returned with valuable information of the enemy's movements'.

Second Lieutenant Cecil Patrick Healy
1912 Olympics Stockholm
Australia
Swimming
Gold, Silver, Bronze
19th Battalion Australian Infantry
Died 29 August 1918 aged 36

'Honoured Swimmer'

Cecil Patrick Healy was born on 28 November 1881 in Darlinghurst, an inner-city suburb of Sydney Australia. The family later moved to the rural town of Bowral, where he received his education at the J. Lee Pullings's school. He was the third son of native-born parents Patrick Joseph Healy, barrister, and his wife Annie Louisa, née Gallott.

His talent as a swimmer quickly developed and in 1895 he won a 66-yard handicap race at the old Sydney Natatorium. He returned to Sydney in 1896 and joined the East Sydney Amateur Swimming club, becoming friends with another great Australian swimmer, Frederick Lane. He was also a member of the North Steyne Surf Lifesaving Club and a keen water polo player. He was also an early pioneer of the Australian crawl style known as freestyle and of the technique of side-breathing. When not swimming, he worked as a commercial traveller.

With a first class club and training Healy improved quickly. In 1904 Healy swam the quickest time ever in the 100 yards freestyle, completing it in 58 seconds. The following year, 1905, at Balmain he won the 100 yards state championship in 61.1 seconds, followed by equalling the world record in the 110 yards freestyle and winning his first Australian title. In 1906 he was selected to attend the Intercalated Olympic Games in Athens. He won a very creditable bronze medal in the 100 metre freestyle being defeated by the America swimmer Charles Daniel, the 1904 Olympic champion, and the famous Hungarian swimmer and 1904 Olympic silver medallist Zoltan Halmay.

Remaining in Europe he went on to win the Kaiser's Cup in Hamburg, followed by the Amateur Swimming Association 220-yard British Championship in 2 minutes 37.4 seconds. He was however defeated in the 100 yards by his old enemy the American Charles Daniel, coming in second. Returning to Australia he was unable to attend the 1908 Olympic Games in London due to a lack of funding. In 1909 and 1910, he again successfully defended his Australian championships and in the following year inflicted the first defeat on the Australian legendary swimmer Frank Beaurepaire in any race, beating him in a 440-yard race.

In 1912 Healy qualified for the 1912 Olympic Games in Stockholm. He swam in the 100 metres reaching the final where he took the silver medal, being beaten to the gold by the American swimmer Duke Kahanamoku. Kahanamoku had been disqualified in an early heat but thanks to Healy's support during an appeal he was reinstated. Healy's honesty cost him the gold medal. In the 400 metres freestyle, despite setting a new world record in his heat he only managed fourth in the final. Swimming the opening leg of the 4×400 metres freestyle, together with Harold Hardwick, Leslie Boardman and Malcolm Champion, the young Australian held off the much fancied American team to win the gold. Once again remaining in Europe he took three seconds off Beaurepaire's world record time in the 220 yards while racing in Scotland. Covered in laurels he returned to Australia.

He became a lifesaver on Manly Beach and was awarded the Royal Humane Society's silver medal for saving the lives of numerous swimmers caught in the surf and tides. He also became vice-president of the New South Wales Amateur Swimming Association and of the Surf Bathing Association of New South Wales. An excellent surfer, he was a founder, captain and gold honour badge holder of the Manly Surf Club and prominent in the fight to deregulate bathing laws.

In September 1915 he enlisted into the Australian Defense Force, serving with the Army Service Corps. Promoted to quartermaster sergeant he saw service in Egypt and France. Selected for a commission, he was sent to the Officer Training School at Trinity College Cambridge. While there he swam, rowed, boxed and played rugby. He was commissioned as a second lieutenant into the 19th Sportsman Battalion on 1 June 1918. He was killed in action during his very first engagement, at the battle of Mont St Quentin, attacking a German machine gun emplacement on 29 August 1918. Healy was, and still remains, the only Australian Olympic gold medallist to be killed on the battlefield.

WARRANT OFFICER
CECIL HEALY
SWIMMER

He is buried in Assevillers New British Cemetery (France), grave reference II. F. 6.

A requiem mass for him was celebrated in St Mary's Cathedral, Sydney. He is commemorated by the Healy shield for life-saving in New South Wales. In 1981 he was honoured by the International Swimming Hall of Fame at Fort Lauderdale, Florida where he became an 'Honoured Swimmer'.

Second Lieutenant Joseph Frank Dines
1912 Stockholm
Great Britain
Football
Gold
13th Battalion The King's Liverpool Regiment
Died 27 September 1918 aged 32

The Smiling Footballer

Joseph Frank Dines was born on 12 April 1886 in King's Lynn, Norfolk. Joseph Dines was the youngest of four sons of Frank and Josephine Dines of 4 Whitefriars Terrace. An intelligent man he trained as a teacher in Peterborough later becoming an assistant master at St Margaret's School in the Millfleet. Dines was described at the time as being 'a thoughtful young man, a commanding half-back and a master of the art of dribbling.'

He represented Lynn All Saints before moving to Lynn United and then being offered terms with Lynn Town making his first team debut on 13 February 1904 against Peterborough Loco in the Dereham Charity Cup. In all he made 149 appearances for Lynn, scoring twenty-eight goals for them. He also played against Aston Villa in the 1906 FA Cup. Winning his county colours he played in the Norfolk eleven that won the Southern Counties Championship in 1908, as well as making appearances in both Norwich and Woolwich Arsenal Reserves.

Moving from Norfolk in 1910 he accepted a teaching position at the Highlands School, Ilford. He also found time to marry Ethel Henrietta Eugenie Dines of 176 Chigwell Road, South Woodford. Selected to play for England he went on to receive twenty-seven amateur caps. He also turned out for Queens Park Rangers, Millwall and captained Ilford. A gifted centre-half Dines also turned out for Liverpool in their third match of the 1912/13 season away to Chelsea which Liverpool won 2–1. This appearance caused consternation at Ilford FC as this report from *The Staffordshire Sentinel* published on the 24 August 1912, shows: 'The news that Joe Dines, the English amateur international footballer, has signed forms for Liverpool caused some dismay out Ilford way, as he had been one of the mainstays of the Ilford FC for some years. Dines will not altogether desert his old club.'

In 1912 he was selected to be a member of the England team that travelled to Stockholm to take part in the Olympic Games. He played half-back in all three of Great Britain's matches. They defeated Hungary 7–0 and Finland 4–0 before finally defeating the mighty Denmark 4–2 in the final on 4 July 1912, winning the gold medal (which they retained as they had won it during the 1908 London Olympics as well).

So personable was Dines that he became known as 'The Smiling Footballer'. Although offered terms by several clubs he always refused to turn professional.

Joe and two of his brothers volunteered to join the army in November 1915. He served with the Ordnance Corps, the Middlesex Regiment, the Machine Gun Corps and the Tank Corps, before finally being commissioned as a second lieutenant into 13 battalion of the King's Liverpool Regiment. After officer training he was sent to the front where he survived for eleven days. On 27 September 1918, while leading an attack against a German machine gun position, Dines was cut down and killed by machine gun fire. The attack was considered a great success and the battalion took over 600 German prisoners. However this was at a cost of 6 officers and 125 men. Alas Joseph Dines was one of the fallen officers.

He is buried in the Grand Ravine British Cemetery, Havrincourt, grave reference A. 42.

Later a slate plaque was erected on the house where Dines was born, a fitting tribute to one of Norfolk's greatest sons.

Lieutenant Hanns Braun
1908 London; 1912 Stockholm
Germany
Athletics
Silver, Bronze
Imperial German Air Service
Jasta 1 and 34b
Died 9 October 1918 aged 31

'Considered to be the first of Germany's great international Athletes'

Hanns Braun was born on 26 October 1886 at Wernfels (Spalt), Bayern, Germany. His father was the famous German painter Louis Braun (1836–1916), famous for his military paintings. Not surprisingly he studied art in Munich becoming a fine sculptor and architect in Berlin.

A natural athlete and excellent runner at several distances he not only represented his country but also the Munich Sports Club and the Berliner Sport-Club. He became the German champion at 400 metres in 1909, again in 1910 and once again in 1912. He became the German champion in the 800 metres while running in Leipzig on 28 May 1908 when he finishing in a time of 1:57.4. He also became the British AAA champion in 1909, 1911, and again in 1912. On 7 February 1909 he set the indoor world record in the 1,000 metres in Berlin in a time of 2:39.0.

Selected to run for Germany in the 1908 London Olympics he came third in the 800 metres in a time of 1:55.2. Although his time was 0.8 of a second faster than the previous Olympic record it was alas three seconds slower than that of the gold medal winner the American runner Mel Sheppard. Braun was also part of the German medley relay. The event consisted of 1,600 metres being run by four athletes per team. Interestingly the athletes had different distances to run. In the medley, the first two runners each ran 200 metres. The third runner ran 400 metres and the fourth ran 800 metres. The German team consisted of Arthur Hoffmann, Hans Eicke, Otto Triloff and finally Hanns Braun who ran the last 800 metres. Running against teams from the USA and Hungary it looked for a while that they were only going to manage third. Braun began his leg of the race five yards behind the Hungarian runner Ödön Bodor. Digging in, he managed to pass Bodor, the Americans however were too far ahead and the German team took silver in a time of 3:32.4 (the American team took the gold in a time of 3:29.4). Braun also competed in the 1,500 metres but failed to advance to the final (he had been the German record holder at this event in 1907).

Continuing with his athletics in 1909 he became the German 110 metre hurdles record holder and then the following year, 1910, he became the German 100 metre record holder as well as the 400 metre hurdles record holder.

In 1912 he was selected once again to take part in the Olympics, this time being held in Stockholm. Running in the 400 metre final against four Americans, Charles Reidpath, Edward Lindberg, Ted Meredith and Caroll Haff, he managed to split the American team up and come second in a time of 48.3 (the America Charles Reidpath taking the gold in a time of 48.2 and his team mate Edward Lindberg bronze in a time of 48.4). He also ran in the 800 metre race coming sixth.

In 1914 at the beginning of the First World War he enlisted into the Volunteer Replacement Infantry battalion of the German Life Guards. He then joined the Imperial German Flying Corps (after 1916 named the Imperial German Air Service) as a sergeant serving on the ground staff. Selected to become a pilot after training he joined Jasta 1 in October 1916. He became a flying instructor and was commissioned in January 1917. He joined Jasta 34b on 15 September 1918. He was killed a month later in a mid-air

Braun winning his silver medal during the 1912 Olympic games.

collision with an aircraft from his own Jasta at 11am on 9 October 1918, crashing at Croix Fonsomme, Cambrai.

He is buried in the military cemetery in Vladslo, Belgium, grave location block 3, grave 2170.

In 2008 he was inducted into the German sports Hall of Fame.

The Hanns Braun Memorial Award is presented every year for outstanding achievement in sport.

He is also commemorated on his father's grave in the Northern Cemetery in Munich, grave location 3-1-20.

Lieutenant Imre Mudin
1908 London; 1912 Stockholm
Hungary
Athletics
101st Infantry Regiment
Died 23 October 1918 aged 30

'One of Hungary's finest athletic brothers'

Imre Mudin was born on 8 November 1887 in Ketegyhaza, Hungary. He was the son of Albert Mudin, a French hatmaker, who had moved to Hungary looking for work, and marriage. His mother was Róza Hécsel. Imre was the youngest of six siblings, all of whom, with the exception of his brother István, died while they were still young. After attending a local elementary school he went to Arad to study civil engineering and teaching. He graduated in 1911 and took up a position at a boy's school in Nagyatad. He taught mathematics, physics and natural history and put together an insect collection of 200 butterflies. He was also keen on his boys becoming involved in physical fitness and any number of sports. In 1912 he organized the first sports competition for boys' schools in the region, which later turned into a traditional contest.

Imre was a member of the famous Magyar Atletikai Sporting Club. Under the guidance of his brother Istvan, who had taken a silver and bronze in the 1906 Games in Athens, he specialized in the shot put. Among his athletic successes were nine national titles in the shot put (1908–14 and 1916–17), two in the discus throw (1910 and 1916) and the javelin throw (1916–17). He broke the Hungarian national record at an Olympic test event in June 1908 with a throw of 12.88 metres. As a result he was selected to represent Hungary in the 1908 London Olympics. He took part in the freestyle javelin, Greek discus throw and the discus throw, however he failed to win a medal in any event. His brother István was flagbearer for Hungary at these games. Four years later in 1912, he was selected once again to take part in the Olympics this time in Stockholm. Once again he failed to win a medal. In 1916 and 1917 and despite being in the army he took part in the Hungarian Athletics Championship winning the discus throw, javelin throw, shot put in 1916, and in the following year won both the javelin throw and the shot put. In 1915 he also found time to marry Melina Pavlovlits, an opera singer. They had no children. After Imre died Melina never married again and died in 1991.

Imre took a commission in the Hungarian Army on 11 August 1914 serving as a sub lieutenant and later lieutenant with the 101st Infantry Regiment. A good officer and soldier he was decorated with the Silver Medal of Bravery 1st Class in 1915. He was killed in action on 23 October 1918 during the battle for control of the Monte Grappa massif on the Italian front. Accounts of the time said he was shot by a sniper while retiring to a safer position. His body was never identified and he has no known grave.

His brother and double Olympic medallist István was killed in action on 22 July 1918.

The sports stadium at Nagyatad was named after Imre Mudin. The sports hall at Ketegyhaze was named in honour of the two brothers in 2008.

Sergeant William Jones Lyshon
1912 Stockholm
America
Wrestler (Featherweight)
135th Infantry Regiment
Died 13 October 1918 aged 30

'William was so popular that the works at the Bell Company paid for
him to go to the Olympics, First Class'

William Jones Lyshon was born on 30 December 1887 in Philadelphia, Pennsylvania, USA. He was educated at and graduated from Girard College, Philadelphia. A gifted wrestler he became the Middle Atlantic AAU champion as well as representing the Germantown Boys Club and the Pennsylvania Railroad YMCA. Such was his talent that for a time he was taken on by Pennsylvania University as a volunteer wrestling coach.

In 1912 he started to work as service inspector for the Philadelphia Bell Telephone Company and it was because of this he was able to go to the 1912 Olympics in Stockholm. Initially Lyshon wasn't selected for the 1912 American wrestling team because he couldn't afford to pay his fare to Sweden. However, being a young man of resolve, he offered to work his passage to Stockholm. Working for the Philadelphia Bell Telephone Company he also became a member of the Spare Pair Society, which was composed of members of the Bell Company. When the members heard of his plight, and realizing what a great honour it was, the members raised enough funds for Lyshon not only to travel to the games, but to travel first class.

Fighting in the men's featherweight, Greco-Roman wrestling competition, he was pinned and beaten in his first fight by the Hungarian wrestler József Pongrácz and then again in his second fight by the Swedish Wrestler Anders Sigfrid Hugo Johansson, ending his games. He wasn't to have another chance for a medal.

During the First War Lyshon joined the ranks of the 315th Infantry Regiment eventually becoming a Sergeant with G company. He was shot in the head by a German sniper and killed on 13 October 1918. His body was later returned to the USA and buried in Fernwood Cemetery, Pennsylvania, with full military honours.

Sous-Lieutenant Alfred Philippe Ferdinand Joseph Motté
Chevalier of the Legion of Honour
1908 London; 1912 Stockholm
France
Athletics
234ᵉ Regiment Infantry
Died 31 October 1918 aged 31

The Longest Jumper in France

Alfred Motté was born on 2 June 1887 in Roubaix, France. He was one of five children born to Albert Marie Motté and Leonie Clemence Marguerite Lepoutre. A keen athlete he competed for Racing Club de Roubaix. Predominantly a popular football club it also had an athletics department. Motté specialized in the men's standing high jump and standing long jump and was selected to compete for the French athletics team in the 1908 London Olympic games.

The men's standing long jump was held on 20 July 1908 at the White City Stadium, London. It was eventually won by the American Ray Ewry with a jump of 10 feet 11¼ inches (3.33 metres). The silver was taken by the Greek jumper Kostas Tsiklitiras with a jump of 10 feet 7¼ inches (3.22 metres) and the bronze by another American, Martin Sheridan, with a jump of 10 feet 7 inches (3.22 metres). Motté's distance isn't known but he finished well down the field. In the men's standing high jump Motté did much better, coming seventh with a jump of 4 feet 10 inches (1.47 metres). This gold was also taken by Ray Ewry with a leap of 5 feet 2 inches (1.57 metres), the silver by another American, John Biller, with a jump of 5 feet 1 inch (1.55 metres), and the bronze by Tsiklitiras.

Four years later Motté was selected again to represent France in the men's standing long jump, this time in Stockholm. Despite jumping a distance of 3.10 metres he

still finished well down the field. The gold was taken by the Greek Kostas Tsiklitiras with a jump of 3.37 metres, the silver by the American Platt Adams with a jump of 3.36 metres, and the bronze by his brother Ben Adams with a distance of 3.28 metres.

During the First World War Motté served as a sous-lieutenant with the 234e French Infantry and was killed in action shortly before the end of the war on 31 October 1918 at Sézanne, Marne, France.

Captain Arthur Yancey Wear
1904 St Louis USA
America
Tennis
Bronze (Doubles)
356th Infantry Regiment
6 November 1918 aged 38

'Refused to leave his regiment despite being gravely ill'

Arthur Yancey Wear was born on 1 March 1880 in St Louis, USA. He was one of five children (having two brothers and two sisters) born to James Hutchinson, who ran a wholesale dry goods business, and Nannie, née Holliday. From a long established American family he was descended from Jonathan Wear of Tennessee who, with four brothers, served in the Revolutionary War, all of them being participants in the battle of King's Mountain. One of his uncles, also named Jonathan Wear, fought under General Jackson at New Orleans in the War of

1812. He was educated at the Smith Academy St Louis before in 1898 going up to Yale University. He was a member of the Freshman, College, and University Baseball teams, and served as secretary and treasurer of the Freshman Football Association. He graduated and in 1903 joined his family business of Wear Brothers.

A noted and talented lawn tennis player he was selected to play tennis for the USA in the 1904 Olympic Games held in St Louis. Playing in the men's doubles together with Clarence Gamble he reached the semi-finals where he was beaten by the eventual winners Beals Write and Edgar Leonard 6–1, 6–2, but still taking the bronze medal. The first time Olympic medals were issued for tennis was in 1904. His brother Joseph also won a bronze medal for tennis in the same games.

On America's entry into the war in 1917 Arthur received a commission into the 356th Infantry company eventually rising to the rank of captain.

In June, 1918, he was posted overseas and participated in the St Mihiel fighting with the 89th Division. On 15 October 1918, Wear was taken seriously ill with duodenal ulcers of the stomach. Although he was told to return home and recover he refused, leading the 2nd battalion of the 356th Infantry, 89th Division, in the Meuse-Argonne operations, continuing in command of the battalion until 6 November 1918 when he collapsed and died.

He is buried in the Meuse-Argonne American Cemetery and Memorial in Lorraine, France, plot B, row 37, grave 13.

Hermann Heinrich Burkowitz
1912 Stockholm
Germany
Athletics
Regiment NK
Died November 1918 aged 26

'A national champion'

Hermann Burkowitz was born on 31 January 1892 in Berlin. A keen runner he represented the SC Charlottenburg sporting club of Berlin. In both 1911 and 1913 he was runner-up in the German 400 metre championship. He was selected to run for Germany in the 1912 Olympic games being held in Stockholm, taking part in both the 400 metre and 4×400 metre relay.

His first event, the 400 metres, was held in the Stockholm Olympic Stadium between 12 and 13 July 1912. Unfortunately Burkowitz was knocked out in the heats, failing to make the final. The race was run by the American runner Charles Reidpath in a new Olympic record; the silver was taken by the German runner Hanns Braun; and another American, Ed Lindberg, took the bronze. Burkowitz's next event was the men's 4×400 metre relay. Once again Burkowitz, together with the German team, was knocked out in the heats. The USA took the gold in a new world record of 3:16.6, France the silver and Great Britain the bronze.

Burkowitz disappeared during the First World War in the fighting around Vlaanderen, Belgium during November 1918.

Physician 1st Class Marie-Charles-André Corvington
1900 Paris
Francce (Haiti)
Fencing
141st Regiment Infantry
Died 13 December 1918 aged 41

World's Fair, Paris.

For his work and outstanding bravery under fire he was posthumously
made a Chevalier of the Legion of Honour

Marie-Charles-André Corvington was born on 19 November 1877 in Aux Cayes, Haiti. Sent to Paris to study, he qualified as a doctor of medicine. In 1910 he married Marguerite Louise Chamerois and they resided with her father at 34 Rue Monge, Paris. An accomplished fencer specializing in the foil, he competed for Salles d'Armes du Palais et Sociétés Savantes, Paris. In 1900 he was selected by France to take part in the 1900 Olympics to be held in Paris.

Fifty-four fencers from ten countries (thirty-nine of them from France) took part in the competition which was held between 14 and 21 May 1900 at the Grand Celebration Hall of the Exposition, Field of Mars, Paris. Sixteen fencers fought their way through to the semi-final. The semi-finals consisted of two pools of eight fencers each, with the top four in each pool advancing to the final. Corvington failed to make it to the semi-final. French fencers took all three medals. The gold was won by Emile Coste who won six of his seven bouts, the silver was taken by Henri Masson who won five of his seven bouts, and the bronze by Marcel Boulenger who won four of his seven matches.

Doctor Marie-Charles-André Corvington was mobilized on 3 August 1914 and attached to the 3/55 military field hospital working as a physician 1st class with the rank of lieutenant. He was later transferred to military hospital 31. Corvington died shortly after the war's end on 13 December 1918. I have been unable to establish if this was as a result of wounds or a medical condition brought on by the effects of war. He is buried in Reims, Champagne-Ardenne, France. In honour of his work as a doctor throughout the war he was posthumously made a Chevalier of the Legion of Honour.

Victor Willems
1908 London Olympics/1912 Stockholm Olympics
Belgium
Fencing (Épée)
Gold (1912) Bronze (1908)
Regiment Unknown
Died 1918

'So little known for such a great competitor'

Victor Willems was born on 19 February 1877. For a man who won two Olympic medals, one gold (1912) and one bronze (1908), I can find very little information on the fencer Victor Willems. Willems was first selected to represent Belgium at the 1908 London Olympics. The épée team event took place just outside the White City Stadium between 20 and 24 July. Willems and the Belgian team came third taking the bronze. The hot favorites, France, took the gold and Great Britain the silver.

In 1912 the Olympic Games were held in Stockholm. Chosen once again to represent Belgium Willems took part in the men's foil, individual, men's épée, individual and men's épée, team. In the men's foil, individual, Willems failed to reach the final being

knocked out in the heats. The great Italian fencer Nedo Nadi took the gold, his Italian team mate Pietro Speciale the silver, and the Austrian fencer Richard Verderber the bronze. In the men's épée, team, Willems and the Belgian team took the gold, a great achievement given the keen competition. Great Britain took the silver and the Netherlands the bronze. In the men's épée, individual, Willems failed to make the final, being knocked out in the early heats. The event was won by a fellow Belgian, Paul Anspach. The Danish fighter Ivan Osiier took the silver and another Belgian, Philippe Le Hardy de Beaulieu, the bronze.

Victor Willems was killed in 1918 during the First World War.

Surgeon Hermann 'Ajax' von Bönninghausen
1908 London Olympics/1912 Stockholm Olympics
Germany
Athletics
5th Lancers and 7th Infantry Regimental Surgeon
Died 26 January 1919 aged 30

'The Last Olympian to Die'

Hermann von Bönninghausen was born on 24 July 1888 in Bocholt, Nordrhein-Westfalen, Germany. His father, August, was a government lawyer. A fine all-round athlete and footballer he played for BFC 1900. Although BFC was one of the founding clubs of the German Football Association in 1900 it wasn't just a football club; it also trained athletes in handball, volleyball, athletics, gymnastics, and ice hockey. Bönninghausen soon came to notice and picked up the nickname 'Ajax'. As well as BFC 1900 he also represented Prussia Duisburg and Turnverein Munchen 1860.

Bönninghausen was also a fine athlete, concentrating on the long jump, the 110 metre hurdles, and the triple jump. In 1907 Bönninghausen set a new German long jump record with a leap of 6.56 metres. Later that year he improved on his own record, jumping 6.80 metres. It wasn't just in the long jump he was setting records either. In 1911 he broke the German 110 metre hurdles record with a run of 16.4 seconds.

He was selected as part of the German athletics squad to take part in the 1908 London Olympics, competing in both the 100 metres sprint and the long jump. He was knocked out in the heats of the 100 metres (the fourteenth heat), having covered the distance in 12 seconds. The gold eventually went to the South African Reggie Walker who won in a time of 10.8 seconds, equalling the Olympic record set by the American sprinters Frank Jarvis and Walter Tewksbury during the 1900 Paris Olympics. The silver went to the American James Rector with 10.9 seconds, the Canadian Robert Kerr collecting the bronze with 11.2 seconds. In the long jump Bönninghausen did not do much better falling outside the top twenty (his distance is unknown). The gold went to the American Frank Irons with a leap of 7.48 metres – a new Olympic record (previously it was held by another American, Myer Prinstein, with a distance of 7.34 in St Louis USA on 1 September 1904). The silver went to the American Daniel Kelly with a jump of 7.09 and the bronze to the Canadian Calvin Bricker with a jump of 7.08.

Bönninghausen was selected by the German athletics team once again to take part in the 1912 Olympics held in Stockholm. This time he competed in the 110 metre hurdles (some records have him competing in both the long jump and the triple jump but I can find no evidence to support that). He got through his first heat with a time of 17.0 seconds but was knocked out in the semi-finals, despite running a full second faster and covering the distance in 16.0 seconds. The final was a one, two, three for the Americans. The gold went to Fred Kelly in a time of 15.1 seconds, the silver to James Wendell in 15.2 and the bronze to Martin Hawkins in a time of 15.3.

During the First World War Bönninghausen served as a surgeon with the 5th Lancers and 7th Infantry Regiment. He was badly wounded in the face towards the latter part of the war but despite the seriousness of his wounds refused to leave his post. Invalided home he died of his wounds on 26 January 1919 in Düsseldorf. He had a brother named Rudolf who was killed on 16 August 1915 with Landsturm-Regiment Nr.8.

Bibliography and Sources

Baker, Keith, *The 1908 Olympics. The first London Olympics*, Sports Books Ltd.

Buckingham, William, *Verdun 1916: The Deadliest Battle of the First World War*, Amberley (2016).

Clutterbuck and Dooner, *The Bond of Sacrifice*, Naval and Military Press (2009)

Conner, Floyd, *The Olympics' most Wanted,* Brassey's Inc. Washington DC

Cooper, Stephen, *The Final Whistle, The Great War in Fifteen players.*

Creagh, Sir O'Moore VC and Humphris, E. M., *The Distinguished Service Order 1886–1923*, Hayward.

De Ruvigny, The Marquis, *The Roll of Honour 1914–1918*, Naval and Military Press (2006).

Drinkwater and Sanders, *The University Boat Race Official Centenary History*, Cassell and Company Ltd.

Frith, David, *Silence of the Heart.*

Fullman, Joe, *The Olympics: Ancient and Modern: A guide to the History of the Games*, Wayland.

Goldblatt, David, *The Games: A Global History of the Olympics*, W.W. Norton (2016).

Harris, Clive and Whippy, Julian, *The Great Game, Sporting Icons who fell in the Great War*, with a forward by Richard Holmes, Pen and Sword Military.

Henshaw, Trevor, *The Sky their Battlefield*, Grub Street.

Lloyd, R. A., *Troop, Horse & Trench – The Experiences of a British Lifeguardsman of the Household Cavalry Fighting on the Western Front during the First World War 1914–18* (2006)

McCrery, Nigel, *Into Touch. Rugby Internationals Killed in the Great War*, Pen and Sword Military.

Military Operations France and Belgium 1914. Official History of the War, Macmillan and Co (1923).

Miller, David, *The Official History of the Olympic games and the IOC: Athens to Beijing 1894–2008*, Mainstream Publishing (2008).

Tibballs, Geoff, *The Olympics' Strangest Games: Extraordinary but True Tales from the History of the Olympic Games* (Strangest Series) Robson Books (2004).

Westlake, Ray, *British Battalions in France and Belgium 1914*, Leo Cooper (1997)

Westlake, Ray, *British Regiments at Gallipoli*, Leo Cooper.

Walker, R. W., *To What End Did they Die? Officers Died at Gallipoli*, Walker.

Other sources
Cambridge University Roll of Service.

The Dragon School.

Dulwich War Record 1914–18.

eBay.

The Golden Games – The History of the Modern Olympics, (DVD) 2004

Great War Forum.

Harrow memorials of the Great War.

Lancing College Memorial.

Medals Forum.

Memorials of Rugbeians who fell in the Great War.

Marlborough College Register.

Oxford University Roll of Service.
Wikipedia.

Regiments:
9th (Queens Own) Lancers
14 London Regiment (London Scottish)
16th Lancers in the Great War
21st Empress of India Lancers
Cheshire Regiment
Coldstream Guards
Devon Regiment
East Yorkshire Regiment
Grenadier Guards
Hampshire Regiment
Honourable Artillery Company (HAC)
Irish Guards
King's Royal Rifle Corps
Lancashire Fusiliers
London Regiment
Manchester Regiment
Royal Army Medical Corps (RAMC)
Royal Artillery
Royal Engineers (RE)
Royal Flying Corps/Royal Air Force
Royal Fusiliers
Royal Garrison Artillery
Royal Horse Artillery
Royal Horse Guards
Royal Marines
Royal Naval Division in the Great War (RND)
Royal Naval Volunteer Reserve (RNVR)
Royal Navy (various)
Royal Sussex Regiment
Royal Warwickshire Regiment
Scots Guards
Staffordshire Regiment
Suffolk Regiment
The Rifle Brigade
West Yorkshire Regiment

Appendix 1:

Olympians in Order of their Date of Death

Name – Country – Olympic Event – Date Died – Award made
G – Gold; **S** – Silver; **B** – Bronze

1914

1. Henri Edmond Bonnefoy, France, 1908, Shooting, 09.8.14, **B**
2. Felix Lucien Roger Debax, France, 1900, Fencing, 25.8.14
3. Robert Merz, Austria, 1912, Football, 30.8.14
4. Oszkár Demján, Hungary, 1912, Swimming, 04.9.14
5. Jean Latrie, France, 1908–1912, Fencing-Modern, Pentathlon, 5.9.14
6. Carl Heinrich Goßler, Germany, 1900, Rowing, 09.8.14, **G**
7. George William Hutson, Britain, 1912, Athletics, 14.9.14, **Bx2**
8. Eduard von Lütcken, Germany, 1912, Equestrianism, 15.9.14, **S**
9. Louis Desire Bach, France, 1900, Football, 16.9.14, **S**
10. Charles Devendeville, France, 1900, Swimming-Water-Polo, 19.9.1914, **G**
11. Leopold Mayer, Austria, 1906, Swimming, 21.9.14
12. Alexander Bouin, France, 1908–12, Athletics, 29.9.14, **S/B**
13. Georges de La Nézière, France, 1896, Athletics, 9.10.14
14. Thomas Gillespie, Britain, 1912, Rowing, 18.10.14, **S**
15. Árpád Pédery, Hungary, 1912, Gymnastics, 21.10.14, **S**
16. Béla Zulawszky, Hungary, 1908–12, Fencing, 24.10.14, **S**
17. Joseph Racine, France, 1912, Cycling, 28.10.14
18. Alphonse Meignant, France, 1912, Rowing, 04.11.14
19. Gerard 'Twiggy' Anderson, Britain, 1912, Hurdling, 11.11.14
20. Jenő Szántay, Hungary, 1908, Fencing, 11.12.14
21. Richard Francis Yorke, Britain, 1908/1912, Athletics, 22.12.14
22. André Six, France, 1900, Swimming, 1914

1915

23. Georg Krogmann, Germany, 1912, Football, 9.1.15
24. Max Hermann, Germany, 1912, Athletics, 29.1.15
25. George Adam Lutz, France, 1908, Cycling, 31.1.15
26. Kenneth Powell, Britain, 1908/1912, Tennis, 18.2.15
27. Edward Radcliffe-Nash, Britain, 1912, Equestrianism, 21.2.15
28. Adolf Kofler, Austria, 1912, Cycling, 13.3.15

29. Wyndham Halswelle, Britain, 1906/1908, Athletics, 31.3.15, **GSB**
30. Geoffrey Barron Taylor, Canada, 1908/1912, Rowing, 24.4.15, **Bx2**
31. Gilchrist Maclagan, Britain, 1908, Rowing, 25.4.15, **G**
32. William Anderson, Britain, 1906, Athletics, 26.4.15
33. Ralph Chalmers, Britain, 1908, Fencing, 08.5.15
34. Henry Mills Goldsmith, Britain, 1908, Rowing, 09.5.15, **B**
35. Anthony Wilding, Australia, 1912, Tennis, 09.5.15, **B**
36. Herman Donners, Belgium, 1912, Water-Polo, 14.5.15, **BS**
37. James Duffy, Canada, 1912, Marathon, 23.5.15
38. Henry Alan Leeke, Britain, 1908, Athletics, 29.5.15
39. Oswald Carver, Britain, 1908, Rowing, 07.6.15
40. Alfred Mickler, Germany, 1912, Athletics, 14.6.15
41. George Fairbairn, Britain, 1908, Rowing, 20.6.15
42. Amon Ritter von Gregurich, Hungary, 1900, Fencing, 28.6.15
43. Jakob Person, Germany, 1912, Athletics, 15.7.15
44. Edward Gordon Williams, Britain, 1908, Rowing, 12.8.15
45. Rudolf Watzl, Austria, 1906, Wrestling, 15.8.15
46. Edmond Wallace, France, 1900, Fencing, 18.8.15
47. Paul Kenna, Britain, 1912, Equestrianism, 30.8.15
48. Fritz Bartholomae, Germany, 1912, Rowing, 12.9.15
49. Arthur Ommundsen, Britain, 1908/1912, Shooting, 19.9.15, **Sx2**
50. Renon Boussière, France, 1912, Marathon, 25.9.15
51. Michel Soalhat, France, 1906, Athletics, 25.9.15
52. Ismael de Lesseps, France, 1908, Fencer, 30.9.15
53. Heinrich Schneidereit, Germany, 1906, Tug-of-War/Weight-lifting, 30.9.15, **G B**
54. Joseph Caulle, France, 1912, Athletics, 1.10.15
55. Béla von Las-Torres, Hungary, 1908/1912, Athletics, 12.10.15, **S**
56. Alfred Staats, Germany, 1912, Gymnastics, 22.10.15
57. Dragutin Tomašević, Serbia, 1912, Athletics, 10.15
58. Lajos Gönczy, Hungary, 1900/1906, Athletics, 4.12.15
59. Edmund William Bury, Britain, 1908, Racquets, 5.12.15, **S**
60. Georg Baumann, Russia, 1912, Wrestling, 1915

1916
61. Hugh Durant, Britain, 1912, Shooting, 20.1.16, **Bx2**
62. Arthur William Wilde, Britain, 1908, Shooting, 21.1.16
63. Geoffrey Horsman Coles, Britain, 1908, Shooting, 27.1.16.
64. Jules Aristide Jenicot, France, 1908, Football, 22.2.16.
65. Walter Jesinghaus, Germany, 1912, Gymnast, 22.2.16
66. Alan Patterson, Britain, 1908/1912, Athletics, 14.3.16
67. Karl Braunsteiner, Austria, 1912, Football, 19.4.16

68. Maurice Raoul-Duval, France, 1900, Polo, 5.5.16
69. Guido Romano, Italy, Athletics, 18.6.16
70. John Somers-Smith, Britain, 1908, Rowing, 1.7.16
71. Alfred Edward Flaxman, Britain, 1908, Athletics, 1.7.16
72. Béla Békessy, Hungary, 1912, Fencing, 6.7.16, **P**
73. William Philo, Britain, 1908, Boxing, 7.7.16
74. Pierre Six, France, 1908, Football, 7.7.16
75. Josef Rieder, Germany, 1912, Cycling, 13.7.16
76. Hermann Bosch, Germany, 1912, Football, 16.7.16
77. Maurice Salomez, France, 1900, Athletics, 7.8.16
78. John Robinson, Britain, 1908, Hockey, 23.8.16, **G**
79. Robert Finden Davies, Britain, 1912, Shooting, 9.9.16
80. Justin Pierre Vialaret, France, 1908, Football, 30.9.16
81. René Victor Fenouillière, France, 1908, Football, 4.11.16
82. Frederick Septimus Kelly, Britain, 1908, Rowing, 13.11.16, **G**
83. Léon Honoré Ponscarme, France, 1900, Cycling, 24.11.16
84. Louis de Champsavin, France, 1900, Equestrianism, 20.12.16
85. Andrei Akimov, Russia, 1912, Football, 1916
86. Nikolai Kynin, Russia, 1912, Football, 1916
87. Wilhelm Lützow, Germany, 1912, Swimming, 1916

1917
88. Leon Flameng, France, 1896, Cycling, 2.1.17
89. Feliks Leparsky, Russia, 1912, Fencing, 10.1.17
90. Henry Ashington, Britain, 1912, Athletics, 31.1.17
91. Charles Vigurs, Britain, 1908/1912, Gymnastics, 22.2.17
92. Alister Kirby, Britain, 1912, Rowing, 29.3.17
93. Prince Karl of Prussia, Germany, 1912, Equestrianism, 6.4.17
94. Herbert Wilson, Britain, 1908, Polo, 11.4.17
95. Gordon Alexander, Britain, 1912, Fencing, 24.4.17
96. Robert Powell, Canada, 1908, Tennis, 28.4.17
97. Issac Bentham, Britain, 1912, Water Polo, 15.5.17
98. Percy Courtman, Britain, 1908/1912, Swimming, 2.6.17
99. Harold Hawkins, Britain, 1908, Shooting, 16.6.17
100. Henry Gayler, Britain, 1912, Cycling, 23.6.17
101. Percival Molson, Canada, 1904, Athletics, 5.7.17
102. Louis Octave Lapize, France, 1908, Cycling, 14.7.17
103. Waldemar Tietgens, Germany, 1900, Rowing, 28.7.17
104. Noel Godfrey Chavasse, Britain, 1908, Athletics, 4.8.17
105. Wilhelm Brülle, Germany, 1912, Gymnastics, 5.8.17
106. Claude Ross, Australia, 1912, Athletics, 19.8.17

107. James Roche, Britain, 1908, Athletics, 25.8.17
108. George Albert Hawkins, Britain, 1908, Athletics, 20/22.9.17
109. George Butterfield, Britain, 1908, Athletics, 24.9.17
110. Bernhard von Gaza, Germany, 1908, Rowing, 25.9.17
111. Duncan Mackinnon, Britain, 1908, Rowing, 9.10.17
112. Harry Crank, Britain, 1908, Diving, 22.10.17
113. Alexander Decoteau, Canada, 1912, Athletics, 30.10.17
114. Ivan Laing, Britain, 1908, Hockey, 30.11.17
115. Gori Nikitin, Russia, 1912, Football, 1917

1918
116. Juho Halme, Finland, 1908/1912, Athletics, 1.2.18
117. Reginald Pridmore, Britain, 1908, Hockey, 13.3.18
118. Hermann Plaskuda, Germany, 1912, Fencing, 21.3.18
119. Ronald Sanderson, Britain, 1908, Rowing, 17.4.18
120. Kurt Bretting, Germany, 1912, Swimming, 30.5.18
121. István Mudin, Hungary, 1906/1908, Pentathlon/Discus, 22.7.18
122. Albert Rowland, New Zealand, 1908, Sports Walking, 23.7.18
123. Ernest Keeley, South Africa, 1912, Shooting, 23.7.18
124. Henry Macintosh, Britain, 1912, Athletics, 26.7.18
125. Hans Sorge, Germany, 1912, Gymnastics, 6.8.18
126. Thomas Raddall, Britain, 1908, Shooting, 9.8.18
127. Frederick Kitching, Britain, 1908, Athletics, 11.8.18
128. Bertrand de Lesseps, France, 1908, Fencing, 28.8.18
129. Cecil Patrick Healy, Australia, 1912, Swimming, 29.8.18
130. Joseph Frank Dines, Britain, 1912, Football, 27.9.18
131. Hanns Braun, Germany, 1908/1912, Athletics, 9.10.18
132. William Lyshon, USA, 1912, Wrestling, 13.10.18
133. Imre Mudin, Hungary, 1908/1912, Athletics, 23.10.18
134. Alfred Motté, France, 1908, Athletics, 31.10.18
135. Arthur Yancey Wear, USA, 1904, Tennis, 6.11.18
136. Heinrich Burkowitz, Germany, 1912, Athletics, 11.18
137. Andre Corvington, Haiti, 1900, Fencing, 13.12.18
138. Victor Willems, Belgium, 1908, Fencing, 1918
139. Hermann Bönninghausen, France, 1908/1912, Athletics, 26.1.19

Appendix 2:

The Number of Olympians who Died in the First World War by Nation

Great Britain	50
France	29
Germany	22
Hungary	10
Austria	5
Canada	5
Russia	5
Australia	3
USA	2
Belgium	2
South Africa	1
Haiti	1
Serbia	1
New Zealand	1
Finland	1
Italy	1

Appendix 3:

Olympians by Nation

AUSTRALIA (3)

Captain **Anthony Wilding**. Royal Marines. Died 9 May 1915. 1912 Olympics. Tennis. Bronze.

Second Lieutenant **Claude Ross**. RFC (45 Squadron) Died 19 August 1917. 1912 Olympics. Athletics.

Second Lieutenant **Cecil Patrick Healy**. 19 Battalion Australian Infantry. Died 29 August 1918. Swimming. Gold, Silver, Bronze.

AUSTRIA (5)

Lieutenant **Robert Mertz**. Reserve of Infantry Regiment Nr.28. Died 30 August 1914. 1912 Olympics. Football.

Leopold Mayer. Died 21 September 1914. 1906 Olympics. Swimming.

Private **Adolf Kofler**. Cyclist Company, 24 Infantry Battalion. Died 13 March 1915. 1912 Olympics. Cycling.

Rudolf Watzl. Died 15 August 1915. 1906 Olympics. Wrestling.

Karl Braunsteiner. Died 19 April 1916. 1912 Olympics. Football.

BELGIUM (2)

Private 2nd class **Herman Louis Clement Donners**. 1ᵉ Grenadiers. Died 14 May 1915. 1908–1912 Olympics. Water Polo. Silver (1908) Bronze (1912).

Victor Willems. Died 1918. 1908 Olympics. Fencing. Gold and Bronze.

CANADA (5)

Lieutenant **Geoffrey Barron Taylor**. 15 Battalion Canadian Infantry. Died 24 April 1915. 1908 and 1912 Olympics. Rowing. 2 x Bronze.

Private **James (Jimmy) Duffy**. 16 Battalion Canadian Infantry. Died 23 May 1915. 1912 Olympics. Marathon.

Lieutenant **Robert Branks 'Bobby' Powell**. 16/48 Battalion Canadian Infantry. Died 28 April 1917. 1908 Olympics. Tennis.

Captain. **Percival Talbot 'Percy' Molson** MC. Princess Patricia's Canadian Light Infantry. Died 5 July 1917. 1904 Olympics. Athletics.

Private **Alexander Wuttunee Decoteau**. 49th Battalion Canadian Infantry. Died 30 October 1917. 1912 Olympics. Athletics.

Appendix 3

FINLAND (1)
Civilian. **Johan Valdemar (Juho) Halme**. Journalist. Murdered on 1 February 1918. 1908 and 1912 Olympics. Athletics.

FRANCE (28)
Lieutenant **Henri Edmond Bonnefoy**. 133rd Regiment Infantry. Died 9 August 1914. 1908 Olympics. Shooting.

Chef de Bataillon **Félix Lucien Roger Debax.** 240th Infantry Regiment. Died 25 August 1914. 1900 Olympics. Fencing.

Captain **Jean Marie Pierre Xavier de Mas Latrie.** 15ᵉ Chasseurs à Cheval. Died 5 September 1914. 1908 and 1912 Olympics. Fencing, Modern Pentathlon.

Private 2nd Class **Louis Desire Bach.** 128ᵉ Regiment of Infantry. Died 16 September 1914. 1900 Olympic Games. Football. Silver.

Private 2nd Class **Charles Devendeville.** 151ᵉ/1ᵉ Infantry Regiment. Died 19 September 1914. 1900 Olympics. Swimming, Water Polo. Gold.

Private 2nd Class **Alexandre François Étienne Jean Bouin.** 163 Infantry Regiment. Died 9 October 1914. 1908 and 1912 Olympics. Athletics. Bronze and Silver.

Corporal **Georges de La Nézière.** 26ᵉ Infantry Regiment. Died 9 October 1914. 1896 Olympics. Athletics.

Private 1st class **Joseph Racine.** 113ᵉ Infantry Regiment. Died 28 October 1914. 1912 Olympics. Cycling.

Private 2nd Class **Alphonse Adrien Meignant.** 31st Light Infantry Battalion (31ᵉ BCP). Died 4 November 1914. 1912 Olympics. Rowing.

Corporal **André Jules Henri Six.** 24ᵉ Section du COA. Died 1 April 1915. 1900 Olympics. Underwater Swimming. Silver.

Corporal **Georges Adam Charles Lutz.** 106ᵉ Régiment d'Infanterie. Died 31 January 1915. 1908 Olympics. Cycling.

Lieutenant **Edmond Georges Richard Wallace.** 89ᵉ Régiment d'Infanterie. Died 18 August 1915. 1900 Olympics. Fencing.

Renon Boussière. Died 25 September 1915. 1912 Olympics. Marathon.

Private 2nd Class **Michel Léon Marie Soalhat.** 315ᵉ Infantry Regiment. Died 25 September 1915. 1906 Olympics. Athletics.

Ferdinand Ismael de Lesseps. Died 30 September 1915. 1908 Olympics. Fencing.

Sergeant Major **Joseph Louis Alphonse Caulle.** 41st Colonial Infantry Regiment. Died 1 October 1915. 1912 Olympics. Athletics.

Lieutenant **Albert Aristide (Albert) Jenicot.** 165ᵉ French Infantry. Died 22 February 1916. 1908 Olympics. Football.

Captain **Maurice Auguste Raoul-Duval.** 66ᵉ French Infantry. Died 5 May 1916. 1900 Olympics. Polo.

Sous Lieutenant **Pierre Charles Henri Six.** 329th French Infantry. Died 7 July 1916. 1908 Olympics. Football.

Maurice Salomez. 246e Infantry Regiment. Died 7 August 1916. 1900 Olympics. Athletics.

Corporal Quartermaster **Justin Pierre Vialaret.** 16th French Infantry. Died 30 September 1916. 1908 Olympics. Football.

Lieutenant **René Victor Fenouillière**. 2nd Infantry Regiment. Died 4 November 1916. 1908 Olympics. Football.

Léon Honoré Ponscarme Jr. Died 24 November 1916. 1900 Olympics. Cycling.

Commander **Louis Marie Joseph Le Beschu de Champsavin.** 20e Regiment de Chasseurs. Died 20 December 1916. 1900 Olympics. Horse jumping. Bronze.

Sergeant (pilot) **Marie Léon Flameng.** 2nd Aviation group. Died 2 January 1917. 1896 Athens Olympics. Cycling.

Sergeant **Louis Octave Lapize.** 13th Regiment Artillery / French Flying Corps. Died 14 July 1917. 1908 Olympics. Cycling.

Bertrand Marie de Lesseps. Died 28 August 1918. 1908 Olympics. Fencing.

Sous lieutenant **Alfred Philippe Ferdinand Joseph Motté.** 234e Regiment Infantry. Died 31 October 1918. 1908 Olympics. Athletics.

GERMANY (22)

Lieutenant **Carl Heinrich Goßler (Gossler).** Kaiser Wilhelm 2nd Grand Ducal Hessian No.116 in Gießen. Died 9 September 1914. 1900 Olympics. Rowing. Gold.

Lieutenant **Eduard von Lütcken.** Royal Saxon Ulan Regiment Nr.17. Died 15 September 1914. 1912 Olympics. Equestrian. Silver.

Georg Krogmann. Died 9 January 1915. 1912 Olympics. German. Football.

Reservist **Max Herrmann.** No.7 Company 41st Infantry Regiment. Died 29 January 1915. 1912 Olympics. Athletics.

Lieutenant **Alfred Georg Mickler.** Reserve Infantry Regiment 203. Died 14 June 1915. 1912 Olympics. Athletics.

Private **Jakob 'Jacques' Person.** 2 Kompanie / Infanterie-Regiment Nr. 96. Died 15 July 1915. 1912 Olympics. Athletics.

Offizier Stellvertretter (NCO) **Friedrich (Fritz) Bartholomae.** 3 Kompanie / Garde-Reserve-Schützen-Bataillon. Died 12 September 1915. 1912 Olympics. Rowing.

Lieutenant **Heinrich Schneidereit.** German Artillery. Died 30 September 1915. 1906 Olympics. Weight lifting. Tug-of-War.

Einjährig-Freiwilliger **Alfred Heinrich Karl Richard Staats.** Died 22 October 1915. 1912 Olympics. Gymnastics.

Walter Jesinghaus. Died 22 February 1916. 1912 Olympics. Gymnastics.

Josef Rieder. Died 13 July 1916. 1912 Olympics. Cycling.

Hermann Bosch. Died 16 July 1916. 1912 Olympics. Football.

Wilhelm 'Willy' Lützow. Died 1916. 1912 Olympics. Swimming. Silver.

Appendix 3

Prince **Tassilo Wilhelm Humbert Leopold Friedrich Karl of Prussia.** Fliegerabteilung (Artillerie) 258. German Flying Service. Died 6 April 1917. 1912 Olympics. Equestrianism. Bronze.

Lieutenant **Waldemar Tietgens.** Reserve-Feldartillerie-Regiment 49. Died 28 July 1917. 1900 Olympics. Rowing. Gold

Wilhelm Brülle. Died 5 August 1917. 1912 Olympics. Gymnastics.

Oberleutnant **Bernhard von Gaza.** 185th Infantry Regiment. Died 25 September 1917. 1908 Olympics. Rowing. Bronze.

Hermann Plaskuda. Died 21 March 1918. 1912 Olympics. Fencing.

Kurt Bretting. Died 30 May 1918. 1912 Olympics. Swimming.

Hans Eberhard Sorge. Died 6 August 1918. 1912 Olympics. Gymnastics.

Lieutenant **Hanns Braun.** Imperial German Air Service. Died 9 October 1918. 1908 Olympics. Athletics.

Heinrich Heinrich Burkowitz. Died November 1918. 1912 Olympics. Athletics.

Hermann von Bönninghausen. Died 26 January 1919. 1908 1912 Olympics. Athletics.

GREAT BRITAIN (50)

L/9097 Sergeant **George William Hutson**. 'B' Company 2nd Battalion Royal Sussex Regiment. Died 14 September 1914. 1912 Olympic Games. 5,000 metres/3,000 metre team event. 2 x Bronze.

Lieutenant **Thomas Cunningham Gillespie**. 2nd Battalion King's Own Scottish Borderers. Died 18 October 1914. 1912 Stockholm Olympics. Rowing. Silver (Team).

2nd Lieutenant **Gerard Rupert Lawrence 'Laurie' Anderson** **(Twiggy).** 1st Battalion Cheshire Regiment. Died 11 November 1914. 1912 Stockholm Olympics. Athletics.

612 Sergeant. **Richard Francis Charles Yorke**. 14th Battalion London Regiment (London Scottish). Died 22 December 1914. 1908 and 1912 Stockholm Olympics. Athletics.

1832 Private **Kenneth Powell**. Honorable Artillery Company. Died 18 February 1915. 1908 and 1912 Stockholm Olympics. Tennis/110 metre hurdles.

Captain **Edward Radcliffe-Nash**. 16th Lancers. Died 21 February 1915. 1912 Stockholm Olympics. Equestrianism.

Captain **Wyndham Halswelle**. 1st Battalion Highland Light Infantry. Died 31 March 1915. 1906 and 1908 Olympics. Athletics (400 metres). Gold-Silver-Bronze.

Lieutenant **Gilchrist Stanley Maclagan**. 3rd attached 1st Battalion Royal Warwickshire Regiment. Died 25 April 1915. 1908 London Olympics. Rowing. Gold.

21563 Private **William Davidson Anderson**. 5th Battalion Canadian Infantry (Saskachewan Regiment). Died 26 April 1915. 1906 Athens Olympics. Athletics (400 and 800 metres).

Captain **Ralph Chalmers**. 2nd Battalion Suffolk Regiment. Died 8 May 1915. 1908 London Olympics. Fencing.

Lieutenant **Henry Mills Goldsmith**. 3rd Battalion Devonshire Regiment Attached 2nd Battalion Lincolnshire Regiment. Died 9 May 1915. 1908 Olympics. Rowing. Bronze.

Lieutenant **Henry Alan Leeke**. D Company 9th Battalion Royal Warwickshire Regiment. Died 29 May 1915. 1908 Olympics. Athletics.

Captain **Oswald Armitage Guy Carver**. 1/2nd (East Lancs) Royal Engineers. Died 7 June 1915. 1908 Olympics. Rowing. Bronze.

2nd Lieutenant **George Eric Fairbairn**. 10th Battalion Durham Light Infantry. Died 20 June 1915. 1908 London Olympics. Rowing. Silver.

Lieutenant **Edward Gordon Williams**. 2nd Battalion Grenadier Guards. Died 12 August 1915. 1908 London Olympics. Rowing. Bronze.

Brigadier General **Paul Aloysius Kenna** VC DSO General Staff Commanding 3rd Mounted Brigade/21st (Empress of India) Lancers. Died 30 August 1915. 1912 Stockholm Olympics. Equestrianism.

Lieutenant **Arthur Norman Victor Harcourt Ommundsen**. Honorable Artillery Company. Died 19 September1915. 1908 and 1912 Stockholm Olympics. Shooting. 2 x Silver**.**

Captain **Edmund William Bury**. 11 Battalion King's Royal Rifle Corps. Died 5 December 1915. 1908 London Olympics. Racquets. Silver.

Second Lieutenant (formally Squadron Sergeant Major) 4099 **Hugh Durant** RVM. 9th (Queens Royal) Lancers. Died 20 January 1916. 1912 Olympics. Shooting/Modern Pentathlon. 2 x Bronze.

Second Lieutenant **Arthur William Wilde**. 1st Battalion Hampshire Regiment. Died 21 January 1916. 1908 London Olympics. Shooting.

2749 Private **Geoffrey Horsman Coles**. 24th Battalion Royal Fusiliers. Died 27 January 1916. 1908 Olympics. Shooting. Bronze.

Captain **Alan Patterson**. 71st Brigade Royal Artillery. Died 14 March 1916. 1908 London Olympics. 1912 Olympics. Athletics.

Captain **John Robert Somers-Smith** MC. 1/ 5th London Regiment (London Rifle Brigade). Died 1 July 1916. 1908 London Olympics. Rowing. Gold.

Second Lieutenant **Alfred Edward Flaxman**. 1/6 Battalion South Staffordshire Regiment. Died 1 July 1916 (First Day of the Somme). 1908 Olympics. Athletics.

L/7489 Company Sergeant Major **William Philo.** 8th Battalion Royal Fusiliers. Died 7 July 1916. 1908 London Olympics. Boxing (Middleweight). Bronze.

Captain **John Yate Robinson** MC. Adjutant, 7th (Service) Battalion Prince of Wales Own (North Staffordshire Regiment). Died 23 August 1916. 1908 London Olympics. Hockey. Gold.

Captain **Robert Finden Davies**. 9th London Regiment (Queen Victoria Rifles). Died 9 September 1916. 1912 Olympics. Shooting.

Lieutenant Commander **Frederick Septimus Kelly** DSC. Royal Naval Volunteer Reserve (Hood Battalion Royal Naval Division). Died 13 November 1916. 1908 Olympics. Rowing. Gold.

Appendix 3

Captain **Henry Sherard Osborn Ashington**. 7th Battalion East Yorkshire Regiment. Died 31 January 1917. 1912 Olympics. Athletics.

11187 Private **Charles Alfred Vigurs**. 11th Battalion Royal Warwickshire Regiment. Died 22 February 1917. 1908 Olympics, 1912 Stockholm Olympics. Gymnastics. Bronze (1912).

Captain **Alister Graham Kirby**. 5th Battalion London Regiment (London Rifle Brigade). Died 29 March 1917. 1912 Olympics. Rowing. Gold.

Captain **Herbert Haydon Wilson** DSO. Royal Horse Guards. Died 11 April 1917. 1908 London Olympics. Polo. Gold.

Second Lieutenant **Gordon Reuben Alexander**. 2nd Battalion Royal Sussex Regiment, attached 13th Battalion East Surrey Regiment. Died 24 April 1917. 1912 Olympics. Fencing.

56905 Sergeant **Isaac Bentham**. D Battery, 83rd Brigade Royal Field Artillery. Died 15 May 1917. 1912 Stockholm Olympics. Water Polo. Gold.

Private 250755 **Percy Courtman**. D Company 1/6th Battalion Manchester Regiment. Died 2 June 1917. 1908 and 1912 Olympics. Swimming (Breast Stroke). Bronze (1912).

Captain **Harold Ingleby Hawkins**. 2nd Battalion London Regiment. Died 16 June 1917. 1908 London Olympics. Shooting. Silver.

740705 Cyclist **Herbert Henry (Bert) Gayler**. 25th London Regiment (Cyclists). Died 23 June 1917. 1912 Olympics. Cycling. Silver.

Captain **Noel Godfrey Chavasse** VC & bar. Royal Army Medical Corps. Died 4 August 1917. 1908 Olympics. Athletics.

Lieutenant **James Patrick Roche** MC. Indian Army Reserve of Officers, attached 1st King George's Own Sappers and Miners. Died 25 August 1917. 1908 Olympics. Athletics.

96501 Gunner **George Albert Hawkins**. Royal Garrison Artillery (254th Siege Battery). Died 20/22 September 1917. 1908 Olympics. Athletics.

99906 Gunner **George Butterfield (Butt).** Royal Garrison Artillery (230th Siege Battery). Died 24 September 1917. 1908 London Olympics. Athletics.

Lieutenant **Duncan Mackinnon**. 1st Battalion Scots Guards. Died 9 October 1917. 1908 London Olympics. Rowing. Gold.

Second Lieutenant **Harry Crank.** 17th Battalion Lancashire Fusiliers. Died 22 October 1917. 1908 London Olympics. Diving.

Lieutenant **Ivan Laing** MC. 2nd Battalion Coldstream Guards. Died 30 November 1917. 1908 London Olympics. Hockey. Bronze.

Major **Reginald (Reggie) George Pridmore** MC. Warwickshire Royal Field Artillery, C Battery 240th Brigade. Died 13 March 1918. 1908 London Olympics. Hockey. Gold.

Lieutenant Colonel **Ronald Harcourt Sanderson**. 148 Brigade Royal Field Artillery. Died 17 April 1918. 1908 London Olympics. Rowing. Gold.

Captain **Henry Maitland Macintosh**. 1/8 Battalion Argyll and Sutherland Highlanders. Died 26 July 1918. 1912 Stockholm Olympics. Athletics. Gold.

Lieutenant Colonel **Thomas Head Raddall** DSO. 8th Battalion Canadian Infantry (Manitoba Regiment). Died 9 August 1918. 1908 Olympics. Shooting.

Orderly **Frederick Overend Kitching**. British Red Cross Society, Field Ambulance Unit. Died 11 August 1918. 1908 London Olympics. Athletics.

Second Lieutenant **Joseph Frank Dines**. 13th Battalion The King's Liverpool Regiment. Died 27 September 1918. 1912 Stockholm Olympics. Football. Gold.

HAITI (1)
Andre Corvington. Died 13 December 1918. 1900 Olympics. Fencing.

HUNGARY (10)
Private **Oszkár Demján.** Nr.43 Infantry Regiment. Died 4 September 1914. 1912 Olympics. Swimming.

Árpád Pédery. Died 21 October 1914. 1912 Olympics. Gymnastics.

Major **Béla (Vojtech) Zulawszky.** Died 24 October 1914. 1908 and 1912 Olympics. Fencing. Silver.

Captain **Jenő Szántay.** Austro-10 (William) Hussars (Machine-Gun Squad). Died 11 December 1914. 1908 Olympics. Fencing.

Lieutenant Colonel **Amon Ritter von Gregurich.** Imperial and Royal Hussars. Died 28 June 1915. 1900 Olympics. Fencing.

Lieutenant **Béla von Las-Torres.** Kuk Luftfahrtruppen (Austrian Air Force). Died 12 October 1915. 1908 and 1912 Olympics. Swimming. Silver.

Lieutenant **Lajos Gönczy.** 46th Honved Infantry Brigade. Died 4 December 1915. 1906 Olympics. Athletics. Silver and Bronze.

Béla Békessy. Died 6 July 1916. 1912 Olympics. Fencing. Silver.

Lieutenant **István Mudin.** 101 Infantry Reserve. Died 22 July 1918. 1906 and 1908 Olympics. Pentathlon, Greek Style Discus. Silver and Bronze.

Lieutenant **Imre Mudin.** 101st Infantry Regiment. Died 23 October 1918. 1908 and 1912 Olympics. Athletics.

ITALY (1)
Guido Romano. Died 18 June 1916. 1912 Olympics. Gymnastics. Gold.

NEW ZEALAND (1)
32540 Second Lieutenant **Albert Edward MacKay Rowland.** H Coy 3rd New Zealand Rifle Brigade. Died 23 July 1918. 1908 Olympics. Walking.

RUSSIA (5)
Georg Baumann. Died 1915. 1912 Olympics. Greco-Roman wrestling.
Andrei Aleksandrovich Akimov. Died 1916. 1912 Olympics. Football.
Nikolai Dmitriyevich Kynin. Died 1916. 1912 Olympics. Football.

Appendix 3

Captain **Feliks Leparsky**. Died 10 January 1917. 1912 Olympics. Fencing.
Gori Mikhailovich Nikitin. Died 1917. 1912 Olympics. Football.

SERBIA (1)
Sergeant **Dragutin Tomašević.** 18th Infantry Regiment. Died October 1915. 1912 Olympics. Marathon.

SOUTH AFRICA (1)
Ernest James Keeley. 4th Regiment South African Infantry. Died 23 July 1918. 1912 Olympics. Shooting.

UNITED STATES OF AMERICA (2)
Sergeant **William Jones Lyshon**. 135th Infantry Regiment. Died 13 October 1918. 1912 Olympics. Wrestling.
Captain **Arthur Yancey Wear**. 356th Infantry Regiment. Died 6 November 1918. 1904 Olympics. Tennis.

Appendix 4:

History of the Olympic Games

Although this is a brief history of the Olympic Games I have tried to stick to those games that are relevant to the book and they are:

1896 – Athens, Greece. Games of the I Olympiad
1900 – Paris, France. Games of the II Olympiad
1904 – St Louis, Missouri, USA. Games of the III Olympiad
1906 – Athens, Greece
1908 – London, England. Games of the IV Olympiad
1912 – Stockholm, Sweden. Games of the V Olympiad

Although the Olympic Games are now considered to be the world's foremost sports competition, with more than 200 nations participating, it wasn't always so. Their creation was inspired by the ancient Olympic games, which were held in Olympia, Greece, from the eighth century BC to the fourth century AD. They were held in honour of the God Zeus and the Greeks gave them a mythological origin. The first Olympics is traditionally dated to 776 BC. The prizes for the victors were olive leaf wreaths or crowns. In more recent times it was Baron Pierre de Coubertin who established the International Olympic Committee (IOC) in 1894. The IOC is the Olympics governing body with the Olympic charter governing its structure and authority.

1896 Olympics (Games of the I Olympiad)
In 1896 the first modern Olympics were held in Athens. They were staged between 6 and 15 April 1896. The Panathinaikos Stadium Athens was used for the athletics, gymnastics, weightlifting, and wrestling; the Bay of Zea was used for swimming; Athens Lawn Tennis Club for the tennis; Kallithea for shooting; Neo Phaliron Velodrome for cycling and finally Zappeion for the fencing. The 1896 Olympic programme featured 9 sports encompassing 10 disciplines and 43 events. Fourteen nations took part: Australia, Austria, Bulgaria, Chile, Denmark, France, Germany, Great Britain, Greece, Hungary, Italy, Sweden, Switzerland and the USA. 122 medals were awarded in total. The USA topped the medal table with 20 medals: 11 gold, 7 silver and 2 bronze. Greece came second with 46 medals: 10 gold, 17 silver, and 19 bronze. Germany came third with 13 medals: 6 gold, 5 silver, 2 bronze. France was fourth with 11 medals: 5 gold, 4 silver, 2 bronze. Great Britain was fifth with 7 medals: 2 gold, 3 silver, 2 bronze. Hungary came sixth with six medals: 2 gold, 1 silver, 3 bronze. Austria seventh with five medals: 2 gold: 1 silver and 2 bronze. Australia came eighth with two medals, both gold. Denmark

ninth with six medals, 1 gold, 2 silver, 3 bronze. Switzerland came tenth with three medals: 1 gold, 1 silver, 1 bronze. Mixed teams came last with three medals, 1 gold, 1 silver, 1 bronze (mixed teams were allowed at this time and were mostly for tennis doubles matches).

Women were not allowed to compete at the 1896 Summer Olympics, because it was felt that their inclusion would be 'impractical, uninteresting, unaesthetic and incorrect'. Interestingly however the day after the marathon was raced on 11 April 1896 one woman, a Greek, Stamata Revithi ran the marathon course although was banned from entering the stadium. She finished in a time of five hours and 30 minutes. Revithi hoped her achievement would sway the Hellenic Olympic Committee into considering women competitors.

The games, which were watched by over 80,000 people, were considered a great success.

Two Olympians from the 1896 games were killed during the First World War:

1. Georges de La Nezière. French athlete. Died 9 October 1914
2. Léon Flameng. French cyclist. Died 2 January 1917

The 1900 Olympics (Games of the II Olympiad)
The 1900 Olympics were held in Paris. The games commenced on 14 May and concluded on 28 October and became part of the World's Fair also being held in Paris. Largely due to the success of the 1896 games this time 997 competitors took part in 19 different sports. Women were allowed to compete for the first time with sailor Hélène de Pourtalès in the Swiss boat *Lérina* winning a gold medal in the first race of 2–3 ton class and a silver medal in the second race of 2–3 ton class. On 11 July another landmark was reached when Charlotte Cooper, already three times Wimbledon champion, took the singles championship to become the first individual female Olympic champion, also winning the mixed doubles event. The 1900 Olympics also saw for the first time a black competitor in the person of the French rugby player Constantin Henriquez de Zubiera. As the French squad won the rugby tournament he also became the first black man to win a gold medal at the Olympics. There were also some events in the 1900 games which only made one appearance in the Olympics: motorcycling, ballooning, cricket, croquet and Basque pelots (played with a ball using the hand, a racket, a wooden bat or a basket, against a wall). There were some unusual ones: the 200 metre obstacle swimming race, and underwater swimming. It was also the only Olympics in history to use live animals – when pigeons were used for target practice.

There isn't a comprehensive list of participating countries but there appears to have been twenty-eight of them with athletes from three other countries also competing. Argentina, Australia, Austria, Belgium, Bohemia, Canada, Cuba, Denmark, France, Germany, Great Britain, Greece, Haiti, Hungary, India, Iran, Italy, Luxembourg, Mexico, Netherlands, Norway, Peru, Romania, Russian Empire, Spain, Sweden, Switzerland

and the USA with athletes from Brazil, Colombia and New Zealand also taking part.

Most of the winners weren't presented with medals but with trophies or cash. Gold medals were not awarded at all during the 1900 games, only silver for first and bronze for second. However the IOC retroactively awarded gold, silver and bronze medals to first, second and third places. France with the home advantage headed the medal table with 101 medals: 26 gold, 41 silver and 34 bronze. The USA came second with 47 medals: 19 gold, 14 silver, 14 bronze. Great Britain came in third with 30 medals: 15 gold, 6 silver and 9 bronze. Mixed teams, which were still being allowed, won 12 medals: 6 gold, 3 silver and 3 bronze. Switzerland came fifth with 9 medals: 6 gold, 2 silver and 1 bronze. Belgium was sixth with 15 medals: 5 gold, 5 silvers and 5 bronze. Germany seventh with 8 medals: 4 gold, 2 silver, and 2 bronze. Italy eighth with 4 medals: 2 gold and 2 silver. Australia was ninth with 5 medals, 2 gold and 3 bronze; and tenth was Denmark with 6 medals: 1 gold, 3 silver and 2 bronze.

The following fourteen men who took part in the 1900 Olympics died during the First World War:

1. Felix Lucien Roger Debax. French fencer. Died 25 August 1914
2. Carl Heinrich Goßler. German rower. Died 9 September 1914
3. Louis Desire Bach. French footballer. Died 16 September 1914
4. Charles Devendeville. French swimmer. Died 19 September 1914
5. André Six. French swimmer. Died 1914
6. Amon Ritter von Gregurich. Hungarian fencer. Died 28 June 1915
7. Edmond Wallace. French fencer. Died 18 August 1915.
8. Lajos Gönczy. Hungarian athlete (1906). Died 4 December 1915
9. Maurice Raoul-Duval. French polo player. Died 5 May 1916.
10. Maurice Salomez. French athlete. Died 7 August 1916.
11. Léon Honoré Ponscarme. French cyclist. Died 24 November 1916
12. Louis Champsavin. French equestrian. Died 20 December 1916
13. Waldemar Tietgens. German rower. Died 28 July 1917
14. Andre Corvington. Haitian fencer. Died 13 December 1918.

The 1904 Olympics (Games of the III Olympiad)
The 1904 Olympics were held outside Europe for the first time, taking place in St Louis, Missouri in the USA. The games were held between 29 August and 3 September 1904 (although the extended games took place between 1 July and 23 November 1904). A total of 651 athletes (645 men and 6 women) representing 12 countries took part. The events took place at the Washington University in St Louis. Francis Field held the archery, athletics, cycling, football, gymnastics, lacrosse, roque, tennis, tug-of-war, weightlifting, and wrestling; Francis Gymnasium held boxing and fencing; Forest Park held diving, swimming and water polo; and Creve Coeur held rowing. There were 94 events in 17 disciplines, comprising 16 sports. Getting to the US at the time wasn't as

easy at it is today. That, combined with tensions between Russia and Japan, put many European athletes off and only fifty-two athletes from outside Europe competed. Nationalities were as follows: three from Australia, two from Austria, fifty-six from Canada, three from Cuba, only one from France, twenty-two from Germany, six from Great Britain, fourteen from Greece, four from Hungary, eight from South Africa, two from Switzerland, one from Italy, two from Norway, one from Newfoundland and an impressive 526 from America. The medal table was equally impressive with the USA winning 239 medals: 78 gold, 82 silver and 79 bronze, with Germany coming second with a mere 13 medals: 4 gold, 4 silver, and 5 bronze.

The following two competitors who took part in the 1904 games later died in the First World War:

1. Percival Molson. Canadian athlete. Died 5 July 1917
2. Arthur Yancey Wear. American tennis player. Died 6 November 1918

1906 (INTERCALATED) OLYMPICS

These games were held between 22 April to 2 May 1906 in Athens and took place in the same place as the 1896 games: the Panathinaikos Stadium. A very successful games, they introduced many traditions into the modern Olympics. They were not stretched out over months but took a little under two weeks and were not part of any international exhibition. It was the first time nations' athletes marched into the stadium following their national flag; the first time all athletes had to be registered with the NOCs; and it was the first to have an Olympic Village, this time based at Zappeion. They also introduced a closing ceremony and the raising of the national flag to celebrate the winning nation. All these are now accepted as Olympic traditions; however, although the Athens games were accepted as an Olympics at the time and competitors awarded medals, the IOC no longer recognizes it as such and will have nothing to do with it, not even have memorabilia from the games in the Olympic museum. A total of 854 athletes took part in the games (848 men and 6 woman) from twenty countries (including Finland for the first time, who won a gold medal in the discus). This time France headed the medal table winning 40 medals: 15 gold, 9 silver and 16 bronze. The USA came second with 24 medals: 12 gold, 6 silver and 6 bronze. Greece was third with 34 medals: 8 gold, 13 silver, and 13 bronze. Great Britain came in a credible fourth with 24 medals: 8 gold, 11 silver and 5 bronze. A total of 236 medals were awarded.

Eight athletes who took part in the 1906 Olympics were later killed in the First World War:

1. Leopold Mayer. Austrian swimmer. Died 21 September 1914
2. Wyndham Halswelle. British athlete. Died 31 March 1915
3. William Anderson. British athlete. Died 26 April 1915
4. Rudolf Watzl. Austrian wrestler. Died 15 August 1915
5. Michel Soalhat. French athlete. Died 25 September 1915

6. Heinrich Schneidereit. German weightlifting and tug-of-war. Died 30 September 1915
7. Lajos Gönczy. Hungarian athlete. Died 4 December 1915
8. István Mudin. Hungarian pentathlon and discus thrower. Died 22 July 1918

1908 Olympics (Games of the IV Olympiad)

The 1908 Olympics were held in London. They were originally scheduled to be held in Rome but were relocated to London after Mount Vesuvius erupted in 1906 destroying much of Naples; the funding had to be diverted for repairs. The games lasted for a remarkable 187 days (over 6 months), the longest games in modern Olympic history. The games were held at White City once again, together with a major exhibition, this time the Franco-British, which was at the time considered to be a much more important event. The games represented 22 sports, representing 110 events. Twenty-two nations took part in the games (Turkey and New Zealand took part for the first time). With the home advantage, Great Britain, with 676 participants, did well winning a total of 146 medals: 56 gold, 51 silver, and 39 bronze. The USA, with 122 participants, came second with 47 medals: 23 gold, 12 silver, and 12 bronze. Then came Sweden with 25 medals: 8 gold, 6 silver, and 11 bronze. France only managed fourth despite fielding 363 participants, with 5 golds, 5 silvers and 9 bronze.

One of the more bizarre events held during the 1908 Olympics was duelling. The two duellers wore protective clothing and fired wax bullets at each other. Probably the most famous incident in Olympic games history also took place at the 1908 games when the Italian marathon runner Dorando Pietri entered the stadium first but due to total exhaustion had to be helped across the finishing line by games officials. Although Pietri crossed the line first, the American runner Johnny Hayes, who had come second, protested the fact that Pietri had to be helped over the line and Pietri was duly disqualified. The American runner and athlete John Taylor became the first black athlete to win an Olympic gold medal, running as a member of the American medley relay team.

Sixty-one men who took part in the 1908 Olympics later died in the First World War:

1. Henri Edmond Bonnefoy. France, shooting. Died 9 August 1914
2. Jean Latrie. French fencer and modern pentathlon (1912). Died 5 September 1914.
3. Alexander Bouin. French athlete. Died 29 September 1914
4. Béla Zulawszky. Hungarian fencer. Died 24 October 1914
5. Jenő Szántay. Hungarian fencer. Died 11 December 1914
6. Richard Francis Yorke. British athlete. Died 22 December 1914
7. George Adam Lutz. French cyclist. Died 31 January 1915
8. Kenneth Powell. British tennis player. Died 18 February 1915
9. Wyndham Halswelle. British athlete. Died 31 March 1915
10. Geoffrey Barron Taylor. Canadian rower. Died 31 March 1915

11. Gilchrist Maclagan. British rower. Died 25 April 1915
12. Ralph Chalmers. British fencer. Died 8 May 1915
13. Henry Mills Goldsmith. British rower. Died 9 May 1915
14. Henry Alan Leeke. British athlete. Died 29 May 1915
15. Oswald Carver. British rower. Died 7 June 1915
16. George Fairbairn. British rower. Died 20 June 1915
17. Edward Gordon Williams. British rower. Died 12 August 1915
18. Arthur Ommundsen. Britain, shooting. Died 19 September 1915
19. Ismael de Lesseps. French fencer. Died 30 September 1915
20. Béla von Las-Torres. Hungary athletics. Died 12 October 1915
21. Edmund William Bury. British racquets. Died 5 December 1915
22. Arthur William Wilde. Britain, shooting. Died 21 January 1916
23. Geoffrey Horsman Coles. Britain, shooting. Died 27 January 1916
24. Jules Aristide Jenicot. French footballer. Died 22 February 1916
25. Alan Patterson. British athletics. Died 14 March 1916
26. Guido Romano. Italian gymnastics. Died 18 June 1916
27. John Somers-Smith. British rower. Died 1 July 1916
28. Alfred Edward Flaxman. British athletics. Died 1 July 1916
29. William Philo. British boxer. Died 7 July 1916.
30. Pierre Six. French footballer. Died 7 July 1916
31. John Robinson. British hockey player. Died 23 August 1916
32. Justin Pierre Vialaret. French footballer. Died 30 September 1916
33. Rene Victor Fenouillière. French footballer. Died 4 November 1916
34. Frederick Septimus Kelly. British rower. Died 13 November 1916.
35. Charles Vigurs. British gymnastics. Died 22 February 1917
36. Herbert Wilson. British polo player. Died 11 April 1917
37. Robert Powell. Canada tennis player. Died 28 April 1917
38. Percy Courtman. British swimmer. Died 2 June 1917
39. Harold Hawkins. Britain, shooting. Died 16 June 1917
40. Louis Octave Lapize. French cyclist. Died 14 July 1917
41. Noel Godfrey Chavasse. British athletics. Died 4 August 1917
42. James Roche. British Athlete. Died 25 August 1917
43. George Albert Hawkins. British athlete. Died 20/22 September 1917
44. George Butterfield. British athlete. Died 24 September 1917
45. Bernhard von Gaza. German Rower. Died 25 September 1917
46. Duncan Mackinnon. British Rower. Died 9 October 1917
47. Harry Crank. British Diver. Died 22 October 1917
48. Ivan Laing. British hockey player. Died 30 November 1917
49. Juho Halme. Finnish athlete. Died 1 January 1918
50. Reginald Pridmore. British hockey player. Died 13 March 1918
51. Ronald Sanderson. British Rower. Died 17 April 1918

52. István Mudin. Hungarian pentathlon/discus. Died 22 July 1918
53. Albert Rowland. New Zealand sports Walker. Died 23 July 1918
54. Thomas Raddall. Britain, shooting. Died 9 August 1918
55. Frederick Kitching. British athlete. Died 11 August 1918
56. Bertrand de Lesseps. French fencer. Died 28 August 1918
57. Hanns Braun. German athlete. Died 9 October 1918
58. Imre Mudin. Hungary athlete. Died 23 October 1918
59. Alfred Motté. French athlete. Died 31 October 1918
60. Victor Willems. Belgian Fencer. Died 1918
61. Hermann Bönninghausen. German athlete. Died 26 January 1919

1912 Olympics (Games of the V Olympiad)
The 1912 Olympic games were held in Stockholm between 5 May and 22 July 1912. Twenty-eight nations and 2,408 competitors, including 48 women, competed in 102 events in 14 sports. It was the last Olympics to issue solid gold medals to the winners of their events; it was the first time that Japan competed, the first Asian nation to do so; it was the first games to have women's diving and swimming; it was the first games to have the decathlon and new pentathlon; it was the first games to introduce electric timing; it was the first Olympics to introduce an arts competition; it was also the final Olympics where 'private entries' were accepted (not part of a country's officially selected team).

Twenty-eight nations competed in Stockholm. As well as Japan, several other countries made their debut appearance in the games including Egypt, Iceland, Portugal, Serbia (their one and only appearance as a separate country until 2008) and Chile who entered fourteen athletes (although one Chilean athlete did make an appearance during the 1896 games). The first athletes from Armenia also made an appearance, under the flag of the Ottoman Empire.

The USA won the most medals with 63 (174 athletes): 25 gold, 19 silver and 19 bronze. The home nation Sweden, with 444 athletes, came second with 65 medals: 24 gold, 24 silver, and 17 bronze. Great Britain (279 athletes) came third with 42 medals: 10 gold, 15 silver, and 16 bronze.

Seventy-one competitors who competed in the 1912 Olympics were killed in the Great War:

1. Robert Merz. Austrian footballer. Died 30 August 1914
2. Oszkar Demján. Hungarian swimmer. Died 4 September 1914
3. Jean Latrie. France, Fencing and Modern Pentathlon. Died 5 September 1914
4. George William Hutson. British athlete. Died 14 September 1914
5. Eduard von Lütcken. German equestrian. Died 15 September 1914
6. Alexander Bouin. French athlete. Died 29 September 1914
7. Thomas Gillespie. British rower. Died 18 October 1914
8. Árpád Pédery. Hungarian gymnast. Died 21 October 1914

9. Béla Zulawszky. Hungarian fencer. Died 24 October 1914
10. Joseph Racine. French cyclist. Died 28 October 1914
11. Alphonse Meignant. French rower. Died 4 November 1914
12. Gerard 'Twiggy' Anderson. British hurdler. Died 11 November 1914
13. Richard Francis Yorke. British athlete (1908) Died 22 December 1914
14. Georg Krogmann. German footballer. Died 9 January 1915
15. Max Hermann. German athlete. Died 29 January 1915
16. Kenneth Powell. Britain tennis player. Died 18 February 1915
17. Edward Radcliffe. British Equestrian. Died 21 February 1915
18. Adolf Kofler. Austrian Cyclist. Died 13 March 1915
19. Geoffrey Barron Taylor. Canadian rower. Died 24 April 1915
20. Anthony Wilding. Australian tennis player. Died 9 May 1915
21. Herman Donners. Belgian water polo. Died 14 May 1915
22. James Duffy. Canadian marathon runner. Died 23 May 1915
23. Alfred Mickler. German athlete. Died 14 June 1915
24. Jakob Person. German athlete. Died 15 July 1915
25. Paul Kenna. British Equestrian. Died 30 August 1915
26. Fritz Bartholomae. German rower. Died 12 August 1915
27. Arthur Ommundsen. Britain, shooting. Died 19 September 1915
28. Renon Boussière. French marathon runner. Died 25 September 1915
29. Caulle Joseph. French athlete. Died 1 October 1915
30. Béla von Las-Torres. Hungarian athlete. Died 12 October 1915
31. Alfred Staats. German gymnast. Died 22 October 1915
32. Dragutin Tomašević. Serbian athlete. Died October 1915
33. Georg Baumann. Russia wrestler. Died1915
34. Hugh Durant. Britain, shooting. Died 20 January 1916
35. Walter Jesinghaus. German gymnast. Died 22 February 1916
36. Alan Patterson. British Athlete. Died 14 March 1916
37. Karl Braunsteiner. Austrian footballer. Died 19 April 1916
38. Guido Romano. Italian Gymnast. Died 18 June 1916
39. Béla Békessy. Hungary, sabre. Died 6 July 1916
40. Josef Rieder. German cyclist. Died 13 July 1916
41. Hermann Bosch. German footballer. Died 16 July 1916
42. Robert Finden Davies. Britain, shooting. Died 9 September 1916
43. Andrei Akimov. Russia footballer. Died1916
44. Nikolai Kynin. Russia footballer. Died1916
45. Wilhelm Lutzow. German swimmer. Died 1916
46. Feliks Leparsky. Russian fencer. Died 10 January 1917
47. Henry Ashington. British athlete. Died 31 January 1917
48. Charles Vigurs. British gymnast. Died 22 February 1917
49. Alister Kirby. British rower. Died 29 March 1917

50. Prince Karl of Prussia. German equestrian. Died 6 April 1917
51. Gordon Alexander. British fencer. Died 24 April 1917
52. Issac Bentham. British water polo. Died 15 May 1917
53. Percy Courtman. British swimmer. Died 2 June 1917
54. Henry Gayler. British cyclist. Died 23 June 1917
55. Wilhelm Brülle. German gymnast. Died 5 August 1917
56. Claude Ross. Australian athlete. Died 19 August 1917
57. Alexander Decoteau. Canadian athlete. Died 30 October 1917
58. Gori Nikitin. Russia footballer. Died 1917
59. Juho Halme. Finnish athlete. Died 1 January 1918
60. Hermann Plaskuda. German fencer. Died 1 March 1918
61. Kurt Bretting. German swimmer. Died 30 May 1918
62. Ernest Keeley. South Africa, shooting. Died 23 July 1918
63. Henry Macintosh. British athlete. Died 26 July 1918
64. Hans Sorge. German gymnast. Died 6 August 1918
65. Cecil Patrick Healy. Australia swimmer. Died 29 August 1918
66. Joseph Frank Dines. British footballer. Died 27 September 1918
67. Hanns Braun. German athlete. Died 9 October 1918
68. William Lyshon. American wrestler. Died 13 October 1918
69. Imre Mudin. Hungarian athlete. Died 23 October 1918
70. Heinrich Burkowitz. German athlete. Died November 1918
71. Hermann Bönninghausen. German athlete. Died 26 January 1919

The Olympics would not take place again until 1920. The next games should have been held in Berlin in 1916 but due to the war it was cancelled. The peace treaty signed after the war, the Treaty of Versailles, affected the Olympics in several ways. New states were created out of the failed old ones. Sanctions were implemented on several countries, while others seen as having been responsible for starting the war faced outright bans. These included Hungary, Germany, Austria, Bulgaria and the Ottoman Empire. Germany remained banned until 1925. The 1920 games (Games of the VII Olympiad), the first to be held after the war, were held in Antwerp. Twenty-nine nations took part, including many of the new states now able to compete in their own right such as Estonia and Czechoslovakia. It is also worth remembering that, although this book is about the Olympians that died during the First World War, thousands of others were injured, their wounds not allowing them to continue with their sporting careers.

Appendix 5:

Casualties Who Won Olympic Medals

1896

Léon Flameng. French. Cyclist. Died 2.1.17. **Gold-Silver-Bronze**

1900

Carl Heinrich Goßler. German. Rowing. Died 09.8.14. **Gold**
Louis Desire Bach. French. Football. Died 16.9.14. **Silver**
Charles Devendeville. French. Swimming, Water Polo. Died 19.9.14. **Gold**
Andre Six. French. Swimming. Died 1914. **Silver**
Maurice Raoul-Duval. French. Polo. Died 5.5.16. **Bronze**
Louis Champsavin. France. Equestrian. Died 20.12.16. **Bronze**
Waldemar Tietgens. German. Rowing. Died 28.7.17. **Gold**

1904

Arthur Yancey Wear. American. Tennis. Died 6.11.18. **Bronze**

1906

Wyndham Halswelle. British. Athletics. Died 31.3.15. **Silver-Bronze**
Rudolf Watzl. Austrian. Wrestling. Died 15.8.15. **Gold-Bronze**
Heinrich Schneidereit. German. Tug-of-War/Weight-lifting. Died 30.9.15. **Gold-Bronze x2**
Lajos Gönczy. Hungary. Athletics. Died 4.12.15. **Bronze-Silver**
István Mudin. Hungarian. Pentathlon/Discus. Died 22.7.18. **Silver-Bronze**

1908

Henri Edmond Bonnefoy. France. Shooting. Died 09.8.14. **Bronze**
Alexander Bouin. France. Athletics. Died 29.9.14. **Bronze**
Béla Zulawszky. Hungary. Fencing. Died 24.10.14. **Silver**
Wyndham Halswelle. British. Athletics. Died 31.3.15. **Gold**
Geoffrey Barron Taylor. Canadian. Rowing. Died 24.4.15. **Bronze x2**
Gilchrist Maclagan. British. Rower. Died Died 25.4.15. **Gold**
Henry Mills Goldsmith. British. Rowing. Died 09.5.15. **Bronze**
Oswald Carver. British. Rowing. Died 07.6.15. **Bronze**
George Fairbairn. British. Rowing. Died 20.6.15. **Silver**
Edward Gordon Williams. Britain. Rowing. Died 12.8.15. **Bronze**

Arthur Ommundsen. British. Shooting. Died 19.9.15. **Silver**
Bele von Las-Torres. Hungary. Athletics. Died 12.10.15. **Silver**
Edmund William Bury. British. Racquets. Died 5.12.15. **Silver**
Geoffrey Horsman Coles. British. Shooting. 27.1.16. **Bronze**
John Somers-Smith. British. Rowing. Died 1.7.16. **Gold**
William Philo. British. Boxing. Died 7.7.16. **Bronze**
John Robinson. British. Hockey. Died 23.8.16. **Gold**
Frederick Septimus Kelly. British. Rowing. Died 13.11.16. **Gold**
Herbert Wilson. British. Polo. Died 11.4.17. **Gold**
Harold Hawkins. British. Shooting. Died 16.6.17. **Silver**
Louis Octave Lapize. France. Cyclist. Died 14.7.17. **Bronze**
Bernhard von Gaza. Germany. Rower. Died 25.9.17. **Bronze**
Duncan Mackinnon. British. Rower. Died 9.10.17. **Gold**
Ivan Laing. British. Hockey. Died 30.11.17. **Bronze**
Reginald Pridmore. British. Hockey. Died 13.3.18. **Gold**
Ronald Sanderson. British. Rowing. Died 17.4.18. **Gold**
Hanns Braun. German. Athletics. Died 9.10.18. **Silver-Bronze**
Victor Willems. Belgium. Fencer. Died 1918. **Gold-Bronze**

1912
George William Hutson. Britain. Athletics. Died 14.9.14. **2x Bronze**
Eduard von Lütcken. German. Equestrian. Died 15.9.14. **Silver**
Alexander Bouin. France. Athletics. Died 29.9.14. **Silver**
Thomas Gillespie. British. Rowing. Died 18.10.14. **Silver**
Árpád Pédery. Hungary. Gymnastics. Died 21.10.14. **Silver**
Anthony Wilding. Australian. Tennis. Died 09.5.15. **Bronze**
Herman Donners. Belgium. Water Polo. Died 14.5.15. **Silver-Bronze**
Fritz Bartholomae. German. Rower. Died 12.8.15. **Bronze**
Arthur Ommundsen. British. Shooting. Died 19.9.15. **Silver**
Hugh Durant. British. Shooting. Died 20.1.16. **Bronze**
Guido Romano. Italian. Gymnastics. Died 18.6.1916 **Gold**
Wilhelm Lutzow. German. Swimmer. Died 1916. **Silver**
Charles Vigurs. British. Gymnastics. Died 22.2.17. **Bronze**
Alister Kirby. British. Rowing. Died 29.3.17. **Gold**
Prince Karl of Prussia. German. Equestrian. Died 6.4.17. **Bronze**
Percy Courtman. British. Swimming. Died 2.6.17. **Bronze**
Henry Gayler. British. Cycling. Died 23.6.17. **Silver**
Henry Macintosh. British. Athletics. Died 26.7.18. **Gold**
Cecil Patrick Healy. Australia. Swimming. Died 29.8.18. **Gold-Silver-Bronze**
Joseph Frank Dines. British. Football. Died 27.9.18. **Gold**

"We have a responsibility to our fellow countries armed forces who have invested in our security, to help when they leave this great service.

Remembering a few fall with Broken Bodies, Broken Minds and Broken lives.

Let's help and heal together."

Goose Cryer M.C. – Care after Combat